Enriching Your Marriage

Enriching Your Marriage

DRS. CLAUDIO AND PAMELA CONSUEGRA

Pacific Press®
Publishing Association
Nampa, Idaho | www.pacificpress.com

Cover design by Gerald Lee Monks
Cover design resources from iStockPhoto.com | anyaberkut
Inside design by Aaron Troia

The authors assume full responsibility for the accuracy of all facts and quotations as cited in this book.

Purchase additional copies of this book by calling toll-free 1-800-765-6955 or by visiting adventistbookcenter.com.

Library of Congress Cataloging-in-Publication Data
Names: Consuegra, Claudio, author. | Consuegra, Pamela, author.
Title: Enriching your marriage / Claudio and Pamela Consuegra.
Description: Nampa, Idaho : Pacific Press Publishing Association, [2020] | Summary: "Practical, biblical instruction for a rich, long-lasting marriage relationship"— Provided by publisher.
Identifiers: LCCN 2020046189 (print) | LCCN 2020046190 (ebook) | ISBN 9780816366866 (paperback) | ISBN 9780816366873 (e-book edition)
Subjects: LCSH: Marriage—Religious aspects—Christianity.
Classification: LCC BV835 .C636 2020 (print) | LCC BV835 (ebook) | DDC 248.4—dc23
LC record available at https://lccn.loc.gov/2020046189
LC ebook record available at https://lccn.loc.gov/2020046190

October 2020

Dedication

We dedicate this book to our parents, who believed in the commitment and permanence of marriage and gave us an example of what love is, as God designed it to be.

Fernando Consuegra
January 20, 1922–January 5, 1973

Cecilia Consuegra
June 1, 1924–March 2, 2000

Fernando and Cecilia Consuegra
Married June 29, 1945

George Washington Napier
October 4, 1930–August 28, 1993

Sadie June Napier
June 20, 1935–October 11, 2006

George and June Napier
Married July 7, 1956

Contents

Introduction

Why write this book? The market is saturated with self-help books on every topic, and a lot of books on marriage have already been written. So, again, why write yet another book on marriage? The simple answer is that this is *our* book on marriage. We have written books for parents and grandparents, books on discipleship, devotional books, and even a Bible-study guide. But as we conduct couples' retreats and conferences around the world, we are often asked if we have a book that goes along with our presentation—only to respond that we do not. In this book, we simply share what we have learned and taught through the years, what has been helpful, and the good and bad lessons we have learned on our own marriage journey.

At the very core, this book is our story, a story we have shared with hundreds around the world and now want to share with you, our kind reader. Our prayer is that as you journey with us through the pages of this book, you will find something helpful, something humorous, something encouraging, something inspiring, and something you can apply to your personal life so that your marriage will be a blessing to you individually, to you as a couple, and to your family. So welcome to our home, welcome to our life, and welcome to our story.

We don't presume to tell you that this is the ultimate marriage book, the best there is, or the final word on the subject. All we want to do is to share with you what we have learned through almost four decades of marriage, countless couples' retreats, premarital and marriage counseling sessions and from our experience teaching classes, preaching sermons, reading books, learning from others, and continuing to learn every day. Those attending the retreats have often told us they enjoyed our presentations, and many couples have said the information made a positive difference in their marriage. In fact, many have told us that their marriage was saved by attending our marriage retreat.

We don't take any credit. All the credit and praise goes to our heavenly Father, our Lord and Savior Jesus Christ, and our Guide and Counselor, the Holy Spirit. It is God who heals us, changes us, and makes us daily into His image. At the same time, God has chosen to use us as His instruments, so if through our words people have been helped, we feel blessed, privileged, and honored to have been used by Him.

OUR STORY

Our love story began one morning in late May 1978 on the campus of what was then Columbia Union College, now Washington Adventist University, in Takoma Park, Maryland.

HIS STORY

I had enrolled during the spring semester to take a lighter class load, as I was still learning English. I was born and raised in Colombia. Spanish is my first language, and I had come to the United States shortly after graduating from high school in late 1975. Late in 1976, I accepted Jesus' sacrifice on my behalf and was baptized into God's family. In 1977, while taking classes in English as a second language, I also enrolled in the premed program at a local community college. But in the summer of that year, I received another invitation from God; this time, He was asking me to make a drastic life change, and instead of becoming a physician—a life dream of mine—I realized that He wanted me to become a pastor. That's how I ended up transferring from the community college to Columbia Union College in the middle of the academic year.

Pamela graduated high school from Shenandoah Valley Academy in central Virginia a few days before we met, arrived on campus that morning in May, and was given a job at the college bookstore. It was summer vacation, and I had no reason to be on campus; however, I was looking for a particular item a friend suggested might be available at the college bookstore.

I walked into the store, and the first person I saw was this divinely beautiful girl with long, blond hair, brilliant green eyes, and the most radiant smile standing by the counter. The student body at Columbia Union College was relatively small, fewer than a thousand, so it was easy to get to know everyone (or at the very least recognize them as students at the college). So when I first laid eyes on this amazingly cute girl, I immediately knew I had not seen her before.

What a lot of people don't know about me is that not only am I a typical introvert but also, to top it off, I am a very shy person. Normally, it would take me days, weeks, or even months to muster enough courage to approach a girl to initiate a conversation with her, and often, by the time I did, some other guy had swept in before me. But this morning, as if being carried forward by some unseen Power (I wonder who that might have been?), I walked up to Pamela and asked, "You're new here, aren't you?" Still flashing that sparkling smile, she responded, "Yes, it's my first day." My heart was pumping so hard and fast it seemed as if it were about to burst. With a tightness in my throat, I somehow mustered enough courage to quickly come up with the best pickup line I could think of, and I said, "Great! Would you like me to show you around Washington, DC?" And just like that, in the twinkling of an eye, she fell madly in love with me.

HER STORY

History, or at least *his story*, sounds quite credible, but perhaps I need to explain further as I tell you my side of things. I grew up in the beautiful Blue Ridge Mountains of Virginia, so that makes me a southern girl in every sense of the phrase. In fact, you may remember the television show called *The Waltons*. Well, that area of rural Virginia was home to me. My mother grew up with John-Boy Walton, and the television series frequently mentioned places and people that I was very familiar with. Family was everything to me—with all four of my grandparents living nearby, along with a host of aunts, uncles, cousins, two brothers, and one sister. Home meant lots of people and laughter, and there was always an extra place set at our table.

I made the decision to attend college to become a teacher. At that time, leaving home to go to college was a *big* deal. There were preparations to be made, goodbyes to be said, and advice was freely handed out. However, my dear southern mama had only one word of advice for me: "Now, Pam, you must find a good southern boy to marry." That was it! There was no mention of studying hard or getting a good education. Nope, her only desire was for me to meet and marry a "southern boy."

I arrived on campus, unpacked our family car, watched my mama and daddy drive off, and headed to the college bookstore where I was to begin work. I met the manager, was given brief instructions, and took my place near the front checkout area.

Within minutes of walking into that store, someone else walked in. Yes, he was tall, dark, and handsome. And the part about him offering to show me around Washington, DC, is true. I accepted that invitation and, thus, had a date within a very short time of arriving on that campus.

I telephoned my mama after giving my parents time to make the drive back to Virginia and shared with her that I already had a date. She asked one question and one question only: "Is he a southern boy?" I thought for a moment and decided that his birthplace of Colombia qualified him as a "southern boy." So, I replied, "Yes, mama, he is from farther down south than we are. He's from Colombia." My dear mama interpreted my response to mean Columbia, South Carolina, so she was very pleased indeed!

So, with mama's approval, I dated my "southern boy" for three years and said "I do" in our senior year of college. And for the record, "I do, *still.*"

OUR STORY AFTER "I DO"

Despite slightly different views of the details, that's how we began to write our life story together more than forty-one years ago. We dated during the first three years of college and were married in our senior year. Instead of evening dates at the college library, we were now studying together in our small apartment in the basement home of some dear friends. That first year, God began to work a series of amazing miracles in our lives that have not stopped taking place, even as we write this book. God has opened doors we never could have imagined and has blessed us beyond what we deserve. He has shown us His love in more ways than we could write about in hundreds of thousands of pages. Like the apostle John, we could say about what Jesus has done in our life and marriage, "And there are also many other things that Jesus did, which if they were written one by one, I suppose that even the world itself could not contain the books that would be written" (John 21:25).

As we reflect on more than forty-one years together, more than thirty-eight of those as a married couple, we are truly amazed and humbled. We have been blessed with two gorgeous, smart, kind, and loving daughters, and He has brought into our family two handsome, talented, strong, and supportive sons-in-law whom we love as our own children. We have lived in eight states (a couple of them more than once), and we have traveled to every state in the United States, every province in Canada, and more than fifty countries around the world. We have written ten books (including the *Adult Sabbath School Bible Study Guide* for the world church for the second quarter of 2019); hosted a live radio program for several years; recorded many television programs; held countless baptisms and couples' retreats; and we have trained hundreds of pastors and teachers; and, through it all, we have truly received more in our lifetime than we have given. With the psalmist, we gladly shout, "The LORD has done great things for us, and we are glad" (Psalm 126:3).

With all of these amazing blessings poured out since we first met, you may be thinking our life has been nearly perfect. Unfortunately, that's hardly the case. About ten years into our marriage, we went through a very difficult time. We decided early in our life together that divorce would never be an option for us. We would work through, and fight through, whatever challenges came our way. The late Ruth Bell Graham, the wife of renowned preacher and evangelist Billy Graham, made a statement about their marriage that resonates with us even today: "I've never considered divorce. Murder, yes, but not divorce."[1] Well, we can assure you that neither of us has ever considered murder, but we, like Graham, also said divorce would not be part of our vocabulary.

While going through that difficult time in our life, we read a book that served as the catalyst for a complete turnaround in our marriage. Shortly after, we attended a couples' training event and began offering our own couples' weekend retreats. We saw and heard evidence of people's lives and marriages being changed and positively affected. Every time we hear of changed lives, we are humbled and quickly remind people that we have no power to make such changes—only God can. At the same time, we are grateful to have the opportunity to be His instruments in the healing of relationships.

ARE YOU QUALIFIED?

Some time ago, we were asked, "What qualifies you to do what you do?" While we don't like to wave our credentials around for others to see, please allow us to tell you just a little about ourselves.

Pamela is a lifelong educator, having taught at every level from kindergarten to doctoral classes. She holds a bachelor of science degree in elementary education, a master of science degree in curriculum development and instruction, and a PhD in educational leadership. Perhaps the most important qualification is that she has been a great wife and mother. She has helped navigate this ship through troubled waters and led us to shore masterfully.

Claudio is a pastor and marriage and family counselor. He obtained a bachelor of arts degree in theology, a master of science degree in counseling psychology, and a doctor of ministry degree in family ministries. He has been a law enforcement and hospital chaplain, church pastor, department director, and church administrator for nearly forty years.

At the time of this writing, we serve in team ministry as the Family Ministries directors for the North American Division of the Seventh-day Adventist Church in Columbia, Maryland. We have been directly involved in the work of families for more than a quarter of a century and have helped countless couples prepare for marriage or deal with marital challenges. The bottom line, however, is that our biggest and most important qualification is that God called us to the gospel and educational ministry, and, later, He called us again to ministry with families. He called us, He enabled us, and He has empowered us to serve and help others. As long as He still uses and directs us, we will continue to do His bidding.

We pray that through the reading of this book, you will be blessed and will share what you learn with others who may be struggling in their own marriage. We are truly blessed when we bless others.

Claudio Consuegra, DMin
Pamela Consuegra, PhD

---

1. Kristen Driscoll, "Ruth Bell Graham: A Life Well Lived, Part 2," *Decision*, July 24, 2007, https://decisionmagazine.com/ruth-bell-graham-a-life-well-lived-part-2/.

Chapter One

Two Becoming One

*For this reason a man will leave his father and mother
and be united to his wife, and the two will become one flesh.
This is a profound mystery—but I am talking about Christ and the church.*
—Ephesians 5:31, 32, NIV

What would you say is the purpose of marriage? Why was marriage established? Having been immersed in family ministries for more than twenty years, we can tell you with certainty that most people see marriage as a means or a gateway to happiness. But one day, when they find themselves at the end of their marital rope, they come to us as if to justify their desire to leave their relationship and ask, "Don't I have the right to be happy?"

Happiness. Is that the purpose for which God designed marriage? Is that why God created a man and a woman and brought them together to become one flesh? What is the purpose of marriage anyway? As you may recall in the story of Creation (Genesis 1; 2), God first created Adam and gave him the task of naming all of the animals. But as the beasts came to him, Adam noticed a pattern: for each kind, there was a male and its female counterpart. Quickly he realized there was no such mate for him. This didn't catch God by surprise. It had been a part of His plan for Adam. It was important for Adam to notice that being alone was not good or healthy as he felt the void of something—or rather someone—missing from his life. Consider these words: "Adam's study of the animal creation supplied him with considerable knowledge, but did not satisfy his longing for companionship with another being, his equal. This fact indicates the equal partnership that the woman should enjoy with the man. No real companion could be found for Adam among creatures inferior to him."[1]

"The LORD God said, 'It is not good that man should be alone; I will make him a helper comparable to him'" (Genesis 2:18). While God made the animals to be the man's companions, they were still not the perfect companion. Only the creation of someone like him would provide true completeness and satisfaction. God didn't make for Adam some other lower creature like the animals. God made from Adam an equal to himself.

Several Bible translations and versions have used different terms to try to illustrate the equal relationship between Adam and Eve. We find words like "corresponding" (ISV, CSB); "suitable" (NASB, NIV); "a[n] help meet" (KJV, ASV); "a helper fit" (ESV); and "just right" (NLT). The emphasis in all these examples is of a companionship, an equality, and a mutuality in the spousal relationship. We also find that theme in other places in the Bible. For instance, in Song of Solomon, the bride, the Shulamite, shouts with joy, "My beloved is mine, and I am his," and, "I am my beloved's, and my beloved is mine" (Song of Solomon 2:16; 6:3). We also read about this relationship of mutuality in the first letter Paul wrote to the Corinthians, in which he tells them, "The wife does not have authority over her own body, but the husband does. And likewise the husband does not have authority over his own body, but the wife does" (1 Corinthians 7:4). Another place where the Bible illustrates the principle of mutuality in marriage is found in one of the most significant passages in the New Testament dealing with the marital relationship. In Ephesians, the apostle Paul tells husbands and wives to "submit to one another out of reverence for Christ" (Ephesians 5:21, NLT).

In God's plan, equality means complementarity. The Jewish Study Bible explains, "The creation of the woman after the man and from a part of his body need not imply the subordination of women to men."[2] God could have made woman the same way He made man. He could have made a second clay model, breathed into her nostrils, and given her life. But the method God employed to create Eve, from the side of Adam, shows the intimate relationship He intended for married couples to have. As Matthew Henry stated, "The woman was made of a rib out of the side of Adam; not made out of his head to rule over him, nor out of his feet to be trampled upon by him, but out of his side to be equal with him, under his arm to be protected, and near his heart to be beloved."[3]

We can only imagine what happened when God brought Eve to Adam as he awakened from divine surgery. Perhaps he rubbed his eyes to make sure he was not still sleeping, that he was not seeing a mirage of sorts. But the moment he realized this beauty was the companion he had longed for, Adam burst into the first poem of human history:

> Here is someone like me!
> She is part of my body,
>   my own flesh and bones.
> She came from me, a man.
>   So I will name her Woman! (Genesis 2:23, CEV).

Again, reflect on this moment when Adam met Eve: "Instinctively, or as the result of divine instruction, he recognized in her part of his own being. He was henceforth to love her as his own body, for in loving her he loves himself."[4]

UNEXPECTED MATH: 1 + 1 = 1

American journalist Mignon McLaughlin is often attributed with stating, "In the arithmetic of love, one plus one equals everything, and two minus one equals nothing."[5] Even before entering school, a child is able to discern that one plus one equals two. The events described in Genesis 2 are not only about some divine surgery God performed to remove part of Adam's side and turn it into another human being. They also illustrate an interesting mathematical calculation. The union of a husband to his wife results in two becoming one. Marriage, as God intended, is the process of a man and a woman becoming one—and by doing so, reflecting the relationship between Christ and His bride, the church (Ephesians 5).

God says that when it comes to marriage, one plus one really does equal one. The areas of weakness in one become intertwined with the areas of strength in the other. But how do we get to the point of two becoming as one? How do we, in our marriages, make God's math a reality?

At first glance, many assume that this text refers only to sexual intimacy. Indeed, that is one part of what it means for a husband and wife to become one. However, it is so much more than that. When married, a husband and wife become one physically, emotionally, and spiritually. Two lives become united in purpose. To quote Erik Jones:

> Marriage is an exclusive union between *one male* and *one female*. . . .
>
> Marriage forms a unique family unit. The building block of society, in God's view, is the family unit. The nucleus of this family unit is the husband-wife relationship.
>
> The marriage relationship is to be the closest possible relationship on the human plane. The word translated "joined" in the New King James Version is the Hebrew word dabaq, which means "to cling, stick, stay close, cleave, keep close, stick to, stick with" (*Brown-Driver-Briggs Hebrew Lexicon*). This describes the close emotional bond that is to develop between a husband and wife. Later, Christ expounded on this verse by saying, "What God has joined together, let not man separate" (Mark 10:9).[6]

Please do not misunderstand this concept of two becoming one. For many, this has negative implications: *Don't you each have separate lives? What about your own individuality? Why give that up?* It is perfectly acceptable to have things that you personally want to accomplish if your spouse supports you in them. God gave each of you gifts and talents, and you should develop them to their full potential. Becoming one does not mean that you lose the uniqueness of you! Instead, it is possible that you can help in developing the talents and gifts in each other. You can play a crucial supportive role for your spouse and discover that your individual talents and dreams may coincide and lead to the same ultimate goal.

At the time we got married (and even today), one of the customs during the wedding ceremony was to light a unity candle. Usually, the mother of the bride and the mother of the groom would ascend the platform, and each would light a candle. After the vows were pronounced, the bride and groom would take those candles and together light a central, larger candle, the unity candle. Before replacing the two other candles, they would blow them out, signifying that the two were now one. When we got married, however, we decided that, contrary to common practice, we would leave our mothers' candles lit as a symbol that, while we were joining our lives and becoming one, we would also maintain our individuality as we complemented each other.

Some couples discover that each person has separate goals leading in separate directions. It is as if you have a car with two steering wheels, and you are both driving. If you both drive in the same direction, you will be fine; but if you try to drive one way and your spouse is trying to drive the other way, either you will not go anywhere or you will crash. Think about your faith values, your hopes for the future, your dreams, and your goals. Do they align with your spouse, or do you find yourselves pulling in opposite directions?

This does not mean that you must agree on everything or that you must have the same tastes, personal goals, wishes, or desires. Pamela's gifts are in the educational field, one in which she has excelled over the years. Claudio's gifts lean more toward the theological and psychological fields. Pamela would prefer not to have to travel much, whereas Claudio enjoys traveling very much. Claudio would much rather never have to go shopping, while Pamela finds it therapeutic and relaxing. We are different in many ways, but we share more in common than we differ, particularly in the most important areas of life. It is helpful when you can share a vision and ultimate goals together, so you both can work in one accord toward reaching them. It will be extra hard to fulfill that vision if your spouse is not with you or is fighting against you. It is very important to make sure you are on the same page and working together to achieve your hopes, dreams, and goals.

Perhaps the number one way to align your goals and move together is to spend undivided, quality time together. It doesn't happen automatically. You must be intentional about spending quantity and quality time together and communicating about the things that matter most. However, the sad fact remains that most couples today spend more time with technology than they do in face-to-face communication. In an article on ChristianPost.com, authors Mike and Trisha Fox cite some startling statistics, saying that "23% of all couples [spend] less than [one] hour per day with each other," and "of that one hour per day, only three minutes is meaningful conversation!"[7] In addition, Zig Ziglar mentions a survey showing that "more than 90% of the couples who considered their marriages 'strong and close' also said they spent a great deal of time together"; on the other hand, "divorced couples usually had spent little time together before the split."[8]

If there is one word that defines couples of today, it would be *busyness*. We are just too busy. We are consumed with distractions that take us away from each other. Even when we are not at work, it seems that we are not spending time together. It is far too easy to drift apart if we are not intentional about carving out blocks of quality time. Indeed, becoming one is not something that happens overnight. Rather, it happens over time as you discover the intersections of your lives. How could you possibly become one if you spend only three minutes a day in meaningful conversation? As a married couple, you are no longer just looking out for yourselves but should be setting goals for yourselves as a couple. Two can accomplish what is impossible for one. Work together on becoming one in your relationship!

For many years we have shared with couples a simple time formula to help them become more intentional in the quantity and quality of time they spend together. We recommend that this time have no outside technological distractions, such as the cell phone, television, radio, computer, or tablet. We also encourage couples to spend time alone together: no family, children, friends, colleagues, or church members. Spend time getting reacquainted, talking about feelings, and enjoying each other's company, and do not use the time for solving problems, shopping, or completing chores. So, with that in mind, here is a simple suggested time formula to follow. Spend a minimum time together of

- one half hour each night;
- one night each week;
- one day each month; and
- one weekend each quarter.

Sometimes couples look at us, eyes wide open, and ask, "And what are we supposed to do all that time?" We tell them to remember how much time they used to spend when they were dating, when it seemed as if they didn't have enough time to be together, and to follow the same practice. Use the time to come close together as one.

God's math gets even more interesting than just 1 + 1 = 1. Actually, we like to explain to couples that two can become one only if there is a third strand. Yes, that means 1 + 1 + 1 = 1. In his poem, "Marriage Takes Three," Perry Tanksley expresses it beautifully:

> I once thought marriage took
> Just two to make a go
> But now I am convinced
> It takes the Lord also.
> And not one marriage fails
> Where Christ is asked to enter
> As lovers come together
> With Jesus at the center.
> But marriage seldom thrives
> And homes are incomplete
> Till He is welcomed there
> To help avoid defeat.
> In homes where God is first
> It's obvious to see
> Those unions really work,
> For marriage still takes three.[9]

King Solomon understood this principle as well when he wrote:

> It's better to have a partner than go it alone.
> Share the work, share the wealth.
> And if one falls down, the other helps,
> But if there's no one to help, tough!
>
> Two in a bed warm each other.
> Alone, you shiver all night.
>
> By yourself you're unprotected.
> With a friend you can face the worst.
> Can you round up a third?
> A three-stranded rope isn't easily snapped (Ecclesiastes 4:9–12, *The Message*).

A rope of three strands is stronger and harder to break than one with only two strands. That "rope" of three strands consists of you, your spouse, and Jesus. It is only as you add this third strand that you can become a strong cord of one that is difficult to break. In essence, two become one as you add Jesus to the mix, involve Him in all your decisions and goals, and spend time in communion with each other and with Him.

FOR DISCUSSION

1. How much quality time do you spend together each day? Be honest and remember that time spent on technology (including watching TV) does not count as quality time.
2. What steps can you take to increase your quality time together?

THE PURPOSE OF MARRIAGE

Why did God establish marriage? It is not simply a sociological, economic, or legal agreement between two parties. There are businesses, clubs, and other organizations that could meet that criterion. God also intended marriage to be more than just for procreation. In fact, many are now having children without even having sexual intercourse.

Timothy Keller proposes that the purpose of marriage, according to God's design, was for companionship.[10] When God declared, "It is not good for the man to be alone," He didn't just create a whole lot of people to keep Adam company. Instead, God said, "I will make a helper who is just right for him" (Genesis 2:18, NLT). Marriage is not simply a convenient legal agreement between two parties. At the very center of this institution is the fact that marriage, as God intended, is the deepest of friendships and the source of intimate companionship. God planned for this special relationship to provide both parties with close, constant, mutual support, to bear each other's burdens, to build each other up. God fashioned this special arrangement between a wife and her husband, one in which they could be completely vulnerable and transparent with each other, affirm and encourage each other through the battles of life, and enjoy complete emotional intimacy.

But perhaps God created marriage between a man and a woman for a much deeper spiritual reason. In theology, we use three terms to describe what God does for us. When we accept the sacrifice of Jesus on our behalf, at that very instant, we are justified before God. Paul writes to the Romans: "Therefore, having been justified by faith, we have peace with God through our Lord Jesus Christ" (Romans 5:1). We refer to that miraculous experience as *justification*. It is instantaneous as our sins are forgiven and we stand before Jesus justified because of the blood He shed for us on Calvary.

From the moment we accept Jesus as our Savior, we are justified, and there begins a process of preparation to meet Him at His return. Here's what Paul tells the church members in Corinth: "And all of us, with unveiled faces, seeing the glory of the Lord as though reflected in a mirror, are being transformed into the same image from one degree of glory to another; for this comes from the Lord, the Spirit" (2 Corinthians 3:18, NRSV). Step by step, day by day, the Holy Spirit is changing us to be more like Jesus Himself until His return. It is a work that doesn't stop as long as we're alive. We refer to this process of growth and change as *sanctification*. Again, it is the work of the Holy Spirit in us, preparing us, setting us aside, sanctifying us in order for us to be ready for the return of Jesus.

Finally, one day soon, Jesus will return to take us to the place He has been preparing for us (John 14:1–3). At that very moment, "in the twinkling of an eye, at the last trumpet . . . the dead will be raised incorruptible, and we shall be changed. For this corruptible must put on incorruption, and this mortal must put on immortality" (1 Corinthians 15:52, 53). We use the term *glorification* to indicate the amazing transformation we will experience when Jesus returns for us.

The work of salvation, from beginning to end, is God's. It is not in our power to save ourselves because

> we're all sin-infected, sin-contaminated.
>   Our best efforts are grease-stained rags.
> We dry up like autumn leaves—
>   sin-dried, we're blown off by the wind (Isaiah 64:6, *The Message*).

Only God can do that saving work for us. However, we need to go back for a moment to the process of sanctification. We stated that sanctification is the work of the Holy Spirit helping us to become ready for the return of Jesus. Please keep this idea in mind for a moment as we turn briefly to one of the most important passages in the New Testament dealing with the marital relationship. Paul wrote a letter to the members of the church in Ephesus in which he told husbands: "Husbands, love your wives, just as Christ also loved the church and gave Himself for her, that He might sanctify and cleanse her with the washing of water by the word, that He might present her to Himself a glorious church, not having spot or wrinkle or any such thing, but that she should be holy and without blemish" (Ephesians 5:25–27). Sometimes we read those words so fast that we don't realize the treasure floating just under the surface. Please notice three very important elements in Paul's message.

First, he tells husbands how to love their wives: "Husbands, love your wives, *just as* Christ also loved the church" (verse 25; emphasis added). We could replace "just as" with other phrases, such as *in the same way that, exactly like, the same as,* or *in an identical way to the way that.* They all convey the same idea—husbands, your love for your wife should be no different than the love Christ has for His wife (the church).

I (Claudio) have preached on this passage many times and have asked the questions: When did Christ abandon His wife, the church? When did Christ neglect His wife, the church? When was Christ abusive toward His wife, the church? It is preposterous even to think that Christ would ever mistreat His wife, the church, in any way. And that is precisely what Paul wants us to remember. In the same way, it is preposterous and a denial of his faith for a husband to mistreat, abandon, neglect, or abuse his wife in any way.

Second, Paul states, "Christ also loved the church and gave Himself for her" (verse 25). To what extent did Christ give Himself for His wife, the church? To the point of death! Jesus Himself stated, "The greatest way to show love for friends is to die for them" (John 15:13, CEV). Isn't your wife your best friend? Isn't she closer to you than any and all of your other friends? If your greatest declaration of love to your friends is to be willing to die for them, shouldn't that also be your greatest declaration of love for your wife?

Of course, many men might immediately tell us, "I would be willing to die for my wife." As we write this chapter, there was recently a shooting in a church in Texas. A video camera in the church captured the entire incident. Repeatedly, the news reporters made it a point to mention how one of the parishioners had covered his wife with his body to shield her from danger. A real man, a godly man, will do all in his power to protect his wife, even if that means dying for her. But perhaps better questions would be: Are you willing to live for her? Are you willing to tend to her needs? Are you willing to strengthen, encourage, and build her up? Are you ready to respect her, honor her, and be faithful to her?

Third—and this is the main point—Paul tells husbands to love their wives, "just as Christ also loved the church and gave Himself for her, that He might *sanctify* and cleanse her with the washing of water by the word, that He might present her to Himself a glorious church, not having spot or wrinkle or any such thing, but that she should be holy and without blemish" (verses 25–27; emphasis added). Christ loved and even died for the church in order to *sanctify* her. Paul is giving husbands a very strong directive: "Do the same for your wives."

Now, let's make sure we understand what we're trying to say here. Earlier, we stated that sanctification is the work of the Holy Spirit. To paraphrase Paul, "Husbands, love your wives in order to sanctify them, just as Christ did for His wife, the church." We suggest Paul is saying that the ministry or the mission of marriage is the sanctification of your spouse. God has commissioned you, as a husband, to be the Holy Spirit's agent or helper as He prepares your wife for the soon return of Jesus. God is extending a call to husbands to work alongside the

Holy Spirit in the process of sanctification of their wives.

Often, when we make these statements, there are husbands who will ask, "If my role is to help my wife be ready for the second coming of Jesus, who is there to help me?" That's a valid and important question. Paul answers it in his letter to the Corinthians when he writes, "If any brother has a wife who does not believe, and she is willing to live with him, let him not divorce her. And a woman who has a husband who does not believe, if he is willing to live with her, let her not divorce him. For the unbelieving husband is sanctified by the wife, and the unbelieving wife is sanctified by the husband; otherwise your children would be unclean, but now they are holy" (1 Corinthians 7:12–14). While Paul makes specific application to those married to unbelievers, the same is true for those married to believers. The point is that husbands and wives are God's instruments in the hands of the Holy Spirit to help each other be ready for the second coming of Jesus. That's why Gary Thomas asks, "What if God designed marriage to make us holy more than to make us happy?"[11] We don't want to insinuate that marriage should not be a happy union—God forbid! But we are suggesting that happiness should not be the primary reason for us to enter marriage; instead, holiness, sanctification, and preparation for eternity should be.

This concept is not only important for those of us who are married so we can understand and accept God's call to the ministry and mission of marriage. It also is even more critical for those who are not yet married and who are trying to decide whether to take the next step. Perhaps they should ask themselves, *Is the person I'm dating the one I can help be ready for the second coming of Jesus?* Or conversely, *Is the person I'm dating the one who will help me be ready for the second coming of Jesus?* That's why Paul warns, "Don't become partners with those who reject God. How can you make a partnership out of right and wrong? That's not partnership; that's war. Is light best friends with dark? Does Christ go strolling with the Devil?" (2 Corinthians 6:14, 15, *The Message*). In other words, choose someone who will be your marriage ministry partner.

FOR DISCUSSION

1. Husbands, write down your understanding of the Bible verse that says, "Husbands, love your wives, just as Christ also loved the church" (Ephesians 5:25).
2. Wives, write down your understanding of what it means for a wife to submit to her husband (Ephesians 5:22).
3. After you have each written your answers, share them with each other.
4. What does modern culture tell us about these two statements?

5. Does your understanding (and practice) align with the Bible?

CONTRACT VERSUS COVENANT

In today's world, we are all very familiar with contracts. We enter into a contract when we buy a house or a car. We may enter into an employment contract. We usually sign on the dotted line, and the two parties must agree to certain terms before any contract becomes official. Contracts also contain an "out" clause. There are conditions that must be met and, if the terms are broken, the contract may become null and void. In other words, the contractual relationship is no longer binding.

Many view the marital relationship in this manner. It is simply a contract on paper that can easily be considered null and void. If this is the mindset, it becomes far too easy to consider the marriage relationship disposable and one that can be tossed aside for another.

Forgive us for using our sanctified imagination, but in our minds we picture God the Father walking Eve, the most beautiful, perfect bride, down a tree-lined aisle to meet Adam, her groom, and then performing the first-ever wedding ceremony. We imagine listening as the birds provide the special music, the garden provides the most beautiful backdrop, the flowers adorn the scene, and the wedding party of angels is filled with joy. F. D. Nichol further helps our imagination by describing the scene: "God Himself solemnized the first marriage. After making the woman He led her to Adam, who by that time must have awakened from his deep sleep. As Adam was the 'son of God' (Luke 3:38), so Eve could properly be called the daughter of God; and as her Father, God led her to Adam and presented her to him. The marriage covenant, therefore, is appropriately called the covenant of God (Prov. 2:17), a name implying His authorship of that sacred institution."[12]

While contracts require both parties to keep the terms of an agreement for it to remain valid, a covenant is a promise that will be kept without regard of the other party's integrity. An article from LifeWay explains the differences between a contract and a covenant this way:

1. *"Contracts are often made for a limited period of time."* If two parties come to a situation in which the conditions of the contract are not being met, the contract is considered null and void. Although they may repeat the words "till death do us part," often couples interpret those words to mean "as long as the relationship is mutually beneficial."
2. *"Contracts often deal with specific actions."* In other words, our wedding vows express our *intent* to perform certain actions. We state things such as, "I will love and cherish you," "I will stay by your side through

thick and thin," "I will be with you in sickness and in health," "We will eat plenty or starve together," "I will be exclusively yours," and "We're in this till the end."

3. *"Contracts are based on an 'If . . . , then . . . ,' mentality."* Couples that rely on the other spouse for happiness may find that this expectation is not met at times, particularly early in marriage.

4. *"Contracts are motivated by the desire to get something."* For instance, when we need a car, we sign a lease because we want to be able to drive out of the dealership's lot with it. At the same time, the salesperson signed on the dotted line because he or she wants the commission. Often in their interactions, spouses are motivated to get something.[13]

On the other hand, a covenant has different characteristics from those of a contract:

1. *"Covenants are initiated for the benefit of the other person."* Wedding vows are not a declaration of present love but a mutually binding promise of future love. In a covenant relationship, we promise to be loving, faithful, and true to the other person in the future, regardless of how we may feel at the moment or what may be going on around us at the time.

2. *"In covenant relationships people make unconditional promises."* In our wedding vows, we never state that we will do all of those things only if the other person will do likewise. We simply commit to doing our part—unconditionally.

3. *"Covenant relationships are based on steadfast love."* Steadfast love does not rely on feelings; rather, steadfast love is a decision, a choice we make.

4. *"Covenant relationships view commitments as permanent."* When we get married, we vow to stay together, not until love do us part or until the courts do us part or until we just don't want to be together any longer. Instead, we vow to stay together until death alone separates us.

5. *"Covenant relationships require confrontation and forgiveness."* As the article in LifeWay states, "These two responses are essential in a covenant marriage. Confrontation means holding the other person responsible for his or her actions. Forgiving means a willingness to lift the penalty and continue a loving, growing relationship. Ignoring the failures of your spouse isn't the road to marital growth."[14]

God's plan is for us to view marriage as a covenant relationship. There may be some characteristics of a contract within the covenant of marriage, but ultimately it is a covenant. On our wedding day, we made a holy vow that involved not only us as a couple but also Jesus Christ. It is not a vow that is easily tossed aside or discarded. "Till death do us part" was a binding promise made in the presence of our spouse, our family, our friends, and the holy angels—along with Jesus. A contract may easily be considered null and void as there may be numerous loopholes; but a covenant is forever! God's grace and mercy, when given as a gift to each other, smooth over those loopholes.

SO DIFFERENT AND YET SO ALIKE

It shouldn't come as a surprise that men and women are different. We see that every single day. During our marriage retreats, we show several cartoons and pictures to demonstrate, in a humorous way, how different men and women really are. In one of those cartoons, an older, overweight, balding man stands in front of a mirror, but the image he sees is of a much younger, fit man with a head full of hair. On the other side stands a woman, slim and shapely, who looks at her image in the mirror, and the reflection she sees staring back at her is of a woman who is much heavier. Men tend to see themselves better than they are, while women tend to see themselves worse than they are.

In general terms, men and women are different in many areas. Understanding those differences can be a big step forward in having a strong, healthy relationship (we'll talk more about this in chapters 4 and 5). Nowhere is this more important than in the area of roles and responsibilities. If you were brought up in a traditional home, you might have been taught by word and example that the role of the husband is to be the provider for the needs of the home, while the role of the wife is to take care of the day-to-day operations in the home. He is supposed to go to work (outside the home) and bring home the paycheck, while she is supposed to stay home, clean the house, cook, and take care of her husband and children. Again, this is the traditional view of marriage, one still prevalent in some cultures and families today.

On the other hand, many have been raised in a more egalitarian home environment, in which both husband and wife have education and training, both work outside the home, and both contribute to the health and well-being of the family. Today we see many other less traditional arrangements that may work well for individual couples. For instance, it is not uncommon to find a family in which the wife is the one who works outside the home and the husband is the one that stays home to take care of the family. We have also seen homes in which one or both spouses travel extensively or work away from home and are together only for a few days each week or perhaps even each month. Since this is a book on marriage, we won't take the time to talk about such other family arrangements as single parenting, grandparents raising their grandchildren, and so on. (Please see our parenting series, Help! I'm a Parent, and our book, *Grandparenting: Giving Our Grandchildren a* GRAND *View of God*. All are available on AdventistBookCenter.com, Amazon.com, or AdventSource.org in both print and electronic versions.)

So, according to the Bible, what roles do the husband and wife play in their relationship? How can they have a clear understanding of those roles? Understanding each person's role is extremely important. We need to understand two biblical principles all couples would do well to consider:

1. *Practice mutual submission.* Paul wrote to the Ephesians, "Submit to one another out of reverence for Christ" (Ephesians 5:21, NLT).
2. *Don't be selfish.* In his letter to the Philippians, Paul told them, "Do nothing from selfish ambition or conceit, but in humility count others more significant than yourselves" (Philippians 2:3, ESV).

With these two biblical principles in mind, let's look more carefully at the roles the husband and wife play in a healthy relationship.

THE HUSBAND'S ROLE

We can only truly become one if we understand our individual roles in marriage as defined by Scripture. What is the role given to husbands? Paul delineates and defines that role in his letter to the church in Ephesus, where he states, above all, "Husbands, love your wives" (Ephesians 5:25). The love that Christ had for us took Him to the cross; the love of a husband for his wife will involve a similar giving of himself. Such is the nature of true love that it is willing to sacrifice for the loved one. A husband's responsibility is to love his wife without selfishness, without reservation, and without conditions. Love her as Christ loved the church unto death (John 13:1). Love her; seek her best good; sacrifice for her benefit; give yourself to her wholeheartedly; and, when that's all done, love her some more.

But Paul also places the responsibility on the husband to be a spiritual leader of the home. Paul writes to young Pastor Timothy that one chosen to be an overseer, bishop, or deacon should, among other things, "manage his own household well" (1 Timothy 3:4, ESV). B. Reicke expounds on the word "manage" used in the New Testament Greek by explaining that it means to lead in the sense of assisting, protecting, representing, helping, or caring for those under his charge—in this case, the husband's family.[15]

Much like the husband's love for his wife should be like Christ's love for His church, the husband's leadership should also be like Christ's. What kind of leader was Jesus? We find the best example on the night before His death. Jesus and His disciples were gathered to celebrate the Passover service. The custom of the time was that as the guests arrived, and in preparation for the meal, a servant would wash the feet of all those coming into the house. Apparently, arrangements had not been made for a servant to do this, and none of Jesus' disciples took the initiative to even offer to wash His feet, much less any of the others'. But Jesus, leading by example, "put some water into a large bowl. Then he began washing his disciples' feet and drying them with the towel he was wearing" (John 13:5, CEV). The Master became the Servant. Jesus taught and exemplified servant leadership, and a husband should also lead by being willing to serve his wife and family.

To be the leader does not mean to be the ruler, the boss, or a dictator. Instead, husbands are called to influence their wives and families as they are led and influenced by Christ Himself. Ellen White explains this clearly when she writes,

> The Lord Jesus has not been correctly represented in His relation to the church by many husbands in their relation to their wives, for they do not keep the way of the Lord. They declare that their wives must be subject to them in everything. But it was not the design of God that the husband should have control, as head of the house, when he himself does not submit to Christ. He must be under the rule of Christ that he may represent the relation of Christ to the church. If he is a coarse, rough, boisterous, egotistical, harsh, and overbearing man, let him never utter the word that the husband is the head of the wife, and that she must submit to him in everything; for he is not the Lord, he is not the husband in the true significance of the term.[16]

Being the spiritual leader of the home does not mean that the husband should be the leader in every aspect of life. Each spouse has their own gifts, talents, and abilities, which benefit the couple and the family. If the wife is better at handling the finances, perhaps it would be more beneficial to the family if she did so. If the husband is better at cooking and providing healthy, nutritious meals, he should be encouraged to do so. The key is to find out what each person's strengths are and encourage them to exercise those strengths for the betterment of the family.

The role of the husband begins with loving his wife as Christ loves His church and being the spiritual leader of the home, following Jesus' example of servant leadership. But the role of the husband also encompasses being protector and provider. A husband can demand that his wife follow him, and she may feel like she must, but he will never truly have her heart unless he provides for her needs, cares for her well-being, and protects her both physically and spiritually. Paul writes, "If anyone does not provide for his own, and especially for those of his household, he has denied the faith and is worse than an unbeliever" (1 Timothy 5:8). He also tells husbands "Love your wives, and do not be harsh with them" (Colossians 3:19, ESV). The Contemporary English Version takes it even further: "[Do] not abuse her." Even the apostle Peter chimes in when he writes, "In the same way, you husbands must give honor to your wives. Treat your wife with understanding as you live together. She may be weaker than you are, but she is your equal partner in God's gift of new life. Treat her as you should so your prayers will not be hindered" (1 Peter 3:7, NLT). We don't want to miss Peter's final statement, as he seems to indicate that when a husband neglects, mistreats, or abuses his wife, his own prayer life is hindered or completely cut off.

Paul ends his words to husbands the same way he started—by reminding husbands again to "love their wives." Twice in Ephesians 5, Paul tells husbands to love their wives "as their own bodies" and as they love themselves (verses 28, 33). Loving others begins with loving and taking care of ourselves, accepting God's love for us, and becoming the conduits of His love to others. As Ellen White so beautifully states, "The husband is to be as a Saviour in his family. Will he stand in his noble, God-given manhood, ever seeking to uplift his wife and children? Will he breathe about him a pure, sweet atmosphere? Will he not as assiduously cultivate the love of Jesus, making it an abiding principle in his home, as he will assert his claims to authority?"[17]

THE WIFE'S ROLE

Wives also play a very important role. When asked about the wife's role, many immediately quote the verse, "Wives, submit to your own husbands" (Ephesians 5:22). We're often asked, "Why should a woman have to submit to her husband? Why should men have authority? Doesn't this lead to abuse?" It is true that this one Bible verse and other similar ones (Colossians 3:18; 1 Peter 3:1) have been misused repeatedly to support oppression and even abuse of women. Submitting to someone who does not fully understand their role as a husband (as stated in the previous section) is contrary to biblical teaching, and it can be dangerous and perhaps even deadly. Fulfilling our roles in the context of marriage happens only as a wife submits to someone who is leading and loving in the same manner as Christ loved the church.

If we're going to think properly about submission within marriage, we need to think about it within the context of the sacrificial love of Jesus. After all, most would have no problem submitting to someone who loved, led, and served like Jesus. We encourage you to read all of chapter 17 of Ellen G White's *The Adventist Home*, as it is a very clear, descriptive, and balanced presentation on Ephesians 5. Here's a sample of her instructions:

The question is often asked, "Shall a wife have no will of her own?" The Bible plainly states that the husband is the head of the family. "Wives, submit yourselves unto your own husbands." If this injunction ended here, we might say that the position of the wife is not an enviable one; it is a very hard and trying position in very many cases, and it would be better were there fewer marriages. Many husbands stop at the words, "Wives, submit yourselves," but we will read the conclusion of the same injunction, which is. "As it is fit in the Lord."

God requires that the wife shall keep the fear and glory of God ever before her. Entire submission is to be made only to the Lord Jesus Christ, who has purchased her as His own child by the infinite price of His life. God has given her a conscience, which she cannot violate with impunity. Her individuality cannot be merged into that of her husband, for she is the purchase of Christ. It is a mistake to imagine that with blind devotion she is to do exactly as her husband says in all things, when she knows that in so doing, injury would be worked for her body and her spirit, which have been ransomed from the slavery of Satan. There is One who stands higher than the husband to the wife; it is her Redeemer, and her submission to her husband is to be rendered as God has directed—"as it is fit in the Lord."[18]

What if the husband demands submission from his wife? What if he goes on to quote the passages we mentioned? Should she simply quietly obey as if she had no will of her own? White states, "When husbands require the complete subjection of their wives, declaring that women have no voice or will in the family, but must render entire submission, they place their wives in a position contrary to the Scripture. In interpreting the Scripture in this way, they do violence to the design of the marriage institution. This interpretation is made simply that they may exercise arbitrary rule, which is not their prerogative."[19]

The challenge in marriage isn't headship or submission; rather, it's loving God and allowing God's love to transform our homes. Like Christ loved the church, the husband must love and sacrifice for his bride. Like Christ submits to the Father, the wife must submit to her husband. If we are to fulfill the biblical mandate, then both husband and wife will reflect Jesus in their marriage. This kind of mutual, Christlike love provides dignity, honor, and respect for both the husband and the wife.

DEVELOPING YOUR MARRIAGE MISSION STATEMENT

Imagine the impact if everyone who visited your home were to see a marriage mission statement in the entryway. Using all the information in this chapter, we invite you, as husband and wife, to write your own marriage mission statement, frame it, and hang it in your home to serve as a constant reminder. Perhaps you have been part of a group that has developed mission statements for an organization, or maybe this is your first opportunity to engage in the process. Regardless, here are a few ideas—a few borrowed from Dr. Kim Blackham—to help you in the process of developing your own marriage mission statement as a couple:

1. *Set aside a dedicated time.* On the topic of creating marriage mission statements, Dr. Kim Blackham recommends, "Make it a special occasion. You may want to do this over a vacation week or a special getaway. . . . Make it deliberate and intentional." Don't try to squeeze it into an already packed day. Set aside time when this is the only item on your agenda.

2. *Bathe the process in prayer.* Even before the time you have set aside arrives, pray for the process. Pray for wisdom, a listening ear, and an open heart and mind as you write this together.

3. *Identify your marriage legacy.* "What marriage legacy do you want to leave?" asks Blackham. This question will help you zoom in on what's important to you both.

4. *Identify your shared core values.* Blackham offers a series of good questions to consider as you list your core values as a couple: "What matters most to you? What kind of spouse do you want to be? How do you want to resolve conflict? How do you want to treat each other? How do you want your partner to feel because of you? What traditions do you want as part of your family? What do you want your children to learn about relationships by watching you?"

5. *Use short phrases.* Blackham recommends utilizing short phrases such as "To . . . (do something)," "In such a way that (how and in which manner)," and "So that . . . (we gain these results or benefits)."

6. *Write the mission statement.* Be concise. Blackham says the statement should be no more than ten sentences. Continue to rework it until you both are happy. This may take some time, so keep at it and, above all, listen to each other.

7. *Hang the mission statement where you can see it easily.* "So many people write out their mission statement and then tuck it in a drawer and forget about it," says Blackham. "Put yours in a prominent place in your home where you will see it often."

8. *Refer to the mission statement daily.* Blackham notes that "your marriage mission statement should impact your actions on a daily basis. These aren't just good ideas to hang on the wall. These are the core values and

principles that you want to guide your life. Use it!"

9. *Revise the mission statement when necessary.* "Life circumstances change. You get older and wiser. You will learn from your mistakes," Blackham states. She says that it's OK for your marriage mission statement to change too. Marriage is a relationship that needs daily nurturing, so consider it a work in progress—for a lifetime.

10. *Memorize the mission statement.* "This is the reason you want it concise," advises Blackham. "Memorizing your mission statement makes a huge difference! Those words will come back to your mind in moments when you need them most." Commit it to memory and repeat your marriage mission statement together on a daily basis.[20]

COUPLE'S ACTIVITY

1. Dedicate a significant block of time to developing your personal marriage mission statement together.
2. Use the preceding ten steps and all the material you have read in this chapter to assist you.
3. Frame the mission statement and place it in an area of your home where you can view and read it daily.
4. Memorize it, review it frequently, and feel free to change it as needed.

CONCLUSION

God intends that we come together with our wonderful diversity and form a powerful oneness in marriage. Four times we find these words in the Bible: "A man shall leave his father and mother and be joined to his wife, and they shall become one flesh" (Genesis 2:24; see also Matthew 19:5; Mark 10:8; Ephesians 5:31). It is as if God does not want us to miss the point.

In 1 Corinthians 12 and 14, Paul describes the body of Christ as being one but being made up of many individual parts; each is unique in its own function. It is one body with wonderful diversity. A marriage is a team of allies working toward a common goal. Their unity does not generate uniformity; it powerfully creates oneness in the midst of diversity.

Two can become one only as we make Jesus the center of our lives and homes, we become more concerned about the welfare and happiness of each other, and we make it our goal to help each other to be ready for heaven.

Anything that is of value takes dedication to maintain. Be intentional about making your marriage all that God intended, set aside time each day to spend together, don't get discouraged about the rough spots that you encounter, and pray together about your failings and disappointments, as these are opportunities to experience some of the greatest growth.

Marriage is a holy covenant that is not easily broken or discarded, and it looks beyond life here on this earth. May each day bring you closer and closer together as you realize that two have become one, with Jesus binding you together.

Should I remain married to my spouse even though he or she has been unfaithful and therefore rendered the marriage covenant null and void?
The Bible does not dictate that the spouse of someone who has committed the sin of adultery against God and against their own spouse must remain married to them or seek a divorce from them. What Jesus stated are the conditions upon which adultery may be accepted as a reason for a person to choose to divorce their spouse: "And I say to you: whoever divorces his wife, except for sexual immorality, and marries another, commits adultery" (Matthew 19:9, ESV). We want you to notice several things in this text and the greater context.

- *"For any cause?"* Jesus was responding to a question posed to Him by the Pharisees as a test: "Is it lawful to divorce one's wife for any cause?" (Matthew 19:3, ESV). The Pharisees were specifically referring to Moses' teaching in Deuteronomy 24:1. Two rabbinic schools interpreted that passage to allow for divorce. One of them, the school of Hillel, taught that divorce should be allowed for any reason. Similar to this reasoning, today, some places allow a couple to divorce without placing blame on either party and, therefore, refer to it as a "no-fault divorce." On the other hand, the school of Shammai allowed for divorce only in cases where adultery had taken place. In His response, Jesus seemed to have sided with the school of Shammai. However, while Jesus confirmed that adultery would allow the innocent party to seek a divorce, He did not prescribe or dictate that divorce had to take place. We have known many couples who have suffered through this experience, many repeatedly, and yet have chosen to remain married, have rebuilt the broken trust and promises in their relationship, and have recommitted to their relationship. Adultery does not have to be the end of a marriage. What these couples have found is the gift of healing that comes from forgiveness (more on this on chapter 11).

- *The result to both parties.* Now, Jesus takes it one step further by stating that if the person who committed adultery divorces their spouse and marries someone else, they are still living in sin. Furthermore, the person they marry is also guilty of adultery. Not only that but earlier, in Matthew 5:32, we find that Jesus also states that the person at fault is also guilty of causing their former partner, and the person they may choose to marry, to commit adultery. For Jesus, divorce is so serious that even the disciples exclaimed, "If such is the case of a man with his wife, it is better not to marry" (Matthew 19:10, ESV). In other words, getting a divorce is way too difficult. It would be better to not get married at all! The Israelites, like many today, wanted to have an out in case things didn't work out in marriage; but that was never God's plan.

The bottom line is that while the Bible provides a reason for which divorce may be an acceptable course to take, it does not dictate that such a decision must be made. For the sake of the couple, the children, and the family, forgiveness and a recommitment to the marriage vows is a better choice.

1. F. D. Nichol, ed., *The Seventh-day Adventist Bible Commentary*, vol. 1, *Genesis to Deuteronomy* (Washington, DC: Review and Herald®, 1978), 226.

2. A. Berlin and M. Z. Brettler, eds., *The Jewish Study Bible* (New York: Oxford University Press, 2004), 16.

3. Matthew Henry, *Matthew Henry's Commentary on the Whole Bible: Complete and Unabridged in One Volume* (Peabody, MA: Hendrickson Publishers, 1994), 10.

4. Nichol, *SDA Bible Commentary*, 1:226.

5. Mignon McLaughlin, *The Complete Neurotic's Notebook* (Secaucus, NJ: Castle Books, 1981), 105.

6. Erik Jones, "Two Become One," *Daily Bible Verse Blog*, LifeHopeandTruth, accessed July 31, 2020, https://lifehopeandtruth.com/bible/blog/two-become-one/.

7. Mike Fox and Trisha Fox, "The Two Shall Become One," ChristianPost.com, January 26, 2012, https://dev.christianpost.com/news/the-two-shall-become-one.html.

8. Zig Ziglar, *Courtship After Marriage* (Nashville: Thomas Nelson, 1990), 80.

9. Perry Tanksley, "Marriage Takes Three," quoted on The Idea Door, accessed July 15, 2020, https://www.theideadoor.com/other-pages/stories-poems-quotes/marriage-quotes-and-stories-2/marriage-takes-three/.

10. Timothy Keller, *The Meaning of Marriage* (East Rutherford, NJ: Penguin Books, 2013).

11. Gary Thomas, *Sacred Marriage* (Grand Rapids, MI: Zondervan, 2015), 11.

12. Nichol, *SDA Bible Commentary*, 1:226.

13. "Marriage: Covenant or Contract" LifeWay, January 1, 2014, https://www.lifeway.com/en/articles/homelife-marriage-covenant-or-contract.

14. "Marriage: Covenant or Contract."

15. B. Reicke, "προΐστημι," in *Theological Dictionary of the New Testament*, vol. 6, eds., G. Kittel, G. W. Bromiley, and G. Friedrich, Logos electronic ed. (Grand Rapids, MI: Eerdmans, 1964), 700, 701.

16. Ellen G. White, *The Adventist Home* (Hagerstown, MD: Review and Herald®, 1952), 117.

17. White, *Adventist Home*, 117.

18. White, 115, 116.

19. White, 116.

20. Kim Blackham, "Writing Your Marriage Mission Statement," Dr. Kim Blackham, accessed July 31, 2020, https://drkimblackham.com/marriage-mission-statement/.

Chapter Two

Back to the Basics

Be devoted to one another in love. Honor one another above yourselves.
—Romans 12:10, NIV

Have you ever thought that perhaps life is too confusing or complicated today? We find ourselves running hither and yon. And, with easy access to modern technology, you never actually leave the office anymore. Work is as close as your cell phone, and the constant busyness of life pushes out the fundamentals of having a lasting marriage. As we attempt to strengthen our marriages, we need to begin by reminding ourselves of some very simple, basic concepts and ideas that could impact the quality as well as the quantity in years of our lives together as husband and wife. Maybe it's time we get back to the very basics, the foundation upon which to build a strong, lasting marriage.

MARRIAGE IS . . .
Perhaps we need to begin by tackling some erroneous ideas and misconceptions about marriage. Actress Mae West is credited as saying, "Marriage is a fine institution, but I'm not ready for an institution."[1] We laugh about her play on words, but perhaps she had a point. If we feel we are going to be confined or strapped to someone for life as one would be to an straitjacket, why would we choose such a life? If, on the other hand, we look to marriage as a source of ever-growing enjoyment, satisfaction, and emotional and spiritual connection, why wouldn't we want to be part of it? Through the years, we have heard some interesting statements about what marriage is and is not. Let's look at just a few of the things we often misunderstand about marriage:

Marriage is hard work
United States president Theodore Roosevelt made the statement, "Nothing in this world is worth having or worth doing unless it means effort, pain, difficulty."[2] But who wants to hear that making a marriage successful will demand a lot of hard, painful, difficult work? We see couples around us that look naturally

happy and contented, not carrying the tremendous burden of hard work. But we know that by "hard work," what people mean is that it is not as easy as it looks in movies or fairytales. We work hard to manage conflict, to make decisions, to face challenges. We work and save and pay off and plan for our future together—those things don't happen automatically. We work hard at raising a family; spending time together; providing for the physical, emotional, and spiritual needs of our children; vacationing, and enjoying the holidays together.

A closely related idea is that marriage naturally and automatically makes you closer as a couple. Instead of working hard at marriage, this thought says the opposite is true: you don't have to work at all to make your marriage good. Perhaps instead of saying that marriage is hard work or that we don't need to do anything to make it good, what we need to realize is that we must be intentional at making our marriage healthy, strong, and successful. It is not a happenstance. People don't just get lucky.

Marriage takes time. In our fast-paced, hurry-up, get-it-done-now society, we often expect that from day one we will adapt to each other's lifestyle seamlessly and quickly. Even if we have our first minor disagreement shortly after the wedding, as surprised and disappointed as we may be, we expect that it will be the last one. We need to keep in mind that everything in marriage does not have to be resolved in the first month, perhaps not even the first year. There are some things that are important to resolve early on, but there are other issues and difficulties that will need to be worked on throughout your marriage. Don't worry. Remember, you have a lifetime together. You don't have to rush. And the reality is that some things that seem important when you're twenty-five years old won't mean as much when you are fifty years old.

How do you know what those important things are? The simple answer is that you will learn what they are as you live life together. As you live life, you'll learn more about what's most important to you and your spouse. Think of your marriage as a fruit tree. Only time and patience can make the fruit sweet to the taste and pleasant to enjoy. If you pick the fruit before it's ready, it just hasn't had enough time to be at its best. When you nurture your marriage, it will get better with time, and it's never too late to start doing the things that need to be done to ripen your relationship.

Marriage is daily experiencing your wedding day
This is a very idealistic statement. We had a wonderful wedding! A beautiful bride and a handsome groom (if we may say so ourselves), family, friends, music, photos, food, and hardly any expense (many of the elements in our wedding were donated by church members and friends). But the wedding also involved nervousness, some delays, being tired at the end of the day, and even a few dis-

appointments. Who wants to go through it over and over again?

In the movie *Groundhog Day*, Phil Connors is a TV weatherman who thinks that his current job at a local Pittsburgh station is a waste of his talent. Connors is not happy when his bosses send him off to the small town of Punxsutawney, Pennsylvania, to cover the annual Groundhog Day festivities. Phil manages to get through the day by doing the bare minimum to perform his job. But when he tries to head home, a blizzard keeps him in Punxsutawney. Angry and frustrated, Phil spends the night in the small-town hotel, but when he wakes up the next day, he realizes he has to live Groundhog Day all over again, and again, and again, and again to the point of insanity. Occasionally we may wish we could relive one moment or one day of our lives—but perhaps not over and over again ad infinitum.

The truth is that if you get stuck on that one day, you will fail to miss all the other days. And, after being together for more than forty years, we can testify to the fact that we love each other more today than we did on our wedding day. Don't rob yourself of growing together as the years tick by.

Marriage is the killer of your social life
Some people think that once they are married (since they promise to love their spouse exclusively), their social life will come to a screeching halt. While it is true that you will not be looking to have intimate relationships with other people and that you will not place time with others above time with your spouse, it does not mean you can't have friends and that all you will do is stay home with your spouse all day, every day.

Depending on your personality type (extrovert or introvert), you may feel the need to have lots of people around or very few people around. A healthy couple develops friendships with other couples they can spend quality time with. These are friends who can help your during the challenges and difficulties of life and people with whom you can let your hair down, relax, and have good, clean fun. But each spouse may also have friends with whom they enjoy spending time alone. Some ladies have a friend or friends with whom they enjoy shopping, going to the spa, or just sitting and enjoying a hot drink and good conversation. Some guys enjoy having a friend or friends with whom they can go to the gym, play golf, or watch a baseball game. However, it is important to note that no other relationship outside of marriage should take more time, attention, or effort than your own marriage relationship, nor should it interfere with your marriage. As long as proper boundaries and priorities are maintained, other friendships may prove very positive to you as a couple.

Either marriage is perfect or it is a failure
We often have an idealistic view of marriage based on limited knowledge of

someone else's. Often, at our couples' retreats, we hear comments about our marriage from the perspective of others. People tell us, "You guys have such an awesome relationship," "I wish our marriage was like yours," "You have the perfect marriage." While we thank them for their kind comments, we are quick to remind them that what they see is our public image and that we have our share of pain, problems, and shame. In our presentations and as we have tried to do in this book, we are vulnerable in our storytelling. We are just like everybody else—flawed, far from perfect, and extremely finite. However, we're happy to say that we do have a good marriage. Our flaws don't make our relationship a failure or determine our future. Again, we work hard at growing, changing, adapting, apologizing, and forgiving. Thirty-eight years of marriage proves that two imperfect people can still have a good, enjoyable, happy, and fun-filled relationship.

Marriage is ugly

A post has been circulating on social networks for several years. We didn't like the first few words; however, as we read on, we discovered that it paints a realistic view of the journey of married life:

> Marriage is ugly, you see the absolute worst in someone. You see them when they're mad, sad, being stubborn, when they're so unlovable they make you scream. But you also get to see them when they are laughing so hard that tears run down their face, and they can't help but let out those weird gargling noises.
>
> You see them at 3:00 A.M. when the world is asleep except for you two and you're eating in the middle of the kitchen floor. You get to see the side of them that no one else does, and it's not always pretty. It's snorting while laughing; it's the tears when it feels like it's all crashing down, it's the passing gas, it's the bedhead and bad breath, it's the random shouts of joy, it's the anger and the pleasure.
>
> Marriage isn't a beautiful thing, but it is amazing. It's knowing that someone loves you so much and won't leave you even though you said something nasty. It's having someone have your back no matter what. It's fights over stupid things like someone not doing the dishes or picking up after themselves. And it's those nights you fall asleep in the other's arms, feeling like there will never be enough time with them. It's cleaning up their throw-up, or just rubbing their back when they're sick. It's the dirtiest, hardest, most rewarding job there is.
>
> Because at the end of the day, you get to crawl into bed with your best friend, the weirdest, most annoying, loving, goofy, perfect person that you know. Marriage is not beautiful, but it's one amazing ride.[3]

While it is true that marriage is not always a bed of roses; the calm, blue waters of the ocean; or a beautiful, sunshiny day, describing it as ugly only creates fear and dissatisfaction. It is truly during the ugly moments of vomiting and sickness that the beauty of marriage shines through. Beauty in marriage is learning to manage conflict and struggling together to find a workable solution. It is being angry for the right reasons but not lashing out at the other because you are angry. Yes, marriage is indeed one amazing ride!

MARRIAGE IS NOT . . .

As we consider some of what marriage is, we'd like to think about what marriage is not.

Marriage is not rocket science

You don't need an advanced degree in the social sciences to make a marriage work. The principles it's based on are quite simple, commonsense, easy to learn, and easy to put into practice. They begin by performing acts of kindness, being respectful, and remaining loyal. Many of us learned some of these principles as we were growing up—we watched our parents speaking respectfully to each other, holding each other during times of sadness and during times of joy, and remaining committed to their marriage until death separated them from each other.

Marriage is not self-sustaining

Marriage does not thrive on its own. It needs to be nourished daily, carefully, and intentionally. One of the mistakes a lot of couples make is caring for their children and neglecting their spouse. For more than thirty years, studies have shown that having children affects a marriage negatively. An article on the *Fortune* website explains that when "comparing couples with and without children, researchers found that the rate of decline in relationship satisfaction is nearly twice as steep for couples who have children than for childless couples. In the event that a pregnancy is unplanned, the parents experience even greater negative impacts on their relationship."[4] In addition, the decrease in marital satisfaction will likely lead to a change in general satisfaction because the biggest predictor of overall life satisfaction is whether we are satisfied with our spouse. What's also interesting, as the article points out, is that as marriage satisfaction declines, so does the likelihood of divorce.

Part of the problem lies in the fact that children, particularly newborns, need and demand so much attention from their parents. But if all of your focus is on the kids, you are making a costly mistake. Please understand that we are not suggesting you neglect the care of your children in order to have a strong marriage. What we are suggesting, however, is that you find ways to strengthen your marriage even while you take care of your children. Your children will reap the benefits and will react more positively to your healthy relationship than if you neglect it to devote your time exclusively to their care.

Many young couples think that having children will bring them closer together (or at least will not lead to marital distress). We have talked to many couples who are having marital difficulties and yet are considering having children with the mistaken idea that having children will help them solve their problems. "Having children will take the focus off of us and toward them," we were once told. It was only when that couple had children and underwent the additional stress the kids brought with their birth or adoption that the husband and wife understood what we had tried to warn them about. Of course, instead of accepting that our advice had been correct, they began to play the blame game. "My husband doesn't help with the baby," or, "My wife doesn't want to have sex with me like she used to."

We'll say it again: kids are wonderful! We love our daughters, and they have surely enriched our life and our marriage. But having kids doesn't improve a marriage. Instead, having kids will test your marriage's patience and level of commitment in a way that only parenting can. Learning how to have a marriage with kids will improve a marriage—but only if a couple welcomes the challenges of having a family. Once children arrive, letting them get between the relationship you have with your spouse will hurt intimacy.

The bottom line is this: do all in your power to nourish your relationship. Be even more intentional about doing so after the children are born or adopted. Neglecting your marriage in order to care for the children will ultimately hurt both. As we have often said in our couples' retreats, sermons, seminars, and writing, the best gift you can give your children is your marriage. Some have tried to tell us that the best gift we can give our children is faith in God, but we suggest that it is through a healthy marriage that we teach them about a loving God. Children can learn more about God in a healthy home environment than they can in a home where conflict, abuse, or hatred reign.

Marriage is not boring

Two lives woven together can be very exciting! There's something about watching someone very different from you and yet so much like you living their life in a very different way. Pamela and I have had a life that is far from boring. We have lost our parents, grandparents, some siblings, and friends. But we have also had the joy and satisfaction of moving together through our parallel educational pursuits, we have seen our daughters get their degrees, get their jobs, marry our awesome sons-in-law, buy houses and cars, and get a dog . . . or two

... or three. Well, all right, the last part has not been the most exciting for us—but we have even learned to care for those four-legged creatures who bring so much joy to our girls.

We have traveled together, visited some amazing places, met some fantastic people—and the best part is that we have enjoyed it all together. Marriage is not boring at all when you aim to keep it interesting. But we guarantee that even if you don't try, marriage will be anything but boring.

Marriage is not without conflict

This may be a shocking statement to hear, particularly for young unmarried couples. The fact is that conflict is present in every relationship. We're not talking about angry insults, shouting matches, or ongoing abusive language or actions. According to an article from the Gottman Institute, "conflict is a normal and natural part of your 'happily ever after.' "[5] In fact, conflict in marriage is inevitable. The key to a healthy marriage is knowing how to disagree and work through anger and disappointment. The article quotes psychologist and marriage expert Dr. John Gottman:

> Although we tend to equate a low level of conflict with happiness, a lasting relationship results from a couple's ability to manage the conflicts that are inevitable in any relationship. . . .
>
> It's a myth that if you solve your problems you'll automatically be happy.[6]

Instead, we need to learn that some couples may never solve all of their problems, yet they still have a very loving, satisfying relationship. (Read more about conflict management in chapter 7.)

CARING LOVE VERSUS ROMANTIC LOVE

In the introduction, we mentioned that during our tenth year of marriage, we were facing some bumps in the road. During this time, we were introduced to a great book, *His Needs, Her Needs*, written by the Christian psychologist and marriage counselor Willard Harley. As we read through that book every evening during our couple's devotional time, something began to change in our relationship. We will share some of Harley's ideas and concepts throughout this book, but we recommend you read his book for yourselves—as well as his companion book, *Love Busters*.

Harley helped us understand that, in general terms, there are two types of love in a relationship. Those two types of love are (1) romantic love and (2) caring love.

Romantic love is really defined by one key word: *feeling!* It is based on feeling an incredible, unstoppable, and at times indescribable attraction for another person. We frequently make mention of the "starstruck lover." They have met the love of their life, and the feeling of love is in the very air they breathe. They may feel so in love with the other person that they have butterflies in their stomach every time they think of the other person. Sometimes we tell those people that what they feel in the pit of their stomach may not be love but indigestion.

We found a typical portrayal of romantic love in a letter that a young teenage boy sent to a girl he liked. On a piece of notebook paper, with somewhat shaky handwriting and grammar and spelling mistakes, he wrote this to her: "Dear Ashley, would you please be my girlfreind [girlfriend] I like you a lot!"

He then gave her three choices: *yes, no,* or *maybe.* Then he explained on the postscript: "PS. Please circle YES NO or MAYBE."

On the same sheet of paper, Ashley responded with a few grammar and spelling mistakes of her own: "I'm sorry I already have a boyfriend named Kyle. But, when we brake [break] up your [you're] my next choice."

She, too, had a postscript: "PS. That will probably be in a month or two."

Once the romantic feelings left, which Ashley recognized would happen in a month or two, she could move on to the next person that made her feel loved and special and for whom she could have those feelings of attraction and "love." The chances are that the young man probably also moved on to the next girl that responded to him and whom he "loved."

Romantic love is what many movies are made of. What people refer to as "chick flicks" are usually sappy, romantic movies in which boy meets girl, they fall in love, they have fun and laugh together, they get married, and the tears roll down the audience's cheeks when one breaks up with the other, leaves, or dies in some tragic way. It's all about the feelings of euphoria and excitement, the heights of desire and passion, and the rush of happiness and joy. Everything is perfectly choreographed to elicit such feelings from the audience. The light, the music, the camera angle, the weather . . . everything is done to manipulate the audience's emotional reaction.

Unfortunately, many fail to understand that the producers, the directors, and the actors want to evoke such feelings in you so you will come see their movie (and the sequel). And many walk away from these movies wanting and wishing for a similar experience in their own lives. Tony Campolo, the well-known Baptist preacher and sociologist, explains, "The first problem with romance is that it is not very stable. A normal person has at least six romantic experiences prior to marriage." He then adds, "Once you are married, romance often shows signs of rapid decline."[7] No wonder so many divorces take place during the first five years of marriage. As the couple's romantic feelings plummet and their conflict increases, they find themselves disillusioned with their marriage, unhappy with their spouse, trapped in a loveless relationship, and with no hope for ever being happy again. They fly the coop as soon as they can, looking for the next person to bring romance back into their lives, often repeating the same sad cycle again and again.

What happens when those romantic feelings begin to go away? Feelings are not a safe bet on which to base any decision, much less a decision as important as marriage. Chart your own feelings and you will see that they fluctuate from day to day. There are those days that you feel deeply in love with your spouse, and then there are those days when he or she gets on your last nerve. When couples depend on romantic love (or feelings) for their happiness, they will be on a roller coaster of emotions. What often happens is that when the butterflies in their stomach learn to fly in formation and away from the stomach, the person chooses to fly out of the cocoon and into the arms of somebody else who makes them feel the fluttering butterflies in their stomach again.

On the other hand, there is another vital form of love in marriage, which Dr. Harley describes as caring love.[8] Unlike romantic love, caring love is not based on feelings. Rather, it is based on a decision. In other words, I make a conscious decision to love you, knowing full well that we will go through good days and bad days. There will be ups in our relationships as well as downs. We will disappoint each other, and we will not always be in full agreement. And yes, the feelings may even go up and down, but I am committed to loving you.

Remember that covenant relationship we discussed in the previous chapter? That is what we are talking about here. Caring love acknowledges that covenant relationship. It acknowledges those times of feeling so in love as well as those times of disagreement and conflict that will enter our homes. Our marriage vows are not based on how we may be feeling at any particular moment; rather, they are based on a decision. Depending on which vows you may have repeated on your wedding day, in general terms, we vow to take the other person

> from this day forward;
> for better or worse;
> for richer or poorer;
> in sickness and in health;
> till death do us part;
> forsaking all others;
> to love and honor you all the days of your life.

The only feeling expressed in most of the marriage vows, depending on which religious tradition they may be from, is to love. But as we stated before, it is important to understand that true love between a husband and wife as God intended is not a feeling but a decision. We decide that from this moment on, through thick and thin, whether we have a lot of money or no money, whether we are perfectly healthy or sick as a dog, we will have an exclusive relationship, and we will be respectful, kind, and loving as long as life shall last.

In a recent sermon series at our home church, our pastor, Tim Madding, defined love as "seeking the best interest of another, even to one's own detriment or hurt." Love is so much more than a feeling, more than just having butterflies in your stomach when you're with the other person, melting in their presence, or going crazy for them. It is a decision to do the best for them, to meet their most important needs, and to do all in your power to keep them from being hurt or from hurting them. Author and journalist Mignon McLaughlin said it nicely when she wrote, "A successful marriage requires falling in love many times, always with the same person."[9]

GIVE AND TAKE

You may remember seeing commercials on television in which a person is trying to make a decision, one that would carry with it lasting and perhaps negative consequences. Should he quit his job and go to the beach? Should she eat that large piece of chocolate cake? They seem puzzled, confused, and anxious as they try to make decisions by comparing their wishes and desires with all the possible outcomes of their choice.

Sitting on the person's right shoulder is a little, white imaginary angel with wings and a halo telling them not to make the choice: "Don't do it. You need that job to support the family. Vacation time will come later." "Chocolate cake? You've been working hard to lose weight—think of how tight your pants will feel afterward."

Sitting on the other shoulder is a little, red imaginary devil with horns, a goatee, and a tail, who is holding a pitchfork and, with a smirk on his face, tells person, "Oh come on, go ahead. Do it. Quit your job and get the rest you deserve," or, "Eat it. Chocolate is your favorite. It won't hurt you."

We don't have good and bad angels sitting on our shoulders trying to tell us what to do, but we do struggle with two very distinct desires in our life. It is like having two battling personalities, each trying to get us to follow them. One side of our mind or personality is our kind, generous side. It is the side that wants to do what's best for the other, what makes them happy. That side rejoices to see the other person happy, even if it means that side of ourselves is not happy. That side is unselfish and always happy to give because joy and fulfillment come from seeing the other person happy.

Think back to your dating years or the first year of your marriage. If you are like most couples, that time usually found you more willing to give than to take. You constantly found yourself doing all the little things that made your mate happy. Perhaps you cooked the meals your loved one liked best, wore the outfits that were their favorite for special outings, or willingly sacrificed many of your own desires because you knew it would make them happy. Giving was not a burden but a joy to you. Paul appeals to this side of our personality when he writes, "Let nothing be done through selfish ambition or conceit, but in lowliness of mind let each esteem others better than himself" (Philippians 2:3).

The other side of your personality tends to be more self-centered. It wants you to do what feels good to you, what makes you happy, even if it makes the other person not so happy. When dating couples feel this way individually, they are often in conflict, in a tug-of-war to get their way, until one begrudgingly gives in or the partners simply go their separate ways. In the case of married couples, it's a little different. After a few years of marriage and perhaps even the births of a few children, you may have found that you are tired of all the giving. It seems to you as if you're always giving in, always pleasing the other, always doing everything to make them happy and never receiving anything in return. Why is it that you have to be the one to give all the time? Don't you deserve to have some of your own wants and desires met? Isn't it time that you were on the receiving end for once? Paul wrote about this side when he said that "it is from within, from the human heart, that evil intentions come" (Mark 7:21, NRSV).

Christian psychologist Willard Harley refers to these two battling sides of our personality as the Giver and the Taker. As he explains, the Giver is the side of your personality that tells you to do whatever you can to make the other person happy and avoid anything that makes them unhappy, even if it makes *you* unhappy. The Taker, on the other hand, is the side of your personality that tells you to do whatever you can to make *you* happy and avoid anything that makes you unhappy, even if it makes others unhappy.[10]

Successful marriages are filled with moments of give and take with both partners giving and receiving. Although Paul was a theologian, quite often he sounded more like a marriage counselor and teacher. He wrote to the Ephesians, "Submit to one another out of reverence for Christ" (Ephesians 5:20, NLT). Submitting to one another involves mutual giving and receiving. In his farewell sermon to the members of this same church, Paul told them, "By everything I did, I showed how you should work to help everyone who is weak. Remember that our Lord Jesus said, 'More blessings come from giving than from receiving' " (Acts 20:35, CEV). God is guided by the principle of giving: "For this is how God loved the world: He gave his one and only Son, so that everyone who believes in him will not perish but have eternal life" (John 3:16, NLT). Again, Paul writes to the church members in Ephesus, "Be imitators of God as dear children. And walk in love, as Christ also has loved us and given Himself for us, an offering and a sacrifice to God for a sweet-smelling aroma" (Ephesians 5:1, 2).

STATES OF MIND IN MARRIAGE

According to Harley, couples find themselves in what he calls the "three states of mind in marriage."[11] As each state is discussed, try to discover at which state (or phase) you currently find yourselves.

The first state of mind: Intimacy

This is the premarital or newlywed state that we sometimes call the honeymoon stage, and it is the stage dominated by the giving side of your personality. You both seek to make the other person happy. You feel such incredible love toward the other person, and you truly feel like two have become one. Here are some other defining characteristics:

- Each person finds themselves giving and sacrificing for the happiness of each other.
- Conversation is respectful and nonjudgmental.

We smile understandingly when we see couples nearing the time of their wedding or shortly after that. They hold hands, even when they're eating; look into each other's eyes, lost in thought; hold each other; and don't want to let them go, even if they have to go to the restroom. These couples are so much in love that they find it difficult to make some simple decisions, such as where to go out to eat.

He will ask her, "Where would you like to go?"

She lovingly responds with a sweet smile, "I don't care. Where do you want to go?"

And they go back and forth like that for a while, even if they're starving and would be happy with a cold taco, but they're unable to make a decision because they don't want to be—or even appear to be—selfish. All they want to do is make the other person happy.

In the state of intimacy, each person is not only doing all they can to meet the other person's most important emotional needs (we'll discuss more about emotional needs in chapters 4 and 5) but they are also trying not to cause the other person any unhappiness.

The second state of mind: Conflict

While the giving side of your personality dominates the stage of intimacy, the stage of conflict is dominated by the taking, selfish side of your personality. You start to think it's fine to give sometimes but not all the time. You wonder, *When do I start to receive, when do I get my share, when do I get to decide what I want even if my partner is not happy about it?* The words that used to be loving, sweet, and kind have turned angry, sour, and harsh.

There is a myth that conflict should never occur in a marriage. *After all, if I really love them and they really love me, what is there to have conflict over?* The reality is that if two people live in the same house together, sooner or later, they will disagree over something. The true question has never been *if* you will have a conflict but, rather, *how* you will handle that conflict when it comes your way. You can still have an intimate relationship and have occasional conflict. In this state of mind, however, conflict has become an ongoing, daily struggle and has crossed the line from normal into an unhealthy situation. Here are some characteristics that signal it is unhealthy:

- *Conflict* becomes a word to describe the entire home environment.
- Home is more like a battlefield.
- The couple fights about the same thing today that they fought about yesterday.
- The couple can't seem to find a resolution that both mates can agree on.

Do you remember that loving couple who couldn't decide where to go out to eat? Well, in this stage, they still can't, but the reasons are different.

He asks her, "Where would you like to eat?"

She responds, "Oh, I don't care. You decide."

So, he says, "OK, let's go get pizza."

She then says, "Oh no, not pizza—I'll gain weight."

"Alright, then," he says, "where would you like to eat?"

She states the obvious, "I don't care, you decide."

"How about Chinese?" he says, starting to salivate.

Of course, she responds, "Not Chinese. I don't feel like it tonight."

With his blood pressure rising because he's been over this territory before, he asks, "So where would you like to eat?"

Again she responds with a deceptive smile, "I don't care, you choose."

With pangs of hunger in his stomach, he pleads, "Mexican?"

"No," she says, "it makes me feel bloated."

One more time, he begs, "Then *where* would you like to eat?"

She shrugs her shoulders and tells him, "Anywhere's fine—you decide."

He finally decides to stay home and make himself a peanut butter and jelly sandwich—at which point she cries out, "We never go out anymore."

Every person can identify with this scenario at least once in their married life.

Conflict will come at some point. We hope the conflict will not end in loud arguments, personal attacks, or hurtful reprimands. But when the taking, selfish side of your personality raises its ugly head, it will do all it can to make you happy even if it makes the other person unhappy. In the state of conflict, the individuals are still trying to meet the other person's most important emotional needs, but now they are not as concerned and may indeed be *causing* the other person unhappiness.

While conflict and differing opinions are normal in any relationship, unresolved conflict creates a real problem when you fight about the same thing today that you fought about yesterday. In fact, some couples could save valuable time and record the conversation. Then, when they walk in the door the next day after work, they could play the recording because their argument will only be a repeat. The yelling will ensue, the arguments will be made again, and the ending will be the same—no resolution! Day after day of this scene repeating itself will lead to the next phase.

The third state of mind: Withdrawal

After seemingly unending conflict, many couples reach the place where they stop caring. They stop caring for the other person and they stop caring about their relationship. Some simply walk away from their marriage and get a divorce; or, as some news reports have sadly shown, some go to the extreme of hiring someone to kill their spouse or they kill themselves. Many other couples choose to remain together because they're financially better off that way, because they don't want to cause pain or embarrassment to their families, because they don't want to hurt their children, because they don't want to face the church, or because of countless other reasons. They remain unhappily married. They live under the same roof but in separate bedrooms. A friend told us that she and her husband slept in the same room but in separate beds for several years until they finally divorced. After years of conflict, these couples have moved to the stage of withdrawal.

Withdrawal is exactly as the word denotes. You withdraw from each other and the relationship. It seems easier to step away than it does to continue the destructive behavior. Withdrawal is like an emotional divorce. Here are the indicative signs of withdrawal:

- The partners are so weary of fighting day after day that they shut down and withdraw.
- Very few words are spoken.
- Often couples sleep in separate bedrooms.

- The spouses find themselves living two parallel lives that do not cross.
- The couple may feel it's easier this way because there are no more arguments. (The truth is that they are no longer arguing because they are not even speaking to each other. Home seems more peaceful now! But is it?)

In the state of withdrawal, neither individual is trying to meet the other person's most important emotional needs. Furthermore, even when one tries, the other puts up an emotional barrier, a wall that prevents those attempts from reaching their heart. It goes without saying that at this stage, the end of the relationship is at hand. It may come in the form of an affair. One or both spouses decide to call it quits. Or one person or the other may take drastic measures to end their marriage. For those that seek a divorce, the breakup is not always amicable or pleasant, and the pain of the marriage may follow them for many years, even for the rest of their lives.

A MARRIAGE CONTINUUM

Now, picture these three states of mind in marriage along a continuum. On the far left side of the scale, you find the state of intimacy. On the far right side of the scale, you find withdrawal. In the middle of the scale, picture the state of conflict. If you had to describe your marriage along that continuum, where would it be? What is the state of your marriage?

As marriage and family educators and counselors for more than twenty years, we can tell you that no couple has ever come to us in the state of intimacy to ask for our help. No one has come to us in that state to tell us they are happy, they love each other, they have a strong, healthy relationship, and could we please help them get better? Sadly, in all of those twenty years and the additional fifteen years of pastoral ministry, we have had to work with countless couples dealing with conflict or in the state of withdrawal. Many come to us to tell us they have tried everything, but now they want to give us one last chance. We would rather have had these couples recognize the signs sooner than wait until they were in the state of withdrawal. But regardless, we are always happy when couples come to the place of admitting they need help and are seeking it. Many couples, even in the state of withdrawal, have come to us, have been willing to listen to our guidance and make necessary changes, and have been able to rescue their marriage—and *so can you.*

Maybe you find yourselves in the state of conflict. It seems as if you argue about the silliest things, and the arguments escalate until a molehill quickly becomes an insurmountable mountain. But you're not happy about that, and you want to have a healthier and happier marriage. We can assure you that you can. Or perhaps you have reached that state of withdrawal where you don't even care anymore. At the same time, you long to enjoy intimacy in a relationship with your spouse. You believe in the marriage vows you expressed before God, friends, and family, and you long to live in a healthy, committed relationship with your spouse until death parts you. You look at your children and know that breaking up will break their hearts, and you don't want to do that to them. We are here to tell you that you, too, can turn your marriage around. So if you find yourself in constant conflict or in the state of withdrawal, how do you get back to intimacy?

PLUGGING THE HOLE

Picture in your mind a plastic cup like the ones you can get at some fast food places or hotel exercise rooms. If that cup has a small hole at the very bottom that causes the water to leak out, what must you do in order for the water to stay in that cup? We asked that question at one of our couples' retreats, and someone shouted out, "Get another cup!" But note that we didn't give you that option. Our question was very clear: What must you do in order for the water to *stay* in the cup that has the hole? Don't overthink the question. The answer is very simple: you must plug the hole!

Love can drain out of a relationship one drop, one day at a time. In the beginning, the leak may seem so small that it is hardly noticeable. You stop saying, "I love you." It is small things like not holding hands anymore or not talking without constant interruptions from electronic devices or perhaps not saying thank you after a kind action on the part of the other. Maybe it is just taking each other for granted, not apologizing, or not forgiving. But, as we all know, a slowly leaking pipe can do great damage to a home if left unattended.

Another way to look at the interaction in marriage is as a sort of emotional transaction, referred to as the Love Bank.[12] As Harley explains, we all have an emotional Love Bank, and every person we know has an account in that bank. Your mother and father, your siblings, your spouse, your friends, your coworkers, people at your church, even the janitor at work whom you see every day—everyone has an account in your Love Bank. Every time one of those people does something nice or kind to you, it is as if they are making a deposit in your emotional Love Bank. Conversely, every time anyone does something unkind, rude, or hurtful to you, it is as if they make a withdrawal from your emotional Love Bank. The same is also true for you. Every time you do something nice for someone else, you are making a deposit in your account; and every time you do something unkind to them, you make a withdrawal. It's an emotional transaction of sorts. You either make deposits, or you make withdrawals.

From the very beginning of our relationship, Pamela and I have been making deposits and, at times, withdrawals in each other's emotional Love Bank. After three years of dating, our accounts in that emotional Love Bank were high enough that we felt the desire to spend the rest of our lives together. During the past thirty-eight years together, our accounts have gone up and down—but because the deposits have been exponentially higher than the withdrawals, we continue to enjoy a loving, fulfilling, exciting life together. Please notice that we said there have been withdrawals in our accounts at times. Marriage for us hasn't always been deposits. We have made mistakes; we have not always been kind and loving; we have caused hurt to each other. We are thankful, however, that the deposits have been greater than the withdrawals.

The key is to continue making frequent deposits and minimizing the withdrawals. John Gottman, one of the most influential psychologists of the twentieth century, found in his extensive research and work with couples that "it all comes down to a simple mathematical formula: you must have at least five times as many positive as negative moments together if your marriage is to be stable."[13] In other words, if you have at least five good, positive, thoughtful, loving actions for every negative action, you can have a very good, strong, healthy relationship for the rest of your life. It doesn't mean that you count the good things you do—"One, two, three, four, five . . ."—and then plan on one bad action. No, the point is to maximize your positive interactions (i.e., make deposits in your spouse's Love Bank) and minimize your negative interactions (i.e., minimize or eliminate withdrawals from their Love Bank).

This principle works in many other relationships. Who do you enjoy working with more—the supervisor who is constantly criticizing and harassing you or the one who is always encouraging you? Who do you enjoy spending more time with—the people who are negative and poisonous, or those that are positive and make you feel good about yourself? This same principle is even truer in marriage. Aim to make as many deposits in your spouse's emotional Love Bank as possible while at the same time minimizing or eliminating as many withdrawals as possible.

In the next chapter, we will discuss the specific things, whether intentional or unintentional, that cause leaks in relationships. You see, we cannot stop a leak unless we deal with its underlying cause. We will not be pointing fingers at our spouses, but looking in the mirror and exploring our own destructive behaviors.

CONCLUSION

Do you understand the difference between a covenant marriage and one that is based solely on a contract, a piece of paper? Is your marriage based on mutual giving and receiving? Do you place the interests of your spouse above your own? On the scale of give and take, where do you think you rate? Are you defined more as a giver or as a taker? Remember these words: "Be devoted to one another in love. Honor one another above yourselves" (Romans 12:10, NIV).

Is it possible that we have made marriage more difficult today because we have failed to go back to the basics? Maybe we need to go back to a time when technology did not exist, have more face-to-face conversations, cut things out of our calendars that do not match our family values, and focus on doing things that bring a smile to our loved one's face with no thought of anything in return.

1. "Mae West," *Wikipedia*, updated July 26, 2020, https://en.wikipedia.org/wiki/Mae_West.

2. Theodore Roosevelt, "American Ideals in Education" speech, November 4, 1910.

3. Blogswallop, "Marriage is ugly, you see the absolute worst in someone," Facebook, August 10, 2015, https://www.facebook.com/Blogswallop/posts/marriage-is-not-beautifulmarriage-is -ugly-you-see-the-absolute-worst-in-someone-/1172871552728209/. The wording printed here has been adapted for the audience from the original. The quotation has been edited for clarity and style.

4. The Conversation, "Decades of Studies Show What Happens to Marriages After Having Kids," *Fortune*, May 9, 2016, https://fortune.com/2016/05/09/mothers-marriage-parenthood/.

5. Aaron Jacob and April Jacob, "Conflict Is a Normal and Natural Part of 'Your Happily Ever After,'" The Gottman Institute, September 30, 2016, https://www.gottman.com/blog /conflict-normal-natural-part-happily-ever/.

6. Jacob and Jacob, "Conflict."

7. Tony Campolo, *It's Friday, but Sunday's Comin'* (Nashville: Thomas Nelson, 2008), 47, 48.

8. Willard Harley, *His Needs, Her Needs* (Grand Rapids, MI: Fleming H. Revell, 1994).

9. "Quotes by Mignon McLaughlin," The Best Quotations, accessed July 21, 2020, https:// best-quotations.com/authquotes.php?auth=1122.

10. Willard Harley, *Love Busters* (Grand Rapids, MI: Revell, 2008).

11. "Three States of Mind in Marriage: Intimacy," Marriage Builders, accessed July 28, 2020, https://www.marriagebuilders.com/intimacy.htm; "Three States of Mind in Marriage: Conflict," Marriage Builders, https://www.marriagebuilders.com/conflict.htm; "Three States of Mind in Marriage: Withdrawal," Marriage Builders, https://www.marriagebuilders.com/withdrawal.htm.

12. Harley, *Love Busters.*

13. John Gottman, *Why Marriages Succeed or Fail: And How You Can Make Yours Last* (1994), downloaded August 20, 2020, https://thewildmind.wordpress.com/2010/03/14/some-blogging -positive-reinforcement/.

Chapter Three

Marriage Wreckers

Starting a quarrel is like breaching a dam;
so drop the matter before a dispute breaks out.
—Proverbs 17:14, NIV

As loving and kind as we may try to be, there are times when we will do things that hurt our spouse. Sometimes these things are intentional; other times, we do them out of habit without even thinking. For the health and well-being of our marriage, it's critical that we identify and stop doing the things that, over time, will erode the love. As we ended the last chapter, we spoke about minimizing or eliminating the withdrawals from our spouse's emotional Love Bank and plugging the hole at the bottom of that imaginary plastic cup.

What are those things that destroy our relationships and may, in time, cause the demise of our marriage? What kinds of things constitute withdrawals from our own or our spouse's emotional Love Bank? After all, the first step in addressing the issue lies in identifying it. So we must look at the causes and stop the leaks before we delve into the antidote. In this chapter, we want to talk about those things we have learned and observed, those things that, when we do them, destroy our spouse's love for us. As we explore the things that destroy love in a marriage, it is important to not point fingers. Put that finger down and, instead, look in the mirror. Ask yourself if you have ever practiced or are currently practicing any of these destructive behaviors; if so, determine to eliminate them, knowing that they are contributing to the potential downfall of your marriage.

DESTRUCTIVE PATTERNS

In her two-volume book compilation titled *Mind, Character, and Personality*, author Ellen White writes, "The true principles of psychology are found in the Holy Scriptures."[1] Those principles are not written in any one book as a collection but, rather, are scattered throughout the pages of the Bible, many in the form of stories. The apostle Paul remarked, "The things that happened to those people are examples. They were written down to teach us because we live in a time when all these things of the past have reached their goal" (1 Corinthians 10:11, NCV). One of those stories, and the principles behind their experience, is found in the Old Testament. We want to look at the marriage of a young couple, what caused the demise of their relationship, and the principles we can apply to our marriage and to other relationships so we can prevent the same end this couple experienced.

This is the story of Michal and David. Their relationship began like so many others. Their story reads like some of the best romantic movie scripts from Hollywood. If it were a fairy tale, it would have ended with the words, "And they lived happily ever after." This is one of the few times in the Bible where we read of the love that one person had toward another. For instance, we read that Isaac loved Rebekah (Genesis 24:67), Jacob loved Rachel (Genesis 29:18), Elkanah loved Hannah (1 Samuel 1:5), Samson loved Delilah (Judges 16:4), Rehoboam (a king of Judah) loved Maachah (2 Chronicles 11:21), and King Ahasuerus loved Esther (Esther 2:17). We read of the love of parents toward their children and of the love of God toward us, but the people we just mentioned are the only ones of whom the Bible specifically states that the husband loved his wife. We're not suggesting they are the only men who loved their wives. Certainly, many other stories suggest that there were other husbands who loved their wives, but those are the only people we find in the Bible of whom it is explicitly mentioned. The only other time marital love is mentioned is in the story of the couple we want to take a moment to focus on. We read that "Michal, Saul's daughter, loved David" (1 Samuel 18:20).

Although the Bible doesn't say so, David must have had strong feelings toward Michal as well. Indeed, he loved her enough to go to war for her and return with twice as much of a dowry as her father, the king, required of her prospective suitor (1 Samuel 18:27, 28). Notwithstanding family jealousy and turmoil, their marriage began with good prospects. They loved each other: she was to marry the future king of Israel, and he was loved and admired by the people. But her father hated him. When in-laws do not like their child's potential spouse, it creates a negative dynamic for both the couple and for their own relationship with them. Nevertheless, Michal loved David. In fact, she loved David so much that she was willing to hide him, help him escape, and to lie to her own father to protect him (1 Samuel 19:11–18).

Think about their situation for a moment. The princess and the future king were in love! If romantic love is a good predictor, you might say that future wedded bliss awaited them. Right after they were married, we should read, "And they lived happily ever after." However, this fairy-tale romance ended in bitter disappointment. What happened? Where did Michal and David's relationship go wrong? As we look carefully at their relationship, we can see the slippery slope of their marriage. And many couples today follow the same pattern, which leads them to marital ruin.

Many couples fall into certain patterns that end up sabotaging or harming their relationship. In some cases, these patterns or habits end up destroying their relationship altogether. Interestingly, we see four patterns of behavior illustrated in the relationship between Michal, King Saul's daughter, and King David, her husband. Let's look at their story through the lens of these four patterns so we can learn from their interaction how their marriage ended up in serious trouble and how it eventually fell apart completely.

REPROACH, OR SCOLDING

The first pattern we notice we'll call reproach. After a great victory over the Philistines, King David decided to bring the ark of the covenant to Jerusalem and place it "in the midst of the tabernacle that [he] had erected for it" (2 Samuel 6:17). For David, it was not enough to simply bring the ark back to Jerusalem; he wanted to make sure the occasion would be a high spiritual moment for the people. There were burnt offerings and sacrifices, and the day turned into a spiritual revival. David's wish was that this high experience would continue, so he sent everyone home with bread, meat, and a cake of raisins. But he also wanted his own family to enjoy a worshipful moment, and so he returned to his own home "to bless his household" (2 Samuel 6:20). And what did he encounter when he got home? The Scriptures tell us: "And Michal the daughter of Saul came out to meet David, and said, 'How glorious was the king of Israel today, uncovering himself today in the eyes of the maids of his servants, as one of the base fellows shamelessly uncovers himself' " (2 Samuel 6:20).

Michal met David at the door of their house and reproached him for what she considered behavior unbecoming a king. Reproach is an expression of criticism and disappointment because of something bad that someone has done. It is something you do or say when someone makes you feel ashamed or embarrassed. Often, when you're angry over something someone else has done that mortifies you, your response is to reproach him or her.

Marriage researcher and therapist John Gottman writes about what he calls "the Four Horsemen," as he describes the destructive styles that couples often fall into. He labels this first pattern criticism.[2] Reproach, or criticism, often involves attacking someone's personality or character rather than a specific behavior, and it is usually accompanied by blame.

Gottman notes, "One common type of criticism is to bring up a long list of complaints. I call this 'kitchen sinking' because you throw in every conceivable negative thing you can think of."[3] We remember the story of two men who met while walking downtown in the city where they lived. They had not seen each other in quite a while and were glad to exchange information—where they lived, what they were doing, and how their families were doing. In speaking about his wife, one of the men said, "I love my wife. My biggest complaint about her is that when we argue, she gets historical."

His friend asked for clarification, "Do you mean *hysterical*?"

"No," responded his friend. "She gets historical. She brings up everything bad I have ever done."

Often, criticism in marriage becomes historical when one spouse brings up everything they can remember against their spouse.

Instead of using reproach or criticism against our spouse, we might complain. A complaint is not an attack against the other person but, rather, a comment about something you wish were otherwise. To oversimplify, criticism usually begins with the word *you*, whereas a complaint can and should easily begin with the word *I*. Using an accusatory *you* is why the use of criticism is more likely to make your partner defensive.

As a general rule, a criticism entails blaming, a personal attack, or an accusation, while a complaint is a comment about something you wish were otherwise. Gottman helpfully explains that one of the ways to tell if you've transitioned from complaining to criticizing is if you begin using "global phrases like 'you never' or 'you always.' "[4] However, when you complain, you are simply stating the feelings *you* are experiencing because of a situation, event, or action from your spouse. You can use words such as *anger, displeasure,* or *distress,* not about your spouse but to describe your personal feelings. For instance, you could say something like, "I'm very hurt that you didn't ask me about how my day went today." Or, "I was very hungry when I got home, and when dinner was not ready, I felt neglected." Criticism, on the other hand, is a lot less specific; it is more general in nature and may come with some blame attached to it. This is how the same scenarios would play out if criticism were used: "You never show any interest in me or my work. You just don't care about me." Or, "You never have dinner ready. You don't care if I'm hungry."

It is perfectly all right to complain or express your feelings, wishes, or desires to your spouse. In fact, that is what it means to be assertive, which is one of the ingredients of healthy communication. It is not good, however, to be critical, particularly when you point the accusing finger toward your spouse. Again, the best way to eliminate this first of the Four Horsemen is to begin your conversations with *I* instead of *you*, be specific about the complaint (i.e., reference your feelings), eliminate accusations, and avoid general language such as *always* or *never*.

How does criticism show up in this exchange between Michal and David?

First of all, Michal confronted David in public. She didn't even wait for him to come inside the house where she could talk to him privately about her perception of what had taken place. In addition, she used sarcasm and probably used a mocking tone of voice when she said, "How glorious was the king of Israel today." And, as if that were not enough, she compared him to "one of the base fellows."

Further insight is given as we read, "The dignity and pride of king Saul's daughter was shocked that king David should lay aside his garments of royalty, and lay by his royal scepter, and be clothed with the simple linen garments worn by the priest. She thought that he was greatly dishonoring himself before the people of Israel."[5] Given the benefit of the doubt, perhaps Michal was concerned for David's reputation and saw the possibility that he would lose the respect of the people as their king and leader. Michal could have expressed her concerns privately; but, instead, she attacked David in public and essentially called him a vulgar person, a dirty old man, a mindless fool, a buffoon.

It's one thing to complain to your spouse about something they've done, but it's another to criticize them. It would have been better if she had asked David what he had had in mind when he removed his royal robes instead of making assumptions or ascribing blame for his actions. Marriage researchers Howard Markman, Scott Stanley, and Susan Blumberg label Michal's behavior *negative interpretation*.[6] Negative interpretation is when one spouse believes that the intentions of their spouse are more negative than they really are. They diagnose, label, or pigeonhole their spouse. Michal labeled David as base and shameless. She assumed he was just a careless, stupid man. She accused him of not living up to the proper level of a king because he was really nothing more than a simple shepherd.

Just that interaction alone might not have been enough to derail their relationship. All of us, at one time or another, have probably been critical of our spouse, perhaps even in public. It is not the occasional criticism but rather the repeated pattern of behavior that destroys, a little at a time, even the best of marriages. And, unfortunately, that's not where the negative interactions between David and Michal ended.

SCORN

In the parallel account of this event in the life of David and Michal, we read, "And it happened, as the ark of the covenant of the Lord came to the City of David, that Michal, Saul's daughter, looked through a window and saw King David whirling and playing music; and she despised him in her heart" (1 Chronicles 15:29). *Scorn* (or *contempt*, to use Gottman's term) describes a lack of respect for someone or something, a feeling that someone or something is not good enough to deserve your approval or respect. When Michal scorned David, she showed that she was not willing to accept his actions or even his explanation, because she believed it was stupid, unreasonable, and not good enough for her, the wife of the king of Israel.

Ellen White further describes the motives behind Michal's words: "In the bitterness of her passion she could not await David's return to the palace, but went out to meet him, and to his kindly greeting poured forth a torrent of bitter words. Keen and cutting was the irony of her speech."[7]

The scorn Michal felt toward David was evident in her words and probably her actions. Picture her as she rolled her eyes, crossed her arms, leaned over, bowed in mocking fashion, and with great bitterness spewed her sharp words, "How glorious was the king of Israel today, uncovering himself today in the eyes of the maids of his servants, as one of the base fellows shamelessly uncovers himself" (2 Samuel 6:20).

In this portion of Michal and David's story, we see the intention to insult and psychologically abuse your partner. Scorn means that with words and body language, you're lobbing insults right into the heart of your partner's sense of self. And what fuels these contemptuous actions are negative thoughts about your spouse. In the back of your mind, you feel he is stupid, she is disgusting, he is incompetent, she's a fool.

In a Spanish love song of yesteryear, the composer declared to his former love, "I would rather you hate me than ignore me because scorn hurts less than being forgotten." That may be true in a song; but in real life scornful actions and words hurt—they are devastating, and they may lead to the breakup of a relationship. One of the problems with scorn is that when it begins to overwhelm your relationship, you tend to forget your partner's positive qualities—at least while you're feeling upset. You can't remember a single positive quality or act, and instead, you tend to see only the bad things they say or do.

Nan Silver writes that it's not difficult to identify scorn:

> Recognizing when you or your spouse is expressing contempt is fairly easy. Among the most common signs are:
>
> - Insults and name-calling
> - Hostile humor
> - Mockery
> - Body language—including sneering, rolling your eyes, curling your upper lip.[8]

In the imperfect world in which we live, even the best of couples "may feel overly critical at times,"[9] and it is human to state criticism with a tinge of contempt now and then. What tends to break up otherwise good relationships is when one or both partners focus all their attention on what the other is not or does not do instead of thinking of the good qualities of the other and what attracted them to their partner in the first place.

We have always found it interesting that, for many people, what attracted them to their partner initially becomes the thing they later dislike or even hate about them. The young lady tells us about the young man she's dating or planning to marry, "He's so quiet, pensive, philosophical." A few years into their relationship, she will complain to us, "He never says anything!" A young man would describe the young lady he's in love with by saying, "She's got so much energy. I love her bubbly personality and how she meets new people wherever she goes." Later in their relationship, he will complain that "all she does is talk and flirt with others."

The first thing spouses facing the problem of scorn need to do is to eliminate this destructive pattern and, instead, focus on the good qualities of the other. Also, commend your spouse for all those things they do well and tell them what you appreciate. Affirmation and validation are always better than criticism and contempt. In Gottman's words, "The best way to neutralize your contempt is to stop seeing arguments with your spouse as a way to retaliate or exhibit your superior moral stance. Rather, your relationship will improve if you approach your spouse with precise complaints (rather than attacking your partner's character) and express a healthy dose of admiration—the opposite of contempt."[10]

Markman, Stanley, and Blumberg would describe Michal's negative pattern of interaction as *invalidation*.[11] Invalidation happens when, through words or actions, you devalue your spouse. According to Dr. Kevin Downing and Dr. Peter Robbins, "It includes a wide variety of behaviors including digs, put downs, public humiliation, contempt, bitterness, name calling, . . . and revenge. It can take on subtler forms such as sarcasm and 'joking' about your mate."[12] Can't you almost hear Michal's scorn, sarcasm, and bitterness? "How glorious was the king of Israel today, uncovering himself today in the eyes of the maids of his servants, as one of the base fellows shamelessly uncovers himself" (2 Samuel 6:20). When attacked by their spouse, most people react, and that's exactly what David did.

SELF-DEFENSIVENESS

Here's where the story of David and Michal takes an almost predictable turn. David said to Michal, "It was before the LORD, who chose me instead of your father and all his house, to appoint me ruler over the people of the LORD, over Israel. Therefore, I will play music before the LORD. And I will be even more undignified than this, and will be humble in my own sight. But as for the maidservants of whom you have spoken, by them I will be held in honor" (2 Samuel 6:21, 22).

When David felt his wife's attacks—her criticism and the contempt with which she expressed her feelings—he put up his verbal fists and reacted by defending himself. He did not even attempt to understand where her feelings of anger and bitterness were coming from; instead, David spewed anger and poisonous words toward Michal. If we may paraphrase his response and the feelings behind it, they may sound like this: "Let me remind you, madam [with a sneer and pointing his finger at her a few inches from her face], that you are no longer the king's daughter because he is no longer the king—I am! God rejected your father, and therefore, He rejected his family—that is you, missy—and instead, He chose me! Take that, little lady!"

As Gottman explains, no matter how you express it, defensiveness is fundamentally your attempt to protect yourself and ward off a perceived attack.[13] It doesn't mean that you and your spouse are bad people or that you are intentionally sabotaging your relationship—but if you continue to sabotage your relationship with the Four Horsemen, you will destroy your mutual love and your relationship.

Instead of pausing to try to understand why Michal was so angry, David took the situation to the next level. In the words of Markman, Stanley, and Blumberg, David *escalated* the argument.[14] We don't have a recording of this conversation, but I can imagine David raised his voice above Michal's. His hot temper showed through his reddened face, the veins popping up in his neck, and the downward curve of his eyebrows.

Sadly, defensiveness or escalation is one of the four best predictors of divorce. When spouses respond back and forth with negative, angry remarks, attempting to up the ante, the conversation gets more and more heated. The smallest of negative comments will more than likely raise the level of anger, and soon, what started as a small disagreement escalates into a major fight. As we will explain in the next few pages, annoying behaviors may become the cause of heated battles when the disagreement over those habits escalates over time. It may begin with small things like not putting the toilet seat down, squeezing the toothpaste from the middle of the tube, or not replacing the toilet paper after the roll is finished. As the conversation starts to heat up, the spouses start to become upset until their anger boils over, and before they realize it, they are saying unkind things to each other. Frequently, after these battles have happened many times, one or the other of the spouses bring up the "D word"—threatening to walk away from their marriage.

Solomon wrote, "Sharp words cut like a sword" (Proverbs 12:18, CEV). We might have grown up repeating, "Sticks and stones may break my bones, but words will never hurt me." But that is far from the truth because words do hurt. In fact, sometimes they hurt more than sticks and stones. When emotions escalate, verbal communication often worsens as harsh words and even insults begin to fly back and forth, damaging or even destroying the feelings of love and closeness. All it takes is a few chosen words, piercing and harmful, for oneness and intimacy to be shattered and for the marriage relationship to suffer. In some cases, the damage is irreparable. Research shows that those couples whose marriages have failed often exhibit this pattern of escalation, allowing conversations to intensify and spin out of control.

The good news is that research confirms that successful couples whose marriages last are less prone to let conversations deteriorate into damaging interactions. These couples are able to maneuver out of the nosedive before it ends up in a full-blown crash.

RETREATING, OR STALLING

As the dramatic scene comes to an end, we read, "Therefore Michal the daughter of Saul had no children to the day of her death" (2 Samuel 6:23). Conflict may trigger the fight-or-flight response. *Fight-or-flight* describes a mechanism in the body that enables humans, as well as animals, to mobilize a lot of energy rapidly in order to cope with threats to survival. When they find themselves cornered, some spouses retreat (by leaving the room, for example) or simply put up an emotional wall of protection from the other person's attacks.

Prominent researchers and psychologists use different terms to refer to this pattern in relationships. Gottman calls it *stonewalling*, while Markman, Stanley, and Blumberg refer to it as *withdrawal* and *avoidance*. All these terms describe the ways in which people seek to ignore or get out of tough discussions. Withdrawal can be physical, as when one spouse leaves the room, or less obvious, such as when one spouse gets quiet or simply shuts down completely. It may be the response from a passive-aggressive spouse whose anger toward the other is expressed in silent, sullen behavior. According to Jade Enrique, Heather Howk, and William Huitt, "Avoidance has the same goal, but the emphasis is on preventing the discussion from ever happening in the first place."[15]

Stonewalling may be done through the silent treatment. We have explained during our couples' retreats that stonewalling, or the silent treatment, is particularly hurtful to wives. Because women connect at the emotional level through communication, when a woman's husband gives her the silent treatment, it hurts her deeply. A wife's heart rate goes up dramatically when her husband stonewalls her.

The same is not the case for men. In one of the *Pickles* cartoons, cartoonist Brian Crane shows the main character, Earl, sitting in front of his house with one of his friends. Referring to his wife, Earl tells his buddy, "Opal's mad at me."

"What for?" asks his friend.

"I have absolutely no idea," responds Earl innocently.

"She never tells me why she's mad at me. She just gives me the silent treatment." In the last frame, Earl explains, "That used to bother me, but now I just look at it as a mini-vacation." Yes, men respond differently than women when their spouse gives them the silent treatment. It can be a "mini-vacation"!

In the state of retreat, "spouses no longer feel emotionally bonded or in love, and emotional defenses are raised. Neither one wants to try to meet the other's needs, and both have given up on attempts to get their own needs met by the other," notes Dr. Willard Harley's website, Marriage Builders.[16] In other words, at their wedding, two became one, but being in the state of withdrawal has caused the one to become two again: "They are completely independent, united only in living arrangements, finances and childrearing, although they often have to keep up appearances for neighbors and friends."[17]

This retreat (or stonewalling) happens as one spouse constructs an emotional stone wall as a means of protection against the barbs that may come from the other. Usually, when someone is really listening, he or she reacts to what the speaker is saying, looks at the speaker, and may say, "Uh-huh" or, "Hmm," or reflect on what they are hearing in order to let the speaker know that they are paying attention. But the stonewaller abandons these clues and, instead, replaces them with stony silence. Stonewalling itself is a very powerful act; it conveys disapproval, icy distance, and smugness.

Now, we realize that we're making a big leap here, but we're going to assume the reason Michal didn't have children was that David didn't have anything else to do with her. For all practical purposes, their marriage was over! He withdrew from their relationship. He built an emotional wall, a wall of silence and separation, between himself and Michal. They had nothing more to do with each other. There was no oneness; no intimacy; and, therefore, no real marriage. We read, "To David's rebuke was added that of the Lord: because of her pride and arrogance, Michal 'had no child unto the day of her death.' "[18]

Keep in mind that anyone may occasionally stonewall during an intense marital exchange. The key idea here is that it is *habitual*. Interestingly, these four patterns of reproach, scorn, self-defensiveness, and retreating are not only present in marriages; but you also find them in parenting, in extended families, among friends, at work, and even at church. The questions to ask are: What should you do if you recognize any of these four patterns in your relationship? What can you do to prevent the demise of your marriage?

Gottman explains, "Happiness is not found in a particular style of fighting or making up. Rather, what really separates contented couples from those in deep marital misery is a healthy balance between their positive and negative feelings and actions toward each other."[19] As we explained in chapter 2, maximize the deposits in your spouse's emotional Love Bank and minimize the withdrawals.

THE FOUR ANTIDOTES

Thankfully, you don't have to let the four patterns—reproach, scorn, self-defensiveness, and retreating—destroy your relationship. There are things you can do to stop them in their tracks. Gottman suggests four antidotes that will prevent or stop the destroying effect of these patterns.

The antidote for reproach, criticism, or negative interpretation

A good practice to prevent or halt reproach is to use a "gentle start-up."[20] Leanna Stockard explains: "When we criticize, either intentionally or unintentionally, we often use 'you' statements, which according to Dr. Gottman, 'attacks a person's character.' " Statements that start with *you* tend to be accompanied by the pointed, accusing finger. Instead, writes Stockard, a gentle start-up employs *I* statements with which you declare "how you feel, and what you need, without attacking the other person. An example of this behavior is, 'I am feeling disappointed that the trash was still overflowing after our conversation yesterday that I would be working late tonight' as opposed to, '[Why] didn't you take the trash out? We discussed this yesterday!' "[21] You can get your point across by using gentler language that expresses your feelings and does not attack.

If we consider the situation between David and Michal, it would have been better if she had waited for David to come into the palace instead of going out to meet him. Instead of confronting him in public, she could have asked him to join her in a private room, and she could have said something like, "When I saw you dancing and not wearing an outfit suitable for a king, I was concerned that the public might not appreciate that the king was not in his royal garments." She would not be pointing an accusing finger at David but would be expressing her feelings and concern about what she saw. Complaint without blame is the key.

We have taught countless couples that healthy communication has two ingredients: assertiveness and active listening. Assertiveness is the ability to express what you feel, what you like or dislike, what you want. Sometimes we confuse being assertive with being aggressive. Assertiveness "requires being forthright about your wants and needs, while still considering the rights, needs and wants of others."[22] Assertiveness means getting "your point across firmly, fairly and with empathy." On the other hand, "aggressive behavior is based on winning. You do what is in your own best interest without regard for the rights, needs, feelings, or desires of other people. When you're aggressive, the power you use is selfish. You may come across as pushy or even bullying. You take what you want, often without asking."[23]

Let's discontinue the practice of interacting with our spouse in ways that can be characterized as aggressive, critical, or negatively interpreting their actions or words. Instead, let's replace those actions with assertiveness by lovingly and kindly expressing our feelings and starting with *I* statements rather than *you* statements.

The antidote for scorn, contempt, or invalidation

We invalidate or devalue our spouse when we use contemptuous or scornful words or actions. When we hold contempt for our spouse, we blame them, disrespect them, and attempt to maintain a "superior" role over them. The antidote to this pattern is to build a culture of appreciation. We do this by reminding ourselves of our spouse's positive qualities and expressing gratitude for positive actions. Often, we can catch ourselves being instinctively negative about everything our partner does. We tend to find fault in all they do, and at times, we begin comparing them to others. But this pattern of behavior needs to be challenged by creating a more positive narrative about who our spouse is.

In our work with couples seeking help for their marriage, we tell them to begin by making a list of everything they like and appreciate about their spouse—anytime they do something nice, kind, or loving, add it to the list. And, on those days when negative feelings toward your spouse begin to creep up to the surface, pull out that list and remind yourself about their good qualities, the things you love and appreciate about them. In addition, use the list to affirm your spouse with the specific things on your list. Telling them what you like and appreciate about them is a way to validate them, lift them up, build them up, and strengthen your relationship at the same time. Admiration is the opposite of contempt, which is perhaps one of the most destructive of all the Four Horsemen.

The antidote for self-defensiveness or escalation

Often, when someone criticizes us, we immediately get defensive or provide an excuse as to why we did or did not do something. Unfortunately, this is not helpful, as it invalidates the other person's feelings. When you are feeling defensive, try to use the antidote—take responsibility for your actions. For instance, if your partner complains that you did not take out the trash, attempt to say, "You are correct—we did have this conversation yesterday, and I did not follow through. I will do it right now." This response acknowledges your partner's feelings and shows that you are taking responsibility, which will likely defuse the situation.

This is where the second ingredient of healthy communication comes into play—active listening. In active listening, say Ron Deal and David Olson, "the listener verbally feeds back what he or she hears in order to clarify that the message has been accurately received and interpreted."[24] The goal of the listener is not just to hear what was stated but to try to understand the feelings behind the statement.

Active listening is critically important to derail this third pattern, yet it is something that we are very poor at. Journalist and author Mignon McLaughlin stated, "We hear only half of what is said to us, understand only half of that, believe only half of that, and remember only half of that."[25] No wonder there's so much misunderstanding among people.

In the case of David and Michal, what if David had stopped to consider Michal's feelings? What if he had thought, *She's concerned for my reputation?* Or, *She is acting out of concern for me?* What if he had tried to state what he thought she was feeling? We wonder if perhaps Michal's tone might have changed if she had realized David was really listening to her and trying to understand what she was feeling. Obviously, we will never know what might have happened, but it's not too late for you to try this yourself and see how things may be different in your interaction with your spouse.

The antidote against retreating, stonewalling, or withdrawing

In the heat of an argument, blood floods the brain, which seems to happen faster for men. Fearful that we may say or do something we will regret later, we usually choose the safer option of shutting down and check out either emotionally or physically. Instead of withdrawing or stonewalling, it would be best to let your spouse know that you're feeling flooded or overwhelmed and need to take a break. "Calming down is especially important for men, since as we know, they are more likely to feel physiologically overwhelmed sooner than women during a heated marital exchange," says Gottman.[26] Nevertheless, regardless of your gender, it's virtually impossible to think straight when your blood is pumping furiously and your heart is racing; therefore, it is critically important that we calm down. What's crucial at this point is that you take a break from the conversation for at least twenty minutes.

At the same time, communicate this to your spouse. Let them know you need a break but that you are willing to continue the conversation afterward. If you simply take a break and walk away, you leave your spouse with the impression that you're stonewalling them. If you state that you're taking a break, but without specifying for how long, you leave them with uncertainty. In other words, if you say, "Let's take a break; we can talk about this later," your spouse is left wondering what *later* means: Later in a couple of hours? Later in the week? Later in the future? Whereas if you clearly state, "I need to take a break. Can we sit down tonight, after the kids are in bed, to talk about this?" Or, "Let's sit down calmly in the living room this afternoon at four o'clock to talk about this." A specific, agreed-upon time lets your spouse know you're not just checking out indefinitely but simply taking some needed cooldown time so you can calmly and rationally try to resolve the situation amicably, logically, and lovingly.

It's very important that during this break time you avoid thoughts of righteous indignation (e.g., *I don't have to put up with this anymore*), avoid trying to play the innocent victim (e.g., *Why is he always picking on me?*), and do not take this time to plot your revenge. Instead, do whatever soothes you. While different people are soothed by different things, some things to try include practicing emotional self-care, such as deep breathing; listening to classical, spiritual, or relaxing music; taking a warm shower or bath; or exercising or going for a walk. You can also do some spiritual introspection by praying, reading the Bible, or singing hymns. Don't miss this important point: taking a break from the heated argument is good as long as you don't take that time to develop a plan of attack for when the battle resumes. Instead, take the time off to do something that helps you relax and be better equipped to come back to the conversation.

Our personal experience tells us that it is important to make good use of your own sense of humor and laugh at yourself. Notice we said, "Laugh at yourself," and not, "Laugh at your spouse." Laughing is wonderful medicine to your heart and to your relationship, but laughing at your spouse can be demeaning and devaluing and can actually make things worse. Laugh at yourself because it may help you relax and calm down. Just look at yourself in the mirror, make faces at yourself, smile, and make poses. It's bound to lessen some of the tension you're feeling.

You can also ask yourself, "What difference will this make next week, next month, or in five years?" Sometimes we make a mountain out of a molehill. In the great scheme of things, how important is this conflict? It makes us wonder, had Michal and David been more intentional in making their relationship a strong, healthy one, what the Bible would say about their marriage and where it would have led in the history of Israel. We can't change their history, but we can change ours. Avoid the four patterns that are destructive to your relationship, maintain a strong positive-to-negative ratio, be intentional about keeping your relationship healthy, vibrant, and strong, and learn to laugh together often so, unlike David and Michal, you can live happily ever after. As Robert Browning wrote, "Success in marriage is more than finding the right person: it is being the right person."[27]

DESTRUCTIVE HABITS AND BEHAVIORS

Lying and deception
Because a healthy relationship must be based on trust, lying is one of the most

destructive of all behaviors. We need to know that we can trust what our spouse is telling us. Honesty and trustworthiness are values that should be on our list of nonnegotiables. There is no reason to be dishonest about anything, and even "little white lies" are still lies. King Solomon wrote, "A false witness will not go unpunished, and he who breathes out lies will not escape" (Proverbs 19:5, ESV).

Honesty and trustworthiness in today's world take on new meanings unheard of in days past. In today's world, you can be dishonest to your spouse while sitting in the same room together. In our parents' and grandparents' world, inappropriate and illicit relationships occurred face-to-face. That is no longer the case today, where inappropriate relationships are as close as your cell phone, iPad, computer, or any device that can access the internet.

Participating in inappropriate online behavior is being dishonest and, in effect, lying to your spouse. This includes viewing inappropriate videos or images, engaging in any secretive online chats, sending or receiving texts or photos that you quickly hide or delete, having online "friends" that you do not wish to reveal to your spouse, and so on. The bottom line is this: Are you engaging in any online activity that you would not be comfortable with your spouse viewing alongside you?

Those who have attended our couples' retreat know that we use many comic strips to illustrate the points we're trying to make. We've always said that comic strips are not for children. Rather, they are drawn by adults and are meant for adults. Some of them are intended to just bring a smile or even outright laughter; but, often, we find one that makes a very profound point. One such cartoon depicts Peter standing at the pearly gates, checking people in for admittance to heaven. Peter addresses a man waiting at the gate and tells him: "There's no such thing as the book of life. We make our decisions based on your browser history." Again, while this illustration is intended to be funny, it should give us pause to consider the profound implications. What if that were the case? Would our browser history cause us shame and possibly even shut us out of heaven?

We also have found couples who have dealt with financial dishonesty in their relationship. Not being truthful about how money is being spent; accruing debts without your spouse knowing about it; secretly giving money or gifts to others (including your extended family); and hiding, hoarding, or controlling money are all included in what Scott and Bethany Palmer refer to on their blog as "financial infidelity."[28]

According to new research reported by Lorie Konish, "only 52 percent of individuals believe their significant other is totally honest with them when it comes to money."[29] Think about it! Only 52 percent. That's not even a passing grade. No wonder that, according to Konish, "31 percent of survey respondents said keeping credit cards and other accounts from a partner is worse than physical infidelity." As she goes on to explain, "The reasons for the dishonesty around finances range from failure to communicate to straight up deceit."[30]

Financial professionals say there are telltale signs of financial infidelity to watch for. For instance, you notice that "your mail no longer includes financial statements, such as credit card bills or solicitations and investment account information" writes Konish. Or you notice unusual behavior, such as your spouse "lavishing you with gifts or insisting that you account for every nickel and dime" you spend. Also, watch out for changes in habits in your mate, such as buying new clothes (including underwear), wearing a special aftershave or perfume, dressing differently, or suddenly going to the gym regularly. Experts also suggest being "on the lookout for changes in income or cash flow, including cash withdrawals or checks made out to cash."[31] It's like they say, "Follow the money!"

As with any type of infidelity, lying about finances erodes trust, the very foundation of a healthy relationship. Dishonesty is also a sign of low self-esteem, and it only sinks you lower into that pattern. You may develop a vicious cycle of dishonesty, which leads to even lower self-esteem, which in turn leads to more dishonesty—and so on.

Lying or failing to disclose the truth about money gets worse as the little lies lead to big lies. We met with a couple who asked for our help with their crumbling marriage. He told us that one day after work, as he was driving by one of the many casinos close to the city where they lived, he went into one of them to try his luck. He told me, "Pastor, I know we don't believe in gambling, but since we have been saving money to buy a new house, I thought maybe if I won, it would help us financially." So he stepped into the casino, chose a slot machine near the door, put one quarter in, pulled the lever, and—*clink, clink, clink*—out came $15. He thought to himself, *This could be my lucky day!* (As an aside, a friend of mine who used to work with a state gambling commission told me that slot machines closest to the door of a casino are programmed to pay. They are like a hook to get people to come inside, where they often lose more money. That's exactly what happened to this man.)

The man went further inside the casino and a couple of hours later left the casino $500 poorer. He was ashamed of himself and too embarrassed to tell his wife what he had done. A few days later, he was in the area again and wondered if his luck had changed, so he went into a different casino—no way was he going to go to the same one where he had lost $500 just a few days earlier. He tried the slot machine again and after just a couple of tries—*clink, clink, clink*—out came $50. *Aha*, he thought, *my luck has changed!* Again, he went farther inside the casino, and this time he lost $1,000. He hadn't told his wife about losing $500 the first time, and he surely was not about to tell her that he had lost an additional $1,000.

That's when his wife spoke for the first time. Angry and hurt, she told us, "He did it again and again, and I had no idea until tonight, when he admitted to me that he lost all we have been saving for the down payment on our house—$25,000. We have nothing left." Sad to say, that marriage did not survive. They were the victims of financial infidelity, lies, and dishonesty.

Lack of honesty may begin with good intentions. People who lie to their spouses, or who withhold the truth from them, often rationalize that they don't want to hurt their spouse's feelings. For instance, you tell them you had to work late at the office when the truth is that you walked over to the park with some of your office friends to talk about Sunday's ball game. You were so involved in the conversation that you forgot your wife was fixing dinner and needed you to help her with the kids. You think, *If I tell her what I did, she will be hurt. She will think I value my friends more than I value her and the kids. I don't want to hurt her feelings.* So you hide the truth. That lie helped you avoid a possible argument, so in a sense, you were "rewarded" for lying and will probably rationalize and do it again.

It's interesting that if you ever get stopped by the police for speeding, you think to yourself that everyone else speeds too. You were just the unlucky one that got caught. Don't you also think that most people who tell white lies to their spouses imagine most others also do? That is poor misguided reasoning. Dishonesty is wrong, and there is no rationalizing that will make it right.

FOR DISCUSSION

1. Are there some lies that are more damaging to your relationship than others? Or are they all the same?
2. Here is an exercise to try: Sit down with your spouse and, separately, write down ten things couples may lie about. Share the lists, talk about them, and discuss whether all are significant.

While lying is the most recognizable manifestation of dishonesty, marriage counselor Frank Gunzburg gives examples of other ways we can be dishonest:

- "Avoiding an issue"
- "Distracting your spouse from an issue"
- "Omitting information"
- "Focusing on an insignificant part of an issue"
- "Answering questions with anger to avoid further discussion"
- "Giving the silent treatment as an answer"[32]

Stop and think for a moment. Ask yourself, *Am I being completely honest with my spouse?* Is there anything you are keeping from your spouse, even with the good intention of not hurting them? Being completely honest and truthful may be hurtful in the short run, but lying and dishonesty will hurt more in the long run.

Christian psychologist Willard Harley recommends what he calls the Policy of Radical Honesty.[33] Because dishonesty withdraws love units from your spouse's emotional Love Bank, and honesty makes deposits in the same, we should be sure to be completely honest, all the time. In other words, be transparent with your spouse by sharing with them as much information about yourself as you know. That should include your thoughts and feelings, your likes and dislikes, your personal history and daily activities, and your wishes and plans for the future. To be very clear, Harley suggests that there should be complete honesty in four important areas:

1. *Emotional honesty.* "Reveal your emotional reactions—both positive and negative," Harley writes.[34] If you are happy or upset, if you are angry or concerned, if you are sad or discouraged—whatever your emotions may be at the moment—share those with your spouse. This is particularly important when your spouse (who may perceive that you might be experiencing one of these emotions) asks you about it. Your spouse may ask, "Is there something wrong?" or, "Are you upset about something?" If there is something wrong or you are upset, instead of denying it, why not admit to it and explain the reasons? Now, that demands that your spouse be a good, active listener who will not dismiss your feelings, challenge those feelings, attempt to correct you for feeling that way, or contradict what you are expressing.

2. *Historical honesty.* Harley recommends that you "reveal information about your personal history, particularly events that demonstrate personal weakness or failure."[35] This is particularly important for premarital couples. We have worked with young ladies preparing for marriage who privately reveal to us that they were sexually molested but are afraid to tell their husband-to-be. They have told us, "If I tell him, he may not want to marry me." We have suggested to them that it is better if they know so there are no secrets from the past that may come back to haunt them one day. In fact, just living with those secrets may prevent them from enjoying complete intimacy and be detrimental to their relationship.

    Another situation where historical honesty comes into play is infidelity. Marriage counselors are split on this issue. Some say that admitting to marital infidelity will not only hurt the innocent spouse but also could damage their relationship and make it irreparable. Others say that not disclosing the affair will prohibit the couple from enjoying total intimacy, and at the same time, it allows the spouse who committed the infidelity to not be responsible for their actions and could possibly make it easier for them to repeat the behavior. We believe it is best to disclose infidelity but, perhaps, to do so with the assistance of a professional who will help to navigate those challenging waters and rebuild the trust needed for a strong, healthy marriage.

3. *Current honesty.* "Reveal information about the events of your day," says Harley. "Provide your spouse with a calendar of your activities, with special emphasis on those that may affect your spouse."[36] Spouses in a healthy marriage are glad to share what they are doing and what their plans for the day are so they may be reached if the other needs them. But current honesty also involves having access to each other's electronic media and accounts. We share the same password on our cell phones, computer, tablets, and social media accounts. Either one of us can access the other's equipment or accounts anytime, as there is nothing to hide. We also share one calendar, so we know what we each will be doing throughout the day.

4. *Future honesty.* Harley advises, "Reveal your thoughts and plans regarding future activities and objectives."[37] What goals, dreams, or plans do you have that you would like to reach together? Have you talked about places you would like to visit one day or where you would like to retire? All those are important topics to think about and talk about. Don't harbor a secret desire, but share openly with each other about future hopes and dreams.

A judgmental attitude

Being judgmental can do incredible damage to your relationship. When you are judgmental, you are telling your spouse "that it's *not okay* to be themselves."[38] We usually judge our spouse when we cannot accept their behavior, so we try to impose our standards on them. "This builds resentment in them and will eventually corrode even the most intimate relationships."[39] Jesus warned about the danger to relationships when one person judges another. In Matthew 7:1–5, He taught:

"Judge not, that you be not judged. For with what judgment you judge, you will be judged; and with the measure you use, it will be measured back to you. And why do you look at the speck in your brother's eye, but do not consider the plank in your own eye? Or how can you say to your brother, 'Let me remove the speck from your eye'; and look, a plank is in your own eye? Hypocrite! First remove the plank from your own eye, and then you will see clearly to remove the speck from your brother's eye."

We read these words so often that we fail to remember that the "brother" Jesus is talking about includes those closest to us, particularly our spouse. Let's paraphrase this passage:

Do not judge, so that you are not judged. For with what judgment you judge, you will be judged; and with the measure you use, it will be measured back to you. And why do you look at the speck in your husband's or wife's eye, but do not consider the plank in your own eye? Or how can you say to your husband or wife, "Let me remove the speck from your eye;" and look, a plank is in your own eye? Hypocrite! First remove the plank from your own eye, and then you will see clearly to remove the speck from your husband's or wife's eye.

That passage takes on a different emphasis, doesn't it? What right do we have to correct and to try to straighten out our spouse when we fail to acknowledge how much correction we need ourselves? If we need to make any changes in our relationship, we should start with ourselves, not with our spouse. For that self-examination, we really need outside help: "Look deep into my heart, God, and find out everything I am thinking" (Psalm 139:23, CEV). Paul also declared clearly, "Some of you accuse others of doing wrong. But there is no excuse for what you do. When you judge others, you condemn yourselves, because you are guilty of doing the very same things" (Romans 2:1, CEV). When Jesus and Paul tell us not to judge our spouse, they are telling us to avoid viewing our spouse as less-than because of their imperfections. We judge and find our spouse guilty when we grow frustrated, bitter, or angry over what we see as their inadequacies. When we judge them, we see them as unlovable or undeserving of our love and acceptance. Judging them is antithetical to loving them.

Judging our spouse devalues them, so we need to decide how much we value our spouse. Does he or she feel valued by us? Often, we devalue our spouse without realizing it. Here are some of the ways:

- Making jokes at the other's expense or ridiculing them
- Belittling the other person

- Being judgmental of their opinions and feelings
- Making disrespectful comments
- Using name-calling
- Lecturing or sermonizing
- Threatening them
- Forcing the other person to change their behaviors, beliefs, or attitudes

Pastor and author Patrick Schwenk suggests four ways we can take judgment out of our marriage.

1. *"Start by judging yourself."*[40] That's why Jesus tells us in Matthew 7:5 to "remove the plank" out of our own eye. Schwenk writes that, once we do that, "Jesus says we can 'see clearly' to move toward someone else."[41]

2. *"Turn from your sin in the direction of your Savior."*[42] As Burk Parsons writes, "Repentance is a gift. It is an act that the Holy Spirit works in us resulting in an act that flows out of us."[43] Turning toward the Savior is an act of repentance on our part. Instead of turning toward our spouse's faults, we need to turn toward the faultless Savior.

3. *"Walk humbly."*[44] Schwenk says, "A growing awareness of our own sin and need of God's grace should increasingly produce humility in us."[45] As Ellen White writes, "The nearer we come to Jesus, and the more clearly we discern the purity of His character, the more clearly shall we see the exceeding sinfulness of sin, and the less shall we feel like exalting ourselves."[46] Schwenk notes that when we turn toward Jesus, "we are no longer the standard. Jesus is."[47] When we walk humbly toward Jesus, we recognize that "we cannot hold our spouse to a standard that we fail to meet,"[48] writes Schwenk. When we recognize that we are all sinners in need of His grace, we will be less judgmental and more loving, understanding, and compassionate to each other.

4. *"Love one another in grace and truth."*[49] Understanding our personal need for salvation does not mean we ignore, condone, or avoid dealing with sin or conflict. It means we now deal with it from a different vantage point. As Schwenk puts it: "We deal with it from a place of humility and grace."[50] And we remember that Paul instructs, "Always be humble and gentle. Patiently put up with each other and love each other" (Ephesians 4:2, CEV).

Annoying habits

This is an area that includes intentional as well as unintentional behavior. After all, habits are often those things that we do without giving them much thought.

Perhaps you grew up doing things a certain way in your home as a child. But what if your spouse grew up doing the same thing in a different way? Over time, we do something a certain way so much that it becomes a part of who we are, and we operate like robots in so many of the habits we have. But what if those habits annoy your spouse?

You each have habits, and we can guarantee that you have a habit that is annoying to your spouse. Most likely, it's something small: the way in which you squeeze the tube of toothpaste (I, Claudio, know that the correct way is to squeeze it from the bottom of the tube and roll it a little at a time until all the paste is completely used and the tube is empty); where you leave your dirty clothes; leaving hair in the shower (anyone who knows me, Claudio again, knows I'm incapable of doing this); the way you chew your food; and, yes, how you put the toilet paper on the roll.

On the other hand, if you were to ask Pamela, she would tell you that it is abnormal behavior to get the pliers out of the toolbox in order to squeeze the last microscopic amount of toothpaste out of the tube. Yes, Claudio does that, and, yes, it is annoying to Pamela. To be fair, however, she also annoys him when she throws her toothpaste tube away before he attacks it with his pliers.

And toilet paper? Really? Yes, we once had to be mediators over which way the toilet paper should be placed on the roll. Should it roll over, or should it roll under? Imagine being on the brink of divorce over which way the toilet paper should be placed on the roll!

In case you are wondering, the original patent had a diagram that showed the proper way toilet paper should be placed on a roll (see the sidebar diagram). It was to roll over. There! No need to argue anymore. It's too bad that toilet paper today does not come with instructions, because they would prevent many marital spats.

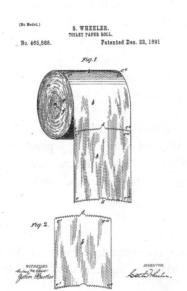

The truth is that many times the little things become *big* things over time. We find that our spouse is doing things that grate on our nerves, but we are often silent until we reach the point of boiling over.

Men often complain about how their wives put their cold feet on them or how they wrap themselves in the blankets and take so much room in the bed. Women complain about how their husbands chew or breathe so loudly and how, when football—or whatever sport—season begins, they lose their husband, and they become sports widows. All of the annoying activities and behaviors your spouse dislikes or even hates make withdrawals in their emotional Love Bank every time you do them.

FOR DISCUSSION

1. What do you do that annoys your spouse? Come on, be honest! We all have annoying traits. If you honestly cannot think of any, just ask your spouse.
2. What steps can you take to change this behavior?

Addictions

Addictive behaviors may or may not have been present before we were married. But as the anniversary years tick by, perhaps there are some addictions that have become more pronounced and destructive over time. Some addictions may seem obvious, but there are others that need to be added to the list. Some of these include the following.

- *Substance abuse.* Drug or alcohol addiction will rapidly cause self-destruction as well as the destruction of your home. According to Jeffrey Juergens on the Addiction Center website, there are important differences between addiction and dependence, and "the terms 'addiction' and 'dependence' are often confused or used interchangeably. While there is some overlap, it's important to understand the major differences between the two."[51]

  Juergens explains that "a dependence is present when a person develops a physical tolerance to a substance."[52] If or when they stop using that substance altogether, they may experience withdrawal symptoms. Often, someone with a substance dependency may be able to resolve it by slowly tapering off the substance.

  "On the other hand," writes Juergens, "an addiction occurs when extensive drug or alcohol use has caused a person's brain chemistry to change. Addictions manifest themselves as uncontrollable cravings to use drugs, despite doing harm to oneself or others. The only way to overcome an addiction is through treatment."[53]

  Addictions don't just happen overnight; rather, they develop over time, slowly and somewhat imperceptibly. "Addictions begin with experimentation with a substance, perhaps out of curiosity, peer pressure, or as a result of stress at home or work," says Juergens.[54]

How would you know if you, your spouse, or someone you know may be struggling with addiction? While everyone is different, here are some warning signs to watch out for, according to Juergens:

- ○ "Ignoring commitments or responsibilities.
- ○ Problems at work, school or at home.
- ○ Unexplained absences.
- ○ Appearing to have a new set of friends.
- ○ Considerable monetary fluctuations.
- ○ Staying up later than usual or sleeping in longer.
- ○ Lapses in concentration or memory.
- ○ Being oddly secretive about parts of personal life.
- ○ Withdrawal from normal social contacts.
- ○ Sudden mood swings and change in behavior.
- ○ Unusual lack of motivation.
- ○ Weight loss or changes in physical appearance."[55]

Research has uncovered the top ten addictions and the approximate number of people in the United States affected by them:

- ○ Tobacco (nicotine): More 40 million
- ○ Alcohol: 18 million
- ○ Marijuana: 4.2 million
- ○ Painkillers (e.g., codeine, Vicodin, and Oxycontin): 1.8 million
- ○ Cocaine: 821,000
- ○ Heroin: 426,000
- ○ Benzodiazepines (e.g., Valium, Xanax, and Klonopin): 400,000
- ○ Stimulants (e.g., prescription drugs like Adderall or Ritalin and illicit substances like meth): 329,000
- ○ Inhalants (e.g., gasoline, household cleaning products, and aerosols): 140,000
- ○ Sedatives (e.g., barbiturates like Lunesta and Ambien): 78,000[56]

The Centers for Disease Control and Prevention has rightly called opioid addiction an epidemic as individuals, families, and communities all across the country are impacted by this crisis.[57] *Opioid* is the umbrella term for medications that relieve acute or chronic pain. What makes opioids so addictive? As explained by the Hazelden Betty

Ford Foundation, "When opioid molecules travel through the bloodstream and into the brain, they attach to opioid receptors on the surface of certain cells. The chemical response triggered in the brain's reward center is the same as the reaction to intense pleasure and reinforces acts such as eating, drinking fluids, caring for babies and having sex—all necessary for survival of the species."[58]

When a person is addicted to alcohol or drugs, they need professional intervention. Getting help does not show that we are weak; rather, it shows an inner strength to admit when we need help, reach out, and get it. When we think about addictions, substance abuse may be one of the first things that come to mind; however, modern times have led to some addictive behaviors that our ancestors never dreamed about.

- *Technology addictions.* Technology addictions are one example of vices that preceding generations did not have to encounter. While technology has been called a modern miracle, it has also proved to be a modern curse to many families. Chances are that you would be surprised to discover how much time you actually spend each day with technology (television, computer, cell phone, and other devices).

   Many of us are addicted to technology and do not even realize it. It has become normal to see families at restaurants together with each family member's head buried in their phones or some other electronic gadget. In fact, it's abnormal to see a family sitting around the table engaged in conversation. A group of friends tried an experiment. They decided that when they went out to eat, they would place their cell phones face down, one on top of the other. If one of the cell phones rang or vibrated, whoever reached out to answer would have to pay the bill for the entire party. They realized they had to take drastic measures to take back the time and joy spent as friends.

   We challenge you to look around the next time you are at a restaurant and test this theory. And we challenge you to start being more mindful of every minute you spend on technology when you are with your family. Those are moments you can never get back: missed opportunities, missed conversations, missed times to bond with each other, missed memories!

   As you do a self-audit, remember to include all forms of technology, such as

   o gaming devices;

- cell phones, computers, tablets;
- social media sites (Facebook, Instagram, Twitter, and others); and
- television.

- *Workaholism.* Do you want to be successful in your career? We hope so. But if your career is your number one goal in life, it can lead to this other addictive and destructive behavior. The problem with the world in which we live is that we never leave the office because our office is as close as our cell phone. We need to set healthy boundaries for work hours in order to protect our family time. Don't give in to the temptation to answer that phone for work-related issues when you are supposed to be spending time with your spouse. In doing so, you are telling your spouse that work, or whoever is calling you, takes priority over time with them. Is that the message you wish to send?

- *Pornography.* Technology has made it much easier and more discreet to access pornography. You no longer need to go to a store and purchase a pornographic magazine. Instead, it is now in the privacy of your home, and it is only a click away. In fact, the number one way that porn is being viewed today is through cell phones. It's easy, discreet, and often free.

Greg Smalley writes about three ways that pornography impacts your marriage:

1. *Intimacy is sacrificed.* Smalley observes, "True intimacy involves being fully known and fully knowing another. It's similar to what the Bible describes in 1 Corinthians 13:12, 'Then I shall know fully, even as I have been fully known.' . . . If you slow the pronunciation of intimacy, you get 'in-to-me-see.' It sounds like being known by another."

2. *Real relationship is forsaken for an imitation.* Smalley goes on to relate a fascinating story: "In the 1950s, renowned researcher Dr. Nikolaas Tinbergen discovered which markings and color patterns on a female butterfly were most irresistible to a male butterfly. He then constructed cardboard dummy butterflies and decorated them with these exaggerated colorations and markings. What he found was astonishing. The male butterflies actually ignored the real female butterflies and kept trying to obsessively mate with the decoys. Porn is no more real than the cardboard butterflies—it's all built on a lie."

3. *The true purpose of sex becomes twisted.* Smalley rightly declares that "sex is a wonderful gift given to a married couple by God as a means

of experiencing physical pleasure together and as a way to experience the deepest, most profound intimacy with a spouse—'and they shall become one flesh' (Genesis 2:24). Unfortunately, pornography twists this true purpose of sex." Smalley goes on to quote these words: "Pornography gives men the false impression that sex and pleasure are entirely divorced from relationships. In other words, pornography is inherently self-centered—something a man does by himself, for himself."[59]

Smalley explains further:

> Because porn is self-centered and self-serving, it doesn't require that husbands be lovers of their wives. In the counterfeit world of porn, sex simply involves an image or video, masturbation and orgasm. The sexual arousal is immediate and gratification is instant—it's all about personal pleasure. In fantasyland, it's easy to pursue a perfectly airbrushed woman who . . . never has a headache, needs no foreplay and requires no ongoing relationship. Porn rewires the brain to focus on "you"—not on intimacy.
>
> God-honoring and marriage-honoring sex is about self-giving love. Righteous sex is about self-sacrifice. It joins two people together in love and should always strengthen a relationship rather than weaken it. The opposite of God's design for sex between a husband and wife can be seen in the use of porn where satisfaction is always at the expense of your spouse—because it's all about you. God created sex to be about love, sacrifice, mutual respect, dignity and care between a husband and wife. Great sex happens when the focus is on serving each other and not on getting our own needs met.[60]

As with other addictions, this is one that is very difficult to deal with on our own. If you have doubts as to whether you are addicted (or are in denial), you may use one of several online tests for pornography addiction, such as the Sexual Addiction Screening Test and the Internet Sex Screening Test. If you know you are addicted, you need to take three important steps for breaking free: (1) attend a twelve-step group, (2) seek professional counseling, and (3) receive marriage counseling. If this is something you or a loved one struggle with, please check out one of our newest resources online at www.newfreedomtolove.org. Everything is free to download and watch in the privacy of your own home.

Abusive behavior

Let's be very clear from the beginning: abusive behavior in any form is unacceptable and inexcusable! God never intended for His son or His daughter to experience abuse at the hands of anyone, let alone someone who is supposed to love, honor, and cherish them. Because abuse is a very extensive topic, we encourage you to visit our website, nadfamily.org and enditnownorthamerica .org for more resources.

Explosions of anger

According to *Psychology Today*, anger in and of itself is simply "one of the basic human emotions, as elemental as happiness, sadness, anxiety, or disgust." It can be very positive and beneficial, or it can become very negative and destructive. "Anger is related to the 'fight, flight, or freeze' response of the sympathetic nervous system; it prepares humans to fight," notes *Psychology Today*. "But fighting doesn't necessarily mean throwing punches." Anger directed in a positive way may "motivate communities to combat injustice by changing laws or enforcing new behavioral norms."[61]

Even the Bible speaks of anger as a very normal and natural emotion. We often quote the words of Paul: "Be angry, and do not sin" (Ephesians 4:26). Neither Paul nor any other Bible writer, forbids anger or considers it bad. What the Bible considers sin is when we allow anger to become harmful to us or others. Solomon wrote, "Control your temper, for anger labels you a fool" (Ecclesiastes 7:9, NLT).

Have you ever been distracted and had someone come from behind and scare you? What is your first reaction after fear itself? Is it anger? A good way to understand anger is by picturing an iceberg. As you probably know, most of the iceberg is hidden beneath the water's surface. In the same way, when we are angry, it's likely that there are "other emotions hidden beneath the surface. It's easy to see a person's anger, but it can be difficult to see the underlying feelings."[62]

In a relationship, one of the things that can be most harmful is explosions of anger. Whether we recognize it or not, we often use anger as a way to control our spouse. Perhaps we have tried some of the other destructive habits and behaviors, such as being judgmental or selfish, or perhaps we have been disrespectful, but we have not gotten the desired results. The next time we get angry, we elicit a response from our spouse and figure out that maybe that's one way to exert control over them.

Do you remember that time you were driving with your wife and an argument ensued? You were losing the battle, and you knew it. So suddenly, you pushed the pedal to the metal and started changing lanes and going around curves faster than what was safe. Your wife got scared and begged you to slow down. Aha! You got her attention, didn't you?

Do you remember that time when you got angry with your husband for coming home late—again? You had told him so many times not to do that or to at least call you when he was going to be late, and yet he did it again! So you got a few dishes and threw them against the wall or took a hammer and broke the television screen or scratched his car. Those explosions of anger were the manifestation of deeper feelings of frustration or helplessness. You may have gotten their attention temporarily, but in the long run, you withdrew a load of points out of your spouse's emotional Love Bank.

Think about the repercussions of an explosion of anger. Anger affects your spouse, your marriage, and your children. Quite often, parents have asked us for help with their children's misbehavior. But as we begin to dig deeper into their relationship, we find out that there's a lot of stress, anger, and unresolved conflict between the parents. In psychology, we refer to this as *triangulation*. For instance, Mom and Dad are continually fighting (yelling, screaming, or giving each other the silent treatment). Their son—who has for the most part had an even temper—picks up on this tension and becomes concerned that his parents may split up as the parents of some of his friends have. In an attempt to keep his parents together, his tactic is to distract them from their conflict. He begins diverting their attention to him by being disobedient, not doing well in school, or doing anything else that will make his parents angry at him and not at each other. They form an unhealthy triangle.

Triangulation may happen in other relationships too. Your coworker complains about you to her supervisor. Then the supervisor talks to you instead of directing your coworker to talk to you directly—thus forming an unhealthy triangle. The deacon at church who does not agree with the elder tells the pastor. If the pastor does not encourage the deacon to talk directly to the elder and instead goes and addresses the issue with the elder himself, he triangulates that relationship. Knowing the relational danger of triangulating, Jesus commanded us to take certain steps: "If your brother sins against you, go and tell him his fault, between you and him alone. If he listens to you, you have gained your brother. But if he does not listen, take one or two others along with you, that every charge may be established by the evidence of two or three witnesses. If he refuses to listen to them, tell it to the church. And if he refuses to listen even to the church, let him be to you as a Gentile and a tax collector" (Matthew 18:15–17, ESV).

In dealing with conflict, Paul is clear: " 'Don't sin by letting anger control you.' Don't let the sun go down while you are still angry" (Ephesians 4:26, NLT). This text is probably the origin of the well-known advice, "Never go to bed angry." There is wisdom in these words.

Stephanie Kirby lists some of the reasons why you shouldn't go to bed angry:

- "It gives you a rough start the next day. . . .

- It allows the problem to grow. . . .
- It does not go away. . . .
- You won't sleep well. . . .
- It can make resolving the situation more difficult."[63]

At the same time, she cautions that there may be times when going to bed angry is OK. She lists the following reasons:

- "It's not something that can be easily resolved. . . .
- Things seem worse at night. . . .
- Alcohol or drugs are involved. . . .
- You aren't thinking clearly. . . .
- You're no longer talking about the real issue."[64]

When he wrote about anger and sin, Paul may have been thinking of Psalm 4:4, where David wrote, "Don't sin by letting anger control you. Think about it overnight and remain silent" (Psalm 4:4, NLT). While both texts from Paul and David have similarities, they also seem contradictory. One says to not let the sun go down on your anger, and the other says to meditate on your bed and be still. We think they both offer good advice. The point is: Don't let anger control you. Try to resolve whatever is causing it as soon as possible. At the same time, you may need to get some rest overnight in order to think about it rationally; but in the meantime, don't sin by adding fuel to the fire by saying hurtful or harmful things. (For more information on how to manage conflict, check out chapter 7.)

CONCLUSION

If we're honest with ourselves, we are all guilty of practicing at least one of these destructive habits. As a reminder, here is the list again:

1. Lying and deception
2. A judgmental attitude
3. Annoying habits
4. Addictions
5. Abusive behavior
6. Explosions of anger

We need to pray that God will reveal to us our shortcomings and that He will help us admit them, seek forgiveness from Him and from our spouse, and commit to refraining from repeating these destructive behaviors in the future.

SOME HOMEWORK

In our couples' retreats, we like to give some homework, which the couples need to begin doing over the weekend event. We want to share the same homework with you so you, too, can begin putting the principles into practice. It is our hope that these simple things will be practiced on a regular basis and become habits in your relationship.

Pray

While it may go without saying, we believe that every marriage will benefit from the practice of daily prayer. Not only do we enlist God's help, but it also brings us closer. We should experience daily, individual communion with our God, but in addition, we recommend praying together as a couple.

We do warn couples, however, to make sure they do not use prayer as a weapon against each other. For instance, gentlemen, it is not appropriate to pray something like, "Please bless my wife and make her a nice, loving person. Help her, so she may not be as mean as she is." That is not a prayer but a hurtful weapon. In the same way, ladies, don't pray for your husband by saying words like, "Bless this miserable husband, rotten scoundrel that he is. Better yet, give me a good one instead." You may smile about these prayers, but believe us, we have heard even worse. Instead, pray out loud for each other's well-being, for health, for safety, for wisdom, for help with challenges, and so on. If you're not used to praying together, you may find it a bit uncomfortable at first, but as you do it regularly, it will become second nature. It will be a joy and a wonderful experience of spiritual intimacy with your mate and with God.

Here are a few tips from Janet Thompson, and some additional ones from us, to help you make the best of your couple's prayer time:

- Pray out loud for each other.
- Pray about each other's concerns, dreams, health, and so on.
- Make praying together a priority in your daily routine.
- Pray in a place where you will not be interrupted.
- Find a mutually agreeable time to pray and set reminders on your phones. If mornings are best, Thompson says, "make it a pleasant time over a cup of coffee or tea." If you decide to pray in the evenings, Thompson advises that you "pray before you get into bed, because both of you probably will be exhausted at the end of the day and it'll be hard to stay awake."
- Take turns. "If one of you is more comfortable than the other praying aloud, have that person start and the other spouse join in or say his or her own prayer," advises Thompson. "Or do

conversational prayer, in which you alternate praying, just like
talking to each other."

- Until you become accustomed to praying together, keep your
prayers short.
- Prepare notes beforehand to jog your memory as your pray. Thompson says, "Write down things you want to remember to pray about.
It's okay to pray with your eyes open so you can look at your notes."
- Enjoy physical closeness as you pray. "Hold hands or embrace while
you pray," encourages Thompson.
- Pray before you leave for work, but also pray before you get in bed.[65]

Remember, prayer is simply having a conversation with God. You don't have
to use big theological terms or sound "spiritual." Just pour out your heart to the
only One who can really help.

Hug

The second bit of homework we want you to begin to practice daily is hugging
to relax. Now, this is not just a quick hug or one from a distance (a.k.a., the
A-frame hug). We learned about the hug to relax by best-selling author and psychologist David Schnarch.[66] Again, you may not be used to doing it. Perhaps
you have not done it since you were dating or early in your marriage. So we'll
explain what we want you to do.

Start by taking a few minutes to slow down, relax, and slow your heart rate.
Then stand facing your partner just a few feet away. You don't have to rush through
this; but, instead, just get a balanced, well-grounded stance. For just a brief moment, close your eyes, take a breath, and relax again. Then, open your eyes, and
when the two of you are ready, move slowly forward while trying to maintain your
relaxed, balanced position until you have one foot between your partner's feet.

If you try a romantic, Hollywood-style hug (her arms around his shoulder, his
arms around her waist as she lifts one leg), it will not be balanced nor relaxing.
Instead, get close enough that you can easily put your arms around your spouse
without feeling off-balance. Find the most comfortable position for both of you.
Are you laughing? Perhaps. That may be the feeling of nervousness as you try
something you have not done in a while.

While holding each other in this relaxed position, concentrate on your breathing. Breathe slowly and simply enjoy the moment and your spouse's embrace.
It is possible, particularly if you have been having tension or conflict in your
marriage, that lots of feelings about your spouse, your relationship, and yourself
may surface. Pay attention to those feelings; but don't stop hugging because of
them. Remain in that position for a few minutes, simply holding each other

comfortably, breathing softly and slowly, and letting time go lightly in each other's embrace. After a few minutes (it may only be one or two minutes at first), talk about the experience with your spouse.

Schnarch explains that it often takes several months of practice, several times a week, but you'll be amazed by the improvements this simple act brings to your marriage. Therefore, this is not a once-in-a-lifetime piece of homework; this is daily homework. In a comic strip, one lady tells her friend, "Wrap your leftovers in plastic to keep your food fresh. Wrap your husband in hugs to keep your marriage fresh." How true that is. The reason hugging to relax is so effective is because the physical closeness releases the pleasure and happiness hormones dopamine, oxytocin, serotonin, and endorphins. The key is not in a quick or a romantic hug but in one that allows us to relax in each other's arms. As another comic described it, "I love the kind of hugs where you can physically feel the sadness leaving your body."

Kiss

The last bit of homework we want to leave with you before we end this chapter is to kiss. Similar to the hug to relax, a kiss that can bring healing and strength to your relationship must last at least ten seconds. We like how Ellen Kreidman explains it:

> When a couple stands at the altar and vows to love each other "till death do us part," they take for granted that they will stay intimately connected forever. The kiss at the end of the ceremony is symbolic of that connection, and throughout the relationship, the kiss remains at the core.
>
> Sadly, as the years pass, staying connected with our mate gradually takes a back seat to all the mundane duties and chores that exist in a marriage. In reality, everything else should take a back seat to our love for each other. . . .
>
> . . . What starts out as a passionate relationship, over time, winds up as a friendship. We are so caught up in our daily routine that we forget all about keeping closeness and passion alive. Many times we're not even aware that this change has occurred, but one day we wake up and realize with a shock that we are living as roommates instead of lovers. . . .
>
> Engaging in a ten-second kiss every day declares that you are lovers—not just roommates. It helps you stay connected. Even though you may tell your mate you love them every day, giving them a ten-second kiss tells them, "I'm still in love with you."[67]

So, starting tonight, do these three pieces of homework: (1) pray together as a couple, (2) hug to relax, and (3) kiss for at least ten seconds. After you finish your homework, if you want to continue with extracurricular activities, it is entirely up to you. *Wink!*

1. Ellen G. White, *Mind, Character, and Personality*, vol. 1 (Nashville: Southern Publishing Association, 1977), 10.

2. Ellie Lisitsa, "The Four Horsemen: The Antidotes," The Gottman Institute, April 26, 2013, https://www.gottman.com/blog/the-four-horsemen-the-antidotes/.

3. John Gottman, *Why Marriages Succeed or Fail* (London: Bloomsbury, 2007), 74.

4. Gottman, *Why Marriages Succeed or Fail*, 75.

5. Ellen G. White, *Spiritual Gifts*, vol. 4a (Washington, DC: Review and Herald®, 1945), 112.

6. Howard J. Markman, Scott M. Stanley, and Susan L. Blumberg, *Fighting for Your Marriage* (San Francisco: Jossey-Bass, 2001).

7. Ellen G. White, *Patriarchs and Prophets* (Mountain View, CA: Pacific Press®, 1958), 708.

8. Nan Silver, "What Makes Marriage Work?" *Psychology Today*, last reviewed on June 9, 2016, https://www.psychologytoday.com/us/articles/199403/what-makes-marriage-work.

9. Silver, "What Makes Marriage Work?"

10. Gottman, *Why Marriages Succeed or Fail*, 84.

11. Markman, Stanley, and Blumberg, *Fighting for Your Marriage*.

12. Kevin Downing and Peter Robbins, "Invalidation in Marriage," accessed July 31, 2020, http://www.turningpointcounseling.org/uploads/1/1/3/5/11359523/_part_3_-_invalidation_in_marriage.pdf.

13. Gottman, *Why Marriages Succeed or Fail*.

14. Markman, Stanley, and Blumberg, *Fighting for Your Marriage*.

15. Jade A. Enrique, Heather R. Howk, and William G. Huitt, *An Overview of Family Development* (Valdosta, GA: Valdosta State University, 2007), 6.

16. "Three States of Mind in Marriage: Withdrawal," Marriage Builders, accessed August 2, 2020, https://www.marriagebuilders.com/withdrawal.htm.

17. "Withdrawal."

18. White, *Patriarchs and Prophets*, 711.

19. Hara Estroff Mirano, "Our Brain's Negative Bias," June 20, 2003. *Psychology Today*, accessed August 20, 2020, https://www.psychologytoday.com/us/articles/200306/our-brains-negative-bias.

20. Lisitsa, "The Four Horsemen."

21. Leanna Stockard, "The Antidotes of the Four Horsemen," Symmetry Counseling, January 21, 2019, https://www.symmetrycounseling.com/marriage-counseling-chicago/the-antidotes-of-the-four-horsemen/#:~:text=Criticism's%20Antidote%20%E2%80%93%20Gentle%20Start%20Up,statements%2C%20which%20according%20to%20Dr.

22. "How to Be Assertive Asking for What You Want Firmly and Fairly," Mended Hearts Therapeutic Center, February 7, 2019, https://mended-hearts.org/how-to-be-assertive-asking-for-what-you-want-firmly-and-fairly/.

23. "How to Be Assertive."

24. Ron L. Deal and David H. Olson, *The Remarriage Checkup* (Bloomington, MN: Bethany House, 2010), 152.

25. "Mignon McLaughlin," Wikiquote, updated on May 13, 2019, https://en.wikiquote.org/wiki/Mignon_McLaughlin.

26. Gottman, *Why Marriages Succeed or Fail*, 176.

27. "Robert Browning," AZ Quotes, accessed February 14, 2020, https://www.azquotes.com/quote/606452.

28. Scott Palmer and Bethany Palmer (The Money Couple), "3 Horrible Outcomes of Financial Dishonesty in Marriage," *The Money Couple* (blog), February 9, 2019, https://themoneycouple.com/3-horrible-outcomes-of-financial-dishonesty-in-marriage/.

29. Lorie Konish, "Tell-Tale Signs That Your Partner Is Guilty of Financial Infidelity," CNBC, January 23, 2018, https://www.cnbc.com/2018/01/23/tell-tale-signs-that-your-partner-is-guilty-of-financial-infidelity.html.

30. Konish, "Tell-Tale Signs."

31. Konish, "Tell-Tale Signs."

32. Frank Gunzburg, "Honesty in Marriage," Frank Gunzburg, PhD, accessed August 2, 2020, https://marriage-counselor-doctor.com/honesty-marriage.

33. Willard Harley, *Love Busters* (Grand Rapids, MI: Revell, 2008).

34. Harley, *Love Busters*, 126.

35. Harley, 126.

36. Harley, 126.

37. Harley, 126.

38. "Judgment—The Ultimate Relationship Destroyer," The Overwhelmed Brain, accessed August 2, 2020, https://theoverwhelmedbrain.com/judgment/; emphasis in original.

39. "Judgment."

40. Patrick Schwenk, "Four Ways to Take Judgement Out of Your Marriage," TheCourage, https://www.thecourage.com/four-ways-to-take-judgement-out-of-your-marriage/.

41. Schwenk, "Four ways to Take Judgement Out of Your Marriage."

42. Schwenk, "Four ways to Take Judgement Out of Your Marriage."

43. Burk Parsons, "The Gift of Repentance," Ligonier Ministries, December 1, 2006 https://www.ligonier.org/learn/articles/gift-repentance/.

44. Schwenk, "Four ways to Take Judgement Out of Your Marriage."

45. Schwenk, "Four ways to Take Judgement Out of Your Marriage."

46. Ellen G. White, *The Acts of the Apostles* (Mountain View, CA: Pacific Press®, 1911), 561.

47. Schwenk, "Four ways to Take Judgement Out of Your Marriage."

48. Schwenk, "Four ways to Take Judgement Out of Your Marriage."

49. Schwenk, "Four ways to Take Judgement Out of Your Marriage."

50. Schwenk, "Four ways to Take Judgement Out of Your Marriage."

51. Jeffrey Juergens, "What Is Addiction?" Addiction Center, updated June 18, 2020, https://www.addictioncenter.com/addiction/.

52. Juergens, "What Is Addiction?"

53. Juergens, "What Is Addiction?"

54. Juergens, "What Is Addiction?"

55. Juergens, "What Is Addiction?"

56. Jeffrey Juergens, "Here Are the 10 Most Common Addictions," Addiction Center, updated July 2, 2020, https://www.addictioncenter.com/addiction/10-most-common-addictions/.

57. "Opioid Overdose: Opioid Basics," Centers for Disease Control and Prevention, accessed August 20, 2020, https://www.cdc.gov/drugoverdose/epidemic/index.html.

58. "Opioid and Heroin Addiction," Hazelden Betty Ford Foundation, accessed August 20, 2020, https://www.hazeldenbettyford.org/addiction/types-of-addiction/opioids.

59. Greg Smalley, "How Pornography Impacts Marriage," Focus on the Family, May 9, 2016, https://www.focusonthefamily.com/marriage/how-pornography-impacts-marriage/.

60. Smalley, "How Pornography Impacts Marriage."

61. "Anger," *Psychology Today*, accessed August 3, 2020, https://www.psychologytoday.com

/us/basics/anger#:~:text=Anger%20is%20one%20of%20the,it%20prepares%20humans%20to%20fight.

62. Kyle Benson, "The Anger Iceberg," The Gottman Institute, November 8, 2016, https://www.gottman.com/blog/the-anger-iceberg/.

63. Stephanie Kirby, "Is Going to Bed Angry Bad for You?" BetterHelp, updated August 27, 2019, https://www.betterhelp.com/advice/anger/is-going-to-bed-angry-bad-for-you/.

64. Kirby, "Is Going to Bed Angry Bad for You?"

65. Janet Thompson, "10 Tips for Praying as a Couple," Crosswalk.com, July 17, 2013, https://www.crosswalk.com/family/marriage/engagement-newlyweds/10-tips-for-praying-as-a-couple.html.

66. David Schnarch, *A Passionate Marriage* (New York: W. W. Norton, 1997).

67. Ellen Kreidman, *The 10 Second Kiss* (New York: Dell, 1998), 19, 22, 23.

Chapter Four

What I Need From Her

However, each one of you also must love his wife as he loves himself,
and the wife must respect her husband.
—Ephesians 5:33, NIV

We want to begin this chapter by giving you some very important, even vital information—something that might revolutionize the way you think: men and women are different! What! You already knew that? OK, we tell that to our couples during a retreat, and they respond with laughter. We know that! But do we really understand just *how* different we are? We show our couples a series of pictures that illustrate the differences, in general terms, between men and women.

The first picture is of a man and woman standing in front of the mirror in their swimwear. She is slim and shapely, but as she looks in the mirror, she sees a woman who is very large and overweight. He, on the other hand, is balding, bulging out of his swim trunks with a large belly protruding in front of him; however, as he looks in the mirror, he sees a much younger version of himself, with an athletic body and a six-pack. In other words, women judge themselves much more harshly than the typical male when it comes to body image.

Another stark difference between men and women is how men and women shop. In general (please notice the word *general*), men do not enjoy shopping. When a man goes to a store like Walmart or Target, he will already know what he wants, and that's all he will be looking for. He will go in the store, take a look around to try to figure out where that item is, and walk directly to the aisle where he thinks he can find the item he came for. Oh, he may have gone to the wrong aisle at first, but he will make a quick course correction and head to the correct aisle where he will find the item, get the item, go straight to the cashier, pay for the item, and leave.

From personal experience, I (Claudio) can testify to the truth of that description. If, for instance, I need a pair of black pants, I will go to a store that sells men's clothing, walk into the store, go directly to the section where I will find the pants, go to the area where the black pants are (because I didn't come looking for blue jeans, white pants, or gray pants), look for a pair in my size, take them to the cashier, and pay for them. I can be in and out of that store within five or ten minutes. When I get home, I'll try the pants on. If they don't fit, I'll ask Pam to go return them for me. In reality, my wife knows me so well and knows what I like and don't like that it's a whole lot easier (and less stressful) for both of us if she buys my clothes. She's happy to go shopping, and I'm happy not to go!

Women, on the other hand, enjoy or even love to go shopping (again, please remember we are speaking in general). Pam says it is therapeutic for her, while it is maddening for me. She will go to the store and go to the section where women's pants are. Now, keep in mind she's not even sure she's looking for pants in the first place. She will look at all the different colors and styles of pants, run her hands through the material, pick them off the rack, look them over, place them back, pick one pair of black pants, go to the fitting room to try the pants on, and then come out; put them back on the rack; and start over again. She will repeat this same scene with the red pants, the pink pants, the white pants, the yellow pants, and, after trying on all the pants in the store, she will move on to the skirt section. There, she will try on several skirts in that section before moving to the blouse section and then to the shoe section and then the purse section, and after three hours, she walks out of that store . . . with nothing. (Pam thinks Claudio should be singing the "Hallelujah Chorus" at this point, since the bank account is untouched!)

Now please understand: I am happy Pam doesn't spend a lot of money shopping. I'm thrilled that she does not come out of that store with several bags and receipts longer than those at a CVS Pharmacy. It's just that spending three hours at a clothing store looking at and trying on clothes is not what we men would usually describe as fun, enjoyable, or therapeutic. Women, on the other hand, tend to use such words to describe going window-shopping or even looking through a clothing catalog, whether it is in print or online.

Now I do want to make something clear: I have always loved and appreciated that Pam dresses very nicely and looks lovely no matter where we're going. But she has managed to do that without spending a lot of money in the process. She has discovered the joy of searching through thrift stores and secondhand stores. She has found some very nice clothes, and donated many of her own, at these stores. Sometimes she has found dresses with the original price tag still on the dress but at a drastically reduced cost.

I remember the day she came home from one of her thrift store excursions, and when she came into the family room, she showed me a dress she had bought at a thrift store in one of the nicest neighborhoods in the Washington, DC, area. With a big smile of satisfaction on her face, she showed me the dress and asked, "Do you like this dress?" She then told me the name of some designer. I have to confess I don't know much about designers, but I think it was something like Ford, Toyota, or something. She proudly told me, "It's a $700 dress!" A few minutes later—when I came to—she said, "No, no, honey; I didn't pay $700 for it—I paid only $3 for it."

Whew, that was certainly a relief! But then she went on to tell me that she had also found a pair of matching designer shoes. She held them up to show me and told me the name of the designer. Again, I don't know much about shoe designers, but I think she said something like Samsung—I don't know. Anyway, she told me they were $200 for the pair, but she had bought them for $2. Imagine that! She was so happy that she had just bought a $1,000 outfit, made by famous designers, but she had only paid $5 for the entire outfit. I, too, was so happy and proud of my wife that I took out my wallet, pulled out a $20 bill, gave it to her, and gladly told her, "Here, babe, buy yourself four more. Don't even worry about bringing me the change." You see, I am very generous with my wife—she can spend it all if she wants (at thrift stores).

I hate shopping, and she loves shopping. And in general terms, that's how most men and women are. Related to shopping, here is how a man and a woman look at clothing. A woman will look at her closet, full of clothes, and will declare with sadness, "I've got nothing to wear . . . again." A man will have a couple of pairs of pants and shirts and one pair of shoes and think, *I'm all set for a long time.*

I have not gone to a barbershop in many years, so I don't know how much a haircut costs, but I know a man goes in with long, unkept hair and comes out with a nice haircut and it costs him somewhere around $20. A woman goes to the beauty salon, and when she comes out, her hair looks exactly the same as when she went in, but she has paid $200 to get it done that way.

Take some time to look at a woman's shower stall. You will find the usual shampoo and conditioner. But you will also find face cleanser, body cleanser, aloe vera cream, micro scrub, macro scrub, apricot cleansing foam, coconut oil body cream, natural toning lotion, and an assortment of stones, towels, sponges, razors, and brushes. A man's shower stall only has one bottle—a three-in-one shampoo, conditioner, and body soap—and he probably uses the same product to wash his dog.

There are many ways in which men and women, in general, are different from each other. We may laugh about the differences (or argue about them), but they are there. And we praise God for those differences. That's what makes us good at what we do, and that's how we complement and love each other. But a very important area in which we are different is in our most important emotional needs. "An emotional need," as Willard Harley defines it, "is a craving that, when satisfied, makes us feel happy and fulfilled and, when unsatisfied, makes us feel unhappy and frustrated."[1] We're not talking about physical needs, such as food, rest, safety, and so on. Nor are we talking about spiritual needs, such as communion with God, salvation, or the Holy Spirit. We are specifically referring to the emotional needs of men and women in this and the next chapter.

FOR DISCUSSION

Before you begin the discovery of the most important emotional needs of men, we would like to ask you, wives, to make a list of what you think are the top three things your husband needs. Husbands, make a list of the top three things you actually need. Don't peek at the other's list until you are finished. Then share with each other and discuss your responses. The list may change after you have read this chapter, but this exercise will help you think about this and compare your thoughts. (Ladies, we will discuss your needs in the next chapter, so your turn is coming.)

1. _____
2. _____
3. _____

Now that you have shared your lists with each other, let's look at the top five things that a husband needs according to research.

1. WIVES, RESPECT YOUR HUSBAND

Some marriage experts have various lists of what a husband needs in marriage; however, we have decided to place respect at the top of the list because it aligns with the scripture that we have chosen to highlight in this chapter (Ephesians 5:33). Scripture makes it clear that wives are called to respect their husbands. It is a fundamental need for men. But what does it mean for a wife to respect her husband? Is it blind allegiance and uncompromising obedience?

Most women do not understand this concept and wonder why a man would choose respect over love. It's because God wired us differently. Women desire love, while men desire respect. To a man, respect is one of the deepest ways that his wife can express love toward him. But women often fail to understand that a man equates his wife's respect and admiration for him with love.

The biblical instruction to respect our husbands has often been misunderstood, and for that reason, it is disliked by many women. Respect does not, in fact, mean blind submission and obedience. If you really want to understand Ephesians 5:33, go back and read the first chapter, paying close attention to the husband's role in marriage. You see, if the husband is leading in the manner that God ordained, then there is no problem with respecting him. If the husband loves his wife "as Christ also loved the church and gave Himself for her" (Ephesians 5:25), then respect will follow naturally.

What does respect mean to a husband? How can you show respect toward your husband? It's actually a lot easier than you think. It does not mean that when your husband comes home from work, you will throw yourself at his feet with great devotion and shout, "The lord and master of this kingdom has returned to his domain. I am at your service, my king. Your wish is my command!" Although I (Claudio) confess that I would not mind if Pam welcomed me home like that. OK, I'm just kidding. In reality, you show respect to your husband when you express appreciation for what he does for you and your family.

Say, for instance, that you ask your husband to hang a picture on a certain wall for you. When he does it, do you say thank you? Or, when he fixes something in the car for you, do you let him know you appreciate it? I remember the day my wife got home from work and noticed I had mowed the grass. As soon as she came into the house, she said to me, "The yard looks really nice." That's all she said—but, boy, did I want that grass to grow so I could mow it again! The fact that she had noticed what I did, and told me about it, made me feel great. No one likes being taken for granted. For us men, what we do to contribute to the health and well-being of our family is important, and it means a lot when our wives let us know how much they appreciate what we do for her and the family.

As we were getting close to paying off our house, I let Pam know when I thought we might be able to do so. I told her once that it would probably be in another couple of years. A few months later, I told her it might be early the next year. And then I told her it looked like we might be able to finish paying for it later that same year, a lot sooner than the length of the mortgage and sooner than either of us anticipated paying the mortgage off. To this day, I remember her telling me, "I'm so happy—you're so good with our finances!" Boy, that felt good. Mind you, I am no financial guru, but I was happy to know she thought I was. That's what we mean by showing respect or appreciation toward your husband.

Perhaps one misconception many people have is that respect has to be earned. But respect is a choice. In other words, you can decide to show respect. Imagine if love had to be earned. Nancy C. Anderson speaks of her personal experience and the time when her marriage was on the brink of divorce. Working with a Christian counselor, she learned that instead of waiting for her husband to earn her respect, she should behave respectfully and watch him grow into the man God designed him to be. She came up with a plan. She would treat him as a VIP:

Verbally: "Cut out complaining . . . and add in compliments."

Intellectually: "Men like to solve problems and fix things. So appeal to
his intelligence by asking him to help you solve a problem."
Physically: "Ask what he would like you to do and then, do it."[2]

There are many other ways in which you can express and show appreciation
to your husband. For instance, recognize that we are all fallible human beings, so
when your husband makes a mistake, he knows it. Don't remind him by telling
him, "I told you so." That's demeaning. Pray that he will learn, that he won't
make the same mistake again, and that things will turn out for the best, and
then focus on what your husband does well. As you begin each day, pray that
God will help you follow the example of Jesus and that He will help you count
your husband's needs as more significant than your own (Philippians 2:1–4).

It's important to do what you can to build your husband up, so speak about
him in positive terms to others. Never belittle him, in person or behind his back,
and never make him feel that he is unnecessary or incapable. Because God has
called men to be and act as the spiritual priests of the home, encourage him
when he gives spiritual direction to your family. This is particularly important to
do in front of your children. Speak to them about their father's positive character
traits both as a husband and as a father. Tell them about his work and sacrifices
for the family and encourage them to express their own appreciation directly to
him. When you do this regularly in front of your husband, it not only shows him
that you respect him but it also helps your children develop a loving, respectful
attitude toward their dad and toward marriage.

A husband who loves his wife in the manner that Christ describes may be
easy to respect. But how do you show respect to your husband if he is unloving
toward you? Our friend and best-selling author Shaunti Feldhahn has an interesting response as to how you can get past this and to a place of respect. She
suggests trying a 30-Day Kindness Challenge:

> First, for the next 30 days *don't say anything negative about your hus-
> band* . . . either to him or about him to someone else. Not your mom,
> not your best girlfriend, *no one*.
>
> Let me repeat that, so you really 'get it': Say nothing negative about
> him. . . .
>
> And second, every day for the next 30 days, find one thing positive
> that he has done that you can praise or thank him for, and tell him,
> and tell at least one other person.
>
> Third, do one small act of kindness or generosity for him daily.[3]

Feldhahn goes on to say, "The beauty of our psychological wiring is that *our feelings follow our words and actions*, and so the more you focus on what you are dissatisfied with, the more dissatisfied you will be. But the more you focus on the positive, the more you will see and be struck by the truly wonderful things about your husband. The more you will, in fact, respect him."[4]

Did you catch that? "Our feelings follow our words and actions." So even if we do not feel like being respectful, we can still act in respectful ways, and our feelings will soon follow. Our goal is not to change our spouse. Let the Holy Spirit do that. But we can change how we view our spouse, with the help of the Holy Spirit.

We have already stated it several times, but we must say it again: both men and women need to be loved and respected. This is not a one-way street. Respect is the way a wife shows love to her husband. But a husband should also show respect to his wife. He may tell her a thousand times that he loves her, but if he is disrespectful to her, particularly in front of the children or in public, those words and actions will cancel out any words of love he expresses to her. As Shaunti Feldhahn reminds us, "What 'I love you' says to a woman, 'thank you' says to a man."[5]

Let's think back for a moment to the principle of the emotional Love Bank. Every time you show and express respect and appreciation for your husband, you are making a deposit in his emotional Love Bank. If you could look inside his emotional Love Bank to determine what your account balance is, would you say it is overflowing? Or is it overdrawn? Would you say that, in this particular area of the need for respect, your husband is fully satisfied, barely surviving, or emotionally thirsty?

Now, for some of you husbands, you may feel emotionally thirsty because you don't hear from your wife often enough the words of respect, admiration, and appreciation that you are craving. At the same time, you are hearing those words from other women. Perhaps a colleague, a friend, your administrative assistant, or a sister from church tells you innocently enough that she likes your tie or that she appreciates the work you do, the message you delivered, or the decisions you make. You hear those words often enough that their account in your Love Bank grows to the point where you begin to feel some attraction toward them. Solomon described such a person: "For the lips of a forbidden woman drip honey, and her speech is smoother than oil" (Proverbs 5:3, ESV). Many men have fallen for that other woman and have left their wife and family for that woman. But Solomon, in his wisdom, also knew that not everything that glitters is gold, as he writes, "But in the end she is bitter as wormwood, sharp as a two-edged sword" (verse 4, ESV).

Just to be clear, we do not blame a wife because her husband has been unfaithful to her. The dynamics of an affair are much more involved than a wife not meeting her husband's needs, or vice versa. At the same time, if we intentionally aim to meet our spouses' most important emotional needs, we will be minimizing the impact of the deposits other people may make in their emotional Love Bank. Be intentional about keeping your relationship fresh and strong. As Solomon encourages husbands: "Drink water from your own well—share your love only with your wife" (verse 15, NLT). And in verse 19, he states, "She is a loving deer, a graceful doe. Let her breasts satisfy you always. May you always be captivated by her love" (NLT).

In *Pickles*, one of our favorite comic strips, Opal says to Earl, "You could be a little more helpful around here, you know, Earl." Earl responds, "What are you talking about? Who cleaned the toilet without being asked?" Opal comes back, "That's right, and then you kept mentioning it every day for a week." Finally, Earl concludes, "Sometimes you have to toot your own horn, or it never gets tooted." If you hear your husband mention the things he has done around the house or the things he has bought or done for the family, he may just be saying indirectly, "I need your affirmation, I need your appreciation—I am starving for your respect."

FOR DISCUSSION

Wives, write three to five specific things that you appreciate, respect, or admire in your husband. Then share them with him:

1. _____
2. _____
3. _____
4. _____
5. _____

Continue to add to this list and continue to express your respect and admiration every day.

2. GOD INVENTED SEX

Sex was a gift given to us by God, our Creator. It is humanity who has marred that gift. The joy of sex within the confines of marriage is God ordained. We're amazed that even in the twenty-first century, there are still so many who believe that sex is a sinful act that came into the world after the fall of Adam and Eve. Many others believe that sex was only intended for procreation, and therefore the moment a woman is no longer able to conceive, she and her husband should cease having sexual intercourse.

In his first letter to the church in Corinth, Paul spoke about sexuality quite extensively, so it was obviously an issue for the church at that time. Chapter 7 of 1 Corinthians is one of the most significant chapters in the New Testament dealing with marriage, and here Paul shares several important principles dealing with sex within the context of marriage. Let's read it as a whole, and then we'll make some specific comments:

> Now concerning the things of which you wrote to me:
> It is good for a man not to touch a woman. Nevertheless, because of sexual immorality, let each man have his own wife, and let each woman have her own husband. Let the husband render to his wife the affection due her, and likewise also the wife to her husband. The wife does not have authority over her own body, but the husband does. And likewise, the husband does not have authority over his own body, but the wife does. Do not deprive one another except with consent for a time, that you may give yourselves to fasting and prayer; and come together again so that Satan does not tempt you because of your lack of self-control (1 Corinthians 7:1–5).

We want you to notice several things. In verse 1, Paul writes that "it is good for a man not to touch a woman." It's at this point when several women will shout, "Amen! Preach, pastor! Tell my husband to leave me alone, not to touch me anymore!" Hold on, sisters; that is not what Paul is talking about. He makes it clear what he's talking about in verse 2 when he continues, "Nevertheless, because of sexual immorality, let each man have his own wife, and let each woman have her own husband." What he's referring to in verse 1 is sex outside of marriage, whether it be premarital sex or extramarital sex. Sex, as intended by God, was meant to take place within the confines of marriage. So men should not be touching a woman, either before they are married or after they are married, unless they are touching their wife.

Paul then explains the obligation husbands and wives owe each other in maintaining a sex life that is regular and mutually satisfying (verse 3). He uses the term "affection" to clearly indicate that sex is not just a physical action but an emotional connection that exists (or should exist) between a husband and his wife, and he also says it is an obligation. The husband should "render to his wife the affection *due* her, and likewise also the wife to her husband" (emphasis added). Mutually agreed on and pleasurable sex is ideal in marriage. Neither party should feel forced to do it nor deprived. A Wikipedia article about the Jewish views on marriage states, "In marriage, conjugal relations are guaranteed as a fundamental right for a woman, along with food and clothing. This obligation is known as 'onah.' Sex within marriage is the woman's right, and the man's duty. The husband is forbidden from raping his wife, they are not to be intimate while drunk or while either party is angry at the other."[6]

Paul then goes on to explain the principle of mutuality and equality in marriage: "The wife does not have authority over her own body, but the husband does. And likewise the husband does not have authority over his own body, but the wife does" (verse 4). We find this principle in other parts of the Bible: "My beloved is mine, and I am his" (Song of Solomon 2:16); "I am my beloved's, and my beloved is mine" (Song of Solomon 6:3); and "Submit to one another out of reverence for Christ" (Ephesians 5:21, NLT).

Finally, Paul gives four very specific, practical principles for couples considering not having sex. He tells couples that they should not deprive their spouses of intimacy, except for the following:

1. *"With consent."* Some versions of the Bible render this expression "by mutual consent" (NIV), "unless you both agree" (NLT), "by mutual agreement" (NET). In other words, if you are going to refrain from having sex, it should be a mutually agreed on decision, not a unilateral one.

2. *"For a time."* According to Paul, abstinence cannot go on indefinitely but only for a time. You both agree that you will refrain from having sexual relations for a certain period of time, but the question is, How long is that period of time? Paul doesn't leave that up to each person or couple but answers it in the next principle.

3. *"That you may give yourselves to fasting and prayer."* The question is, How long can you fast and pray? Paul in his wisdom knew some people might take advantage of the second principle and decide for long periods of time or perhaps indefinitely, so he made it clear that the time agreed upon should be dedicated only to fasting and prayer, and therefore it should not be very long. After all, how long can you fast before it affects you negatively? A few days? Certainly, a week would be too long.

4. *"And come together again so that Satan does not tempt you because of your lack of self-control."* The reason why refraining from sex should not last very long is that it may place one or both spouses in a situation where they may be tempted and fall.

In our work with couples, we have found that, in general, many wives don't understand this critically important aspect of a husband's makeup. As Juli Slattery explains, "Although the average wife acknowledges that her husband's sex drive is stronger than hers, she still tends to underestimate the impact this one aspect has on their relationship. According to a poll of 150 Christian married men, 83 percent stated that they don't believe that women understand a man's sex drive. . . . Husbands feel alone with their secrets and desires; they are at a loss about how to communicate this to their wives. For many men, their attempts to bridge the gap have been met with disinterest or even disdain."[7]

This difference in desire for sex sets the stage for disappointment, misunderstanding, and conflict. Slattery goes on to quote an anonymous woman: "Although we have a pretty good marriage, sex feels like another chore on my list. I hate that my husband thinks about it so much and that he always wants it. I dread going to bed, fearing that he'll ask me for sex. Sometimes I find things to do around the house, hoping that he'll fall asleep before I'm ready for bed. I just wish I could shut him off somehow."[8]

Truth be told, many wives can probably identify with that sentiment. Over time, their sex life has become a burden, and it seems more like an obligation than a desire. They feel guilty for withholding sex, and they also feel a responsibility to meet this desire in order to keep their husband pure. For many women, there is no joy in sex. But it is important for women to realize that sex for a man is much more than a physical release; it is the way they connect at the deepest intimate level with their wife. It is a man's way of showing his wife how much he loves her. It is his deepest expression of love.

Authors Richard and Rita Tate warn that some women may have to give an account to God for the way in which they ignored their husband's sexual needs.[9] Many marriages would blossom overnight if the wife decided to embrace this part of her husband's physical and emotional makeup. When a wife genuinely anticipates meeting her husband's sexual needs, romance can be reborn. When your husband is consistently turned down in his attempts at having sex with you, he will begin to interpret that rejection as a lack of love toward him.

Of course, we understand that there is a time during the month when a woman's body experiences some changes. God provided specific instructions during that time of the month: "Do not have sexual relations with a woman during her period of menstrual impurity" (Leviticus 18:19, NLT). Rabbi Shmuley Boteach wrote that abstaining from sex during a woman's menstrual period is necessary. But he goes on to warn that if you're consistently turning your husband down, particularly with the perpetual headache, you send him the signal that you don't love him.[10]

We remember hearing about a husband who came home with a huge bottle in his hands and presented it to his wife. With a quizzical look, she asked him, "What's this?"

With a grin on his face, he responded, "Aspirin."

Still somewhat confused, the wife retorted, "Aspirin? What for? I don't have a headache."

To which her husband replied with a big smile on his face, "Oh, good!"

As stated earlier, in most marriages, the husband has a stronger sex drive than the wife. Having said that, please know that this is not always the case, and we have heard from many couples for whom this scenario is reversed. So, in addressing this topic, we are speaking in general terms as it applies to most men and women. The key to a healthy sexual relationship is to maintain an enjoyable sexual response in both of you that is frequent enough for both of you.

Couples need to overcome their sexual ignorance and communicate their sexual understanding with each other. We are amazed that in the twenty-first century, when we live in a much more open society and we see and hear things our parents would have never even considered in their lifetime, there's still so much ignorance when it comes to the topic of healthy sexuality. We have asked in many settings at what age sexual education for children should begin, and we have received answers ranging from two to fifteen years of age. Fifteen years of age? If you think your kids don't know about sex when they're fifteen, we recommend you sit with them, pen and paper in hand, and learn from them. You may be surprised at how much they know and understand, although it is often not the correct view of sexuality. They probably have learned from friends, who do not know the correct information; from movies, which don't portray sex correctly; or, worse yet, from pornographic sites. We recommend that sexual education for children begin by educating yourself before they're born. Then utilize that education the moment they are born by using anatomically correct terminology for every part of their bodies, including their penis, breasts, and vagina, and by treating sexuality as normally as we do any other part of life.

I (Claudio) remember distinctly the day I was buying a book from one of my favorite authors, Dr. Kevin Leman. My then sixteen-year-old daughter was with me as I was looking at the book, and with shock on her face, she asked, "Daddy, you're not going to buy that book, are you?" The title of the book was *Sex Begins in the Kitchen*. I casually responded to her, "Yes, honey, because your mom and I are going to be doing a lot more cooking from now on." She walked out of the store, not wanting to be seen with me when I paid for it. In actuality, we have been able to maintain an open conversation about sexuality with our daughters because we have treated it as a very natural, normal part of life. That's not to say we haven't occasionally embarrassed them.

We encourage you to read good, biblically based books on sex, and talk together as a couple about what you are learning. One of the areas in which men still don't understand sex is how women react to their advances. Someone told us that when it comes to sex, men are like matches—they strike, fire, and fizzle quickly. But women are like charcoal—it takes some time to get them going, but once they get started, they will remain warm and glowing for a long time. That's why men need to understand how to get their wives started, what we refer to as foreplay. Now, because there is so much ignorance on this subject, we feel it is necessary to explain to men what foreplay is to their wives. We want to be careful lest someone is offended, but we believe it's important we describe foreplay in as much detail and as graphically as possible so you can understand it and put it into practice. If, at some point, you feel uncomfortable, just skip to the next section. Again, we will be as detailed, as descriptive, as graphic as we can when we describe what foreplay is to a wife. Men, pay attention! Here we go . . .

When you get up out of bed in the morning—make the bed. Brush your teeth (morning breath is only romantic in the movies), take a shower, and don't forget to hang the towel on the towel rack. After you get dressed, go to the kitchen where your wife may be fixing breakfast, come from behind her, wrap her in your arms, kiss her neck, and tell her good morning and that you love her. Enjoy breakfast together without any electronic distractions (such as the TV, cell phones, tablet, computer, radio, and so on). After breakfast, offer to wash the dishes. Have a few minutes for family devotions, and then kiss your wife before you each go your separate ways.

Perhaps at midmorning, you can send her a text message to tell her, "I'm thinking about you," or something similar. Maybe sometime before lunch, you can tell her you want to take her out to her favorite restaurant (hopefully something better than fast food). Well, at midafternoon, you can send her another text message to tell her, "I can't wait to get home to see you," or something like that. On your way home, you can stop by a store and get her some of her favorite flowers, chocolates, or a greeting card. And when you get home, you give her a hug and a kiss and offer to fix dinner or to take care of the kids while she fixes dinner. Oh, and if you don't have kids—this will blow her mind—offer to vacuum the house. After dinner, you can tell her to relax and put her feet up while you wash the dishes, and perhaps you can even fix her a nice, warm bath. You see, men, foreplay for a woman is *not* what happens right before sexual intercourse; rather, it's what happens *all throughout the day*!

Now, to be fair, we also need to explain to you ladies what foreplay is to your husband. Now, in order to be clear, we will need to be very graphic and very detailed in our explanation. We hope you are not uncomfortable or offended by our explicit description of what foreplay is to your husband. If you get to the point where you are offended, please skip our description and go to the next section of this chapter. Here's what foreplay is to your husband . . .

You walk into the room.

That's it! You see, ladies, we like simple things, not too complicated. We love you and want to be with you anytime and anyplace. When we see you walk into the room, we feel that special connection and a deep desire to love you the best way we know how. Don't be offended that we desire you that much. Would you rather your husband had no desire for you at all?

Learn about sex and talk about sex. But also talk about the things that you both enjoy, the things that feel good, and the frequency with which you would like to have sex. And, of course, discuss the things that make you uncomfortable, the things you don't want, like, enjoy, what hurts, and when you would not want to have sex. It is that mutual, clear understanding and agreement that will help you enjoy a satisfying sex life.

Think about these words from Jill Renich, as quoted by Gary Thomas: "A wife may demonstrate her love in innumerable other ways, but it is often negated by her rejection or lack of enjoyment of sex. You may be a great housekeeper, a gourmet cook, a wonderful mother to your husband's children, but if you turn him down consistently in the bedroom oftentimes those things will be negated. To a man, sex is the most meaningful declaration of love and self-worth."[11]

During one of our couples' retreats, we received a question from a husband who wrote: "My wife says that lovemaking is the 'icing on the cake' of our relationship. The problem is—the cake never gets baked, so the cake never gets iced. I am living on bread alone." You have to admire his creativity as he wrote the question, but you also have to feel sorry for his expression of frustration and pain.

We heard a story of a milkman in a town near Kyiv, the capital of Ukraine. He was the only milkman, so he distributed milk, cheese, and butter to everyone in town. Sadly, one day his cow died, so he went to Kyiv and purchased a new cow. But before a cow can produce milk, she must be impregnated. So the milkman got a bull from a nearby town, but every time the bull would come close to the cow, the cow would run away.

Frustrated, the milkman went to his rabbi and told him the story and how frustrated he was that his new cow ran away from the bull every time the bull tried to impregnate her. The rabbi thought for a moment and then asked the milkman, "Did you buy the cow in Kyiv?"

Astonished, the milkman responded to the rabbi, "I did, my rabbi! How did you know that?"

With a mischievous look on his face, the rabbi responded, "My wife is from Kyiv." We're afraid that many wives act like the rabbi's wife, and every time their husbands approach them with their desire to make love, they come up with excuses. Whether they intend it or not, the message they are sending their husband is, "I don't love you." Is that the message you want to send to your husband? The apostle Paul was very wise and inspired when he wrote, "Do not deprive one another" (1 Corinthians 7:5).

Wives, write three specific things you can do meet this important emotional need for your husband:

1. _____
2. _____
3. _____

Now that you have that list, how and when do you plan to implement the items on it?

3. TAKE CARE OF YOURSELF

Another of the most important emotional needs men have is to have a wife that looks nice and takes care of herself. Ladies, go back in your mind to the days of dating the man who is now your husband. Think about how you used to get yourself ready for that date. I (Pam) spent a great deal of time deciding what to wear, how to do my hair, making sure my perfume was the scent that he liked, and so on. I spent more time in exercise, long hot baths, reading, personal devotions, and prayer. As the years of marriage have ticked by, however, I must admit that the scenario has changed somewhat.

All too often I am just happy to get out of bed. Especially on days when I do not have to travel, it is easier to wear the same pajamas during the day that I slept in the night before, forego that shower, swipe a comb through my hair, let that treadmill gather dust, and skip my personal worship time. The years of married life have brought kids; piles of dirty laundry; a house that seems to need daily cleaning (even when we travel, and no one is at home); work responsibilities; and, of course, there's always another meal to prepare. Taking care of myself seems to be low on the list of priorities these days. Those days of nice long bubble baths are very distant memories, and such luxuries cannot be bought today.

We want you to stop! It may be a long time before there is nothing on that to-do list. It is there today, and it will be there tomorrow. If you keep waiting until you have "extra" time to devote to self-care, you will be waiting a very long time. Please remember that some intentional time to take care of yourself will make you a better wife and a better mother. You will also feel better physically, emotionally, and spiritually. And the fact that you feel better will reveal itself.

Why is it important for you to look nice for your husband? One of those amazing details God built into most men is that they tend to be visual. Men are attracted to the physical beauty of a woman. It doesn't mean that they look only at the outside and don't care about the inside, the mind, character, and personality of a woman. Those also are important to men. But what first attracts most men to a woman is their outward physical appearance.

I (Claudio) remember the day I first laid eyes on Pam. I walked into the bookstore of Columbia Union College, where I had already been a student for one semester, and saw this new girl, a freshman, recently arrived on campus and beginning her first day of work. Obviously, I didn't know her; I didn't know where she was from, whether she was intelligent, if she had a good personality, or if she was a committed Christian. I didn't even know her name. All I knew was that in front of me was a beautiful girl with long, golden hair flowing down her back, gorgeous green eyes, and an amazing smile. That's all I saw, and that's all I needed to see to ask her out—and just like that, she fell madly in love with me (that's my story, and I'm sticking by it).

The same thing happened to Adam. When God brought Eve to meet her soon-to-be husband, Adam knew nothing about her. All he knew was that he was lonely, that he had no companion, and that standing in front of him was the most beautiful creature in the entire world. That's all it took for him to burst into the first poem in the history of humanity: "This one is bone from my bone, and flesh from my flesh" (Genesis 2:23 NLT). Men are attracted to the beauty of the female body. It is following that attraction, as we spend time together, that we develop an appreciation for everything else—their intellect, their spirituality, their commitment, their family, and so on.

One of the most fascinating books in the Old Testament is the Song of Solomon. It is the story of a young couple in love and the stages in their relationship, from longing to be married to the wedding day, to the consummation of their marriage, to trouble in their marriage, and to the lifetime commitment they make to each other. In chapter 4, we find the groom's description of his bride-to-be. Let's read it:

> Behold, you are fair, my love!
> Behold, you are fair!
> You have dove's *eyes* behind your veil.
> Your *hair* is like a flock of goats,
> Going down from Mount Gilead.
> Your *teeth* are like a flock of shorn sheep
> Which have come up from the washing,
> Every one of which bears twins,
> And none is barren among them.
> Your *lips* are like a strand of scarlet,
> And your *mouth* is lovely.
> Your *temples* behind your veil

Are like a piece of pomegranate.
Your *neck* is like the tower of David,
Built for an armory,
On which hang a thousand bucklers,
All shields of mighty men.
Your two *breasts* are like two fawns,
Twins of a gazelle,
Which feed among the lilies (Song of Solomon 4:1–5; emphasis
    added).

Please note that as the groom-to-be describes his soon-to-be bride, he uses seven attributes (notice the italicized words in the passage): (1) her eyes, (2) her hair, (3) her teeth, (4) her lips and mouth, (5) her temples, (6) her neck, and (7) her breasts. Since they are not yet married, that's all he can see of her. He begins at the top of her head and moves down to her breasts, where he stops because that's all he can see. In the Bible, the number seven is the number of perfection— the seven days of Creation; the seventh-day Sabbath; the seven branches of the golden candlestick; the seven trumpets and the seven priests who sounded them; the seven-day siege of Jericho; and the seven churches, seven spirits, seven stars, seven seals, seven vials of the book of Revelation. The number seven in the Bible is the perfect number, and what Solomon is trying to tell his bride-to-be is that in his eyes, she is perfect. Imagine how those words must have made her feel!

The end of chapter 4 and the beginning of chapter 5 describe their wedding and the consummation of their marriage. How he addresses her changes from "my sister" to "my spouse" or "my bride." Now that they are married, he is able to see all of her, and in chapter 7, he again describes her, but this time he mentions twelve attributes he notices in her. Again, let's read that portion of the book:

"How beautiful are your *feet* in sandals,
O prince's daughter!
The curves of your *hips* are like jewels,
The work of the hands of an artist.
"Your *navel* is like a round goblet
Which never lacks mixed wine;
Your *belly* is like a heap of wheat
Fenced about with lilies.
"Your two *breasts* are like two fawns,
Twins of a gazelle.
"Your *neck* is like a tower of ivory,

Your *eyes* like the pools in Heshbon
By the gate of Bath-rabbim;
Your *nose* is like the tower of Lebanon,
Which faces toward Damascus.
"Your *head* crowns you like Carmel,
And the *flowing locks* of your head are like purple threads;
The king is captivated by your tresses.
"How beautiful and how delightful you are,
My love, with all your charms!
"Your *stature* is like a palm tree,
And your breasts are like its clusters.
"I said, 'I will climb the palm tree,
I will take hold of its fruit stalks.'
Oh, may your breasts be like clusters of the vine,
And the fragrance of your breath like apples,
And your *mouth* like the best wine!"

"It goes down smoothly for my beloved,
Flowing gently through the lips of those who fall asleep" (Song of
Solomon 7:1–9, NASB; emphasis added).

Please note that in this chapter, the bridegroom mentions twelve attributes of
his spouse (notice the italicized words in the passage). He starts at her feet and
moves all the way up to the top of her head as he describes (1) her feet, (2) her
hips, (3) her navel, (4) her belly, (5) her breasts, (6) her neck, (7) her eyes, (8)
her nose, (9) her head, (10) her hair, (11) her stature, and (12) her mouth. The
number twelve in the Bible is a complete number. We read of the twelve tribes,
the twelve disciples, the twelve gates of the New Jerusalem, and the twelve pillars
upon which it sits. And of course, twelve times twelve equals 144, and 144,000
is the complete number of all the saved. So, by using twelve attributes, Solomon
is telling his wife that she is complete; she lacks nothing.

If there's one lesson men should learn from reading the Song of Solomon,
it's that women loved to be noticed for their appearance, and they enjoy being
told specifically what we like about them. In one of the comic strips we enjoy,
the wife asks her husband, "Have I ever told you how handsome you look
when you're giving me a compliment?" At the same time, women also like for
their husbands to look nice. In another comic strip, the wife asks her husband,
"Explain to me why you dress nice for coworkers you hate and then come home
and dress like a slob for the woman you love?" It's fine to dress comfortably at
home, the place where you come to rest and relax, but dress better when you

leave the house with your spouse. Actually, even at home, you don't have to look your worst for your spouse or family.

FOR DISCUSSION
Ladies, write three specific things you can do to remain attractive to your husband (don't make this too hard, as it's the simple things men enjoy most):

1. _____
2. _____
3. _____

Now that you have that list, what changes do you need to make in order to reach these goals?

4. PRIORITIZE PLAYTIME

Time together was a priority when Pam and I were dating. Other appointments could wait, but time for each other was a given. Is it still a priority today? Why has that changed? We remember as we were dating that we tried to do all we could to maximize the time we could spend together. We were both full-time students in college, and we both had jobs. So, often, our dates consisted of sitting in the college library and holding hands while we studied. I would walk Pam to her dorm when the library closed, and we would spend some more time talking until it was time for her to go in. I would then drive home, call her, and talk a while longer until it was time to go to sleep. And these were our dates before cell phones! Weekends were the best: We would go to church in the morning, and often we went to a park or for a walk or met friends with whom we spent time. Saturday night, we would spend more time together, and, often, it was back to the library to study. Sundays, the same thing happened. So, even though we were busy working and taking classes, we always managed to find ways to spend time together.

Once we got married, some things got a little easier. We could study in our home and spend more time together there. We must also be honest and admit that through the years, there have been times when our jobs have taken precious time away from the family, for which we are sad and sorry. But we also have learned to manage time better so that it does not infringe on our personal and family time. We have learned to enjoy discovering new places together. When we travel, we try to discover interesting facts about the destination. We have spent hours visiting museums and monuments, places of historical importance, and landmarks. As a result, we have been to every state in the United States, every province in Canada, and more than fifty countries around the world. What has made those trips enjoyable is that we have been able to enjoy them together.

Many couples tell us that they used to do such things but that they have very little in common anymore. You may be surprised by how much you still have in common; it's just a matter of discovering what those things are. Do an online search for an interest inventory, and you will discover several you can download for free. Fill them out separately, and then sit together to see which activities you enjoy in common. We did that several years ago. At that time, we were living in New Jersey, and we each completed an interest inventory. When we compared our answers, we found several things that we both liked but had never talked or even thought about doing together. For instance, one of the things we each said we would like to do is snorkeling.

A few weeks later, we received an offer for a timeshare. They offered us three nights in Palm Beach, Florida, two days in the Bahamas, and four days in Orlando. All we had to do was pay $500 each and sit through a timeshare presentation. We have sat through those presentations or sales pitches several times and absolutely hate doing it, but at that price, it seemed worth the pain (considering this was the only way we could afford such a vacation). We spent time in Palm Beach, suffered through the sales presentation and the pressure, and then drove to Fort Lauderdale to get on the cruise ship to the Bahamas.

We had never been on a cruise ship, and we remember driving into the port and seeing the biggest ship we had ever seen in our lives. It was very long, very tall, and very wide. It was amazing—except that, well, that wasn't our cruise ship. Ours was a much smaller one hiding behind the big one. It didn't matter; we were still excited about going on a cruise. When we got to the Bahamas, several vendors waited for the disembarking, hapless tourists to whom they would offer their wares. One of those offers was a three-hour snorkeling trip. Oh boy, were we excited about that! We paid for it, went out on the ocean, and had a blast snorkeling for the first time in our lives. It was not just the warm, clear blue water or the beautiful fish swimming close enough for us to touch them but the fact that all four of us (our girls came along) were enjoying this activity together. It was fantastic!

You may argue that now you are in a place in your life where you must focus more on your career in order to reach the next milestone. Or perhaps you now have children, and their needs take precedence. Pull out your calendar. What appointments have you already scheduled? If you are like most, you may see things like a board meeting, doctor's appointment, church social, softball practice, kids' piano lessons, parent-teacher conferences, and so on. Wait! Do you see "Date night with my spouse" anywhere on your calendar of events?

You see, busyness has pushed out time that you could spend with each other.

There is no time to reconnect, to talk about things that really matter, and enjoy each other's company. No, there is no time for playtime. Why do we consider playtime an extra? We only allow time for that when there is nothing else competing with that time slot. The truth is that we need to be as intentional about scheduling playtime as we are in scheduling that doctor's appointment. It will not happen automatically. It must be added to your schedule, and that time must be guarded and protected as sacred time. If all you offer are the leftovers, your marriage will be starved of the attention it rightfully deserves.

Find something that you both enjoy doing. Take an online interest inventory and compare your responses, choose an activity, make plans, and do it. No more excuses! It matters to your marriage. Rediscover what it is like to just have fun together.

FOR DISCUSSION
Individually, make a list of adjectives that describe your home environment. Use only one- or two-word descriptors. Write down at least three (or as many as you can think of) separately and then compare your lists and discuss why you answered the way you did.

1. _____
2. _____
3. _____

5. MAKE HOME A HAVEN
What adjectives did you each use to describe your home environment? Would they be words such as *hectic, crazy, chaotic, wild, busy, confrontational, loud,* or similar terms? Or would they be words such as *peaceful, calm, secure,* or *a haven*? The reality of today is that many are workaholics not because they love their work so much—rather, they put so many hours in at the office because home is not a haven. They say their homes can be described as *chaotic, loud, conflict-filled,* and *stress-producing*. Who would want to go there?

Home is as close as we will get to heaven here on this earth. Home must be a refuge from the stresses of life. And, for most husbands, this is listed as one of their most important emotional needs. No matter how obstinate our boss, how heavy that rush hour traffic, how much work awaits the next day, a husband needs to know that his home is a haven of peace and rest. He wants to know that his home is a place of tranquility, security, and comfort.

We are not talking about a place where children sit like stone statues and are silent. That is not reality. It should be a place filled with laughter, giggles from little ones, and little feet running to greet you at the door. Home is not a perfect place, but it is a place where forgiveness is offered as needed, hugs are given to console someone whose feelings you may have hurt, "I'm sorry" is heard, and family members pray for each other.

Since this is one of a man's most important emotional needs, we're suggesting that wives help make home such a place for their husbands. In his book, *Men Are From Mars, Women Are From Venus,* John Gray wrote that men need a cave to go into when they get home.[12] Perhaps that's where the idea of a man cave came from. What Gray means is that when a man comes home, he needs a place where he can disconnect from the world, his job, the traffic, the supervisor, and all the pressures outside the home before he can reconnect with his family.

To the wives, we recommend: Give your husband time to go into his cave. Don't wait for him at the door with a list of complaints and problems for him to solve. Give him time to go into his cave before you lay all of your burdens on him. To the husbands, we say: Go into your cave when you get home, but don't stay in the cave. Your wife and family need you to join them. Your wife needs you to help her carry the burdens and responsibilities of the home.

Since this is an important emotional need for most men, we want to share with you wives a few thoughts as to how you can make your homes a haven here on earth. Probably the most important is—don't nag! You may think that, by nagging him, you will get him to do what you want or need him to do, but usually the opposite happens. As a humorous sign stated, "Ladies, if a man says he will fix it, he will. There is no need to remind him every six months about it." The Bible makes two similar statements: "It's better out in the desert than at home with a nagging, complaining wife" (Proverbs 21:19, CEV); and, "The steady dripping of rain and the nagging of a wife are one and the same" (Proverbs 27:15, CEV).

Husbands, if you'd like your home to be a haven, help your wife make it so. Often the wife works outside the home, and when she gets home, her work continues. So offer to help with the children, the cleaning, the laundry. The more you do to help her, the more rested she will be to meet some of your other needs (refer to need number 2). Here's a great marriage tip: your wife won't start an argument with you while you're cleaning the house! Work together to make your home a haven of rest for both you and your family.

CONCLUSION

While addressing the needs of men, this chapter was speaking to the women. So let's ask the men a question by reversing what we asked in the previous chapter. Men, instead of asking what you as a husband need from your wife, perhaps you should ask yourself, *What can I give to her?* For it is in mutually meeting each other's needs that we discover that our own needs are being met in return.

As you reflect on this chapter, do so with meeting your wife's needs at the forefront of your mind. This chapter is not a list to print out and hand to your wife to say, "Here are my needs, so you must meet them." Rather, allow the Holy Spirit to work on your wife's heart as you listen to that Voice speaking to you also.

Is sex on the Sabbath permitted?

We're often asked this question—as there are people who believe that having sex on Sabbath is a violation of the fourth commandment, which forbids secular work during those sacred hours. First, we need to consider the order of Creation. What was the first commandment God gave to humanity? "Be fruitful and multiply" (Genesis 1:22). Perhaps you aren't familiar with Old Testament Hebrew, so please allow us to translate the words from the original text into modern English: "Have sex!" That was the only way that Adam and Eve could be fruitful and multiply. Of course, we must follow the first question with a second one: When did God give that commandment to Adam and Eve? It was on the sixth day of Creation, the day before Sabbath. We don't read anywhere that God told Adam and Eve on the sixth day of Creation, "Be fruitful and multiply, but wait until after the Sabbath."

Some will point out a passage from Isaiah where the prophet writes, "Turn away your foot from the Sabbath, from doing your pleasure on My holy day" (Isaiah 58:13). They tell us that sex is a pleasurable activity, and Isaiah says we should refrain from doing pleasurable things on the Sabbath; therefore, we should not have sex on the Sabbath. My human nature comes out sometimes when I respond, "That's right. Don't do your pleasure on the Sabbath—instead, pleasure your spouse." Sex, within the context of marriage, is for mutual pleasure, for intimate connection—physically, emotionally, and spiritually.

The Jewish religion has much to teach about the responsibility of sex on the Sabbath day. Rabbi Naftali Brawer explains:

> There are two separate mitzvot [laws] in the Torah that involve sexual relations. One is to be fruitful and multiply (Genesis 1:28.) The lesser-known mitzvah is for the husband to ensure he sexually satisfies his wife (Exodus 21:10). This second mitzvah is totally independent from the first and so the obligation to make love to one's wife applies to couples regardless as to whether they wish to, or are capable of conceiving.
>
> The very notion that sexual pleasure can itself—provided it is experienced in the right context—be a mitzvah, underscores the unique Jewish attitude to life. Judaism, on the whole, frowns upon asceticism. It sees the material world not in conflict with sanctity but rather as capable of being sanctified. Nowhere is this more evident than on

Shabbat where the sacred is celebrated through the physical. This holy day is observed not just through prayer and song but also through eating, socialising, relaxing and—for married couples—sexual intimacy. Shabbat illustrates the harmony that can be achieved between the spiritual and the physical. . . .

Friday night, when they step back from the tsunami of pressures that overwhelm them, is an ideal time to reconnect, both personally and physically. Few would define sex as hard work, while it is not just about procreation, and is enjoyed as much by those who are past the age of menopause.[13]

Another Jewish scholar, Dr. Malka Zeiger Simkovich, explains:

Rabbinic literature shows no awareness of a ban or limitation on physical intimacy on Shabbat, and even seems to encourage it. . . .

. . . The Talmud indicates no awareness that the Sabbath is a time of sexual abstinence. To the contrary, marital intimacy is encouraged and making time for it on the Sabbath is praised.[14]

Think about this for a moment. In the Jewish religion, sex on the Sabbath is not an option—it is an obligation. Just for that, I almost became Jewish. (OK, my wife just elbowed me for writing that.)

Theology and history professor Michael W. Campbell provides some insights on Isaiah 58:

The implication of Isaiah 58:13 is that God wants us to lay aside our own agenda and replace it with something far more exquisite. God calls us to live a life of selfless pleasure focused on our relationship with God. The notion that the Sabbath forbids joyous pleasure during the Sabbath hours is basically a misreading of the original text. As Nancy Van Pelt observes, "If this text actually meant to forbid sex because it is pleasurable, then any pleasure including singing hymns, reading the Bible, or eating should also be forbidden. Isaiah was talking about my seeking my own selfish pleasure. If sex is nothing more than 'my pleasure,' it is selfish and therefore wrong not only on the Sabbath but on every other day of the week as well."[15]

Simultaneously enjoying the beauty of the Sabbath and of sex within the context of marriage is one of the most beautiful ways to fully delight in both acts of God's creation.

What does the Bible teach about oral sex and anal sex?

Besides the question concerning sex on the Sabbath, this is another question that we are asked frequently. The short, simple answer is that oral sex is not mentioned at all in the Bible. When people speak about oral sex, they mostly are referring to cunnilingus (which is performed on females) and fellatio (which is performed on males). According to an article on GotQuestions.org, "There are two primary questions that are asked in regards to oral sex: (1) 'Is oral sex a sin if done before [and we would add, 'or outside of'] marriage?' and (2) 'Is oral sex a sin if done within a marriage?' "[16] Again, the Bible does not specifically address either question, but there are some biblical principles that apply.

Let's address the first question: Is oral sex a sin if done before or outside the context of marriage? Many today—particularly young people—have come to believe that oral sex is not really sex and that it is a safer alternative to sexual intercourse, since there is no risk of pregnancy and less risk of sexually trans-mitted diseases (although this last assumption is not necessarily true). The Bible does say, "But among you there must not be even a hint of sexual immorality, or of any kind of impurity . . . because these are improper for God's holy people" (Ephesians 5:3, NIV). The Bible defines "sexual immorality" as any form of sexual contact outside of marriage (1 Corinthians 7:2). In addition, Hebrews 13:4 tells us that only the "marriage bed" is pure and undefiled (NIV). In other words, the Bible is clear that sex is to be reserved for marriage between a man and his wife. So, the short, simple answer to the question as to whether oral sex before or outside the context of marriage is sin is yes.

The second question—Is oral sex a sin if done within the context of marriage?—is not as simple. What makes it more challenging is that, as we stated before, nowhere does the Bible say anything specific about sex between a wife and her husband other than when that intimacy is violated by having sex outside of their relationship (adultery in any form) or even lusting after another person (such as with the use of pornography or online relationships).

While the Bible does not prohibit oral sex within the context of marriage between a husband and his wife, what the couple needs to remember is to follow the principle of "mutual consent" (1 Corinthians 7:5, NIV), as stated by Paul to the members of the church in Corinth. While this text gives four direct principles dealing with whether a couple should abstain from having sex, the "mutual consent" concept is good to apply, in general terms, with regard to oral sex within marriage: "Whatever is done, it should be mutually agreed on between the husband and his wife. Neither spouse should be forced or coerced into doing something he/she is not completely comfortable with. If oral sex is done within the context of marriage and in the spirit of mutual consent, there is not a biblical case for declaring it to be a sin."[17]

Let's take it a step further and see if we can provide a more practical application. Please remember "that God created sex to be a beautiful expression of love" and intimacy between a husband and wife. If either spouse "does not feel that sex is a 'beautiful expression of love,' " then they need to make changes in their sex life. It would seem evident that their "actions are not mutually beneficial to each person."[18] While the Bible does not explicitly condemn oral sex, it may not be appropriate for every couple. So, in deciding whether this is for you, consider these questions:

- "Is oral sex voluntary and have both the husband and wife agreed to it?"
- "Why do you want oral sex? Is it for pure sexual pleasure or is it to fulfill a sexual fantasy derived from porn?"
- "Have you or your spouse been convicted by the Holy Spirit that oral sex is wrong?"
- "Does oral sex edify and fulfill both you and your spouse?"[19]

We have stated several times that the Bible does not explicitly condemn oral sex between a wife and her husband. The question is, Does the Bible condone it? Perhaps the book that hints most directly to oral sex is the Song of Solomon. One way to look at the Song of Solomon is as a beautiful story of a man and woman in love before marriage and all through their lifelong commitment to each other. If viewed in that sense, it can be divided into five scenes:

1. Before the wedding (Song of Solomon 1:1–3:5)
2. The wedding (Song of Solomon 3:6–4:8)
3. Consummation of the marriage (Song of Solomon 4:8–5:1)
4. Distance and conflict in marriage (Song of Solomon 5:2–6:3)
5. A lifetime commitment (Song of Solomon 6:4–8:14)

The passages that hint at oral sex are Song of Solomon 2:3; 4:16; 5:1; and 7:6–8. Let's examine each one:

- Like an apple tree among the trees of the woods,
  So is my beloved among the sons.
  I sat down in his shade with great delight,
  And his fruit was sweet to my taste (Song of Solomon 2:3).

- Awake, O north wind,
  And come, O south!
  Blow upon my garden,

That its spices may flow out.
Let my beloved come to his garden
And eat its pleasant fruits (Song of Solomon 4:16).

- I have come to my garden, my sister, my spouse;
  I have gathered my myrrh with my spice;
  I have eaten my honeycomb with my honey;
  I have drunk my wine with my milk (Song of Solomon 5:1).

- How fair and how pleasant you are,
  O love, with your delights!
  This stature of yours is like a palm tree,
  And your breasts like its clusters.
  I said, "I will go up to the palm tree,
  I will take hold of its branches."
  Let now your breasts be like clusters of the vine,
  The fragrance of your breath like apples (Song of Solomon 7:6–8).

As Kevin Carson explains, "Care must be taken as to whether or not these verses apply to oral sex. At best, they are used in a veiled way to discuss it." He suggests we take two important things into account. First of all, these texts are not a prescription for oral sex. Second, while these texts may imply oral sex, it is "veiled behind the privacy of Solomon and his wife's marriage bed. Therefore, at best, this emphasizes oral sex as private between a husband and his wife."[20]

Taking this into consideration, he suggests his own set of questions for a husband and wife to consider as they contemplate practicing oral sex in the privacy of their marriage bed:

1. *"Is it required or prohibited in the Bible?"* As we have mentioned before, the Bible does not require nor prohibit oral sex within the context of the married relationship between a husband and wife.
2. *"Is it unnatural?"* While most people limit the definition of oral sex to cunnilingus and fellatio, it could be argued that oral sex is any loving contact of the mouth—lips or tongue—with any part of the spouse's body. If it is a loving gesture, then it is not unnatural nor sinful.
3. *"Is it unhealthy or could it cause harm? Is it unloving?"* Keep the principle in mind that true love seeks the highest good of your spouse. Therefore, Carson says, do "whatever is best and that which does not harm [your spouse] physically, mentally, emotionally, or spiritually." Is it unloving? If the wife, for instance, feels forced to do anything that makes her un-

comfortable, she could consider her husband's actions unloving toward her. Please remember the principle of mutual agreement.

4. *"Is it unkind? Is it unloving?"* Carson writes, "Wherever there is anything unkind in the sexual relationship, the lack of kindness or the failure to show love is wrong. If in an effort to be pleased, a husband or wife demands something from the other when the spouse does not want to participate, that would be unkind and unloving. If there is however no demand, and both the husband and the wife would want to participate, then oral sex would not be either unkind or unloving."

5. *"Is it against the conscience of the spouse?"* Carson explains, "If a desired activity by either spouse is not consistent with the conscience of the other spouse, then the request for the sexual act needs to be dropped. If the spouse with the bothered conscience is coerced in participating, the manipulating spouse has encouraged sin. To do anything against one's conscience is sin; in other words, to not be able to do something in faith is sin (Romans 14:19–23)."

6. *"What is your motive? What is the condition of your heart?"* The point of these questions is to do a self-check. The person wanting to have oral sex should ask the following questions, according to Carson: "Why does he or she want to do this? Is it love? Is it motivated by the desire to give? Does it fulfill the purpose of glorifying God? Will it enhance the worship experience of sex together? Or are there other motives? Is it driven by selfishness? Is it driven by the lust of the flesh? Is the spouse who desires this particular act doing so because of pornography, fantasies, regular masturbation, or other experiences which make routine sex with his or her spouse seem boring? Does he or she believe that their typical sex can no longer satisfy? What is your motive? What is the condition of your heart?" Each case is different, but answering these questions for yourself may give you some clarity as to your motives for wanting or asking for oral sex.[21]

"In summary," notes GotQuestions.org, "oral sex before or outside of marriage is absolutely a sin. It is immoral. It is in no sense . . . biblically acceptable."[22] As far as within the confines of marriage, oral sex is free from sin as long as there is mutual consent.

The second part of the original question has to do with anal sex. Unlike oral sex, anal sex is mentioned in the context of the story of Sodom's destruction (Genesis 19). The men of the city went to Lot's house and demanded that the men (i.e., the angels) lodging in his home be handed to them to "know them carnally" (verse 5), a euphemism for having sex with them. Unbelievably, Lot offered to hand over his two virgin daughters so they could do with them what-ever they wanted, but the men refused. They did not want his daughters; they wanted the men. Their clear intent was to have sex with Lot's guests. The term *sodomy*, which derives from this story, refers to anal copulation with a member of the opposite sex, with a member of the same sex, and bestiality (copulation with an animal).[23]

Dr. Clifford and Joyce Penner, international sexual therapists, educators, and authors explain that "anal sex, the penis entering the woman's anus, is dangerous. The anus is highly contaminated, whereas the reproductive tract is sterile in men and clean in women. When the penis enters the anus, there is a high risk of infections and prostate problems. If the penis enters the vagina after having been in the anus, the woman's reproductive tract can easily become infected. In addition, the rectum is not designed for entry and thrusting—the small blood vessels along the wall of the anus and rectum break."[24]

If that is not reason enough, Dr. Douglas E. Rosenau—a licensed psycholo-gist, marriage and family therapist, and certified sex therapist—also explains how "the vaginal tissue, with its lubrication and muscle, was designed for childbirth and intercourse, but the anus was not. . . . Also, the many bacteria in the anus can interfere with the bacteria in the vagina and cause infections."[25]

In Sodom, the intent of the men was to have anal intercourse with Lot's guests. As God was preparing the Israelites to go into the Promised Land, He gave them specific prohibition about sex between two males:

- "You shall not lie with a male as one lies with a female; it is an abomination" (Leviticus 18:22, NASB).
- "If there is a man who lies with a male as those who lie with a woman, both of them have committed a detestable act; they shall surely be put to death. Their bloodguiltiness is upon them" (Leviti-cus 20:13, NASB).

A similar story, which took place in Israel, also reveals that God considered such practice an abomination:

> While they were celebrating, behold, the men of the city, certain worthless fellows, surrounded the house, pounding the door; and they spoke to the owner of the house, the old man, saying, "Bring out the man who came into your house that we may have relations with him." Then the man, the owner of the house, went out to them and said to them, "No, my fellows, please do not act so wickedly; since this man has come into my house, do not commit this act of folly. Here is my

virgin daughter and his concubine. Please let me bring them out that you may ravish them and do to them whatever you wish. But do not commit such an act of folly against this man." But the men would not listen to him (Judges 19:22–25, NASB).

Lest someone say that prohibition against anal sex was an archaic Old Testament regulation, the same condemnation is repeated in the New Testament:

- "Do you not know that the unrighteous will not inherit the kingdom of God? Do not be deceived. Neither fornicators, nor idolaters, nor adulterers, nor homosexuals, nor sodomites" (1 Corinthians 6:9).
- "The law is not made for a righteous person, but for the lawless and insubordinate, . . . for fornicators, for sodomites, for kidnappers, for liars, for perjurers, and if there is any other thing that is contrary to sound doctrine" (1 Timothy 1:9, 10).
- "Just as Sodom and Gomorrah and the surrounding cities, which likewise indulged in sexual immorality and pursued unnatural desire, serve as an example by undergoing a punishment of eternal fire" (Jude 7, ESV).

This last verse clearly shows that the inhabitants of Sodom and Gomorrah engaged in sexual practices that God condemned. In summary, the Bible condemns anal sexual activity between males. But in general, is anal sex a sin between a husband and wife? We can use the same questions from Kevin Carson to help us decide if this should be practiced in marriage:

1. *"Is it required or prohibited in the Bible?"* We need to be very cautious here. Carson cautions that "although though it would be nice to have a specific verse to determine its sinfulness in marriage, there are additional criteria to help us discern if in fact anal sex is a sin."
2. *"Is it unnatural?"* No matter how you may wish to explain it, Carson says, "anal sex would not be considered natural." The Bible declares it unnatural within the context of a homosexual relationship, as it was condemned in Sodom and later in Israel. As far as within marriage between a husband and his wife, it is not in accordance with how "God intended for a man and woman to function; it is not natural." As Carson explains, "The rectum is not designed for entry and thrusting. The muscles around the anal orifice at the opening of the rectum are exclusively intended to push out in order to rid the body of waste. Contrary to the anal orifice, the vaginal orifice was designed for the

vigorous thrusting of intercourse and childbirth, with both its natural lubrication and muscle structure. Clearly one is natural (vaginal intercourse) and the other is not (anal intercourse)."

3. *"Is it unhealthy or could it cause harm? Is it unloving?"* As has already been stated, anal sex can be unhealthy and harmful. Carson writes, "Furthermore, anal intercourse can lead to fecal incontinence, increased risks of anal cancer, tears of the lining of the colon or the rectal tissue, risk of infection, and hemorrhoids. These issues are dangerous and could cause harm." If it is unhealthy for your wife, how could it be loving toward her?

4. *"Is it unkind? Is it unloving?"* Carson notes that "often with anal sex there is increased pain, discomfort, bleeding, risk of infection," and it "rarely produces any kind of orgasm." Asking or forcing your wife to submit to such a practice is far from loving or kind. Why would you want your wife to endure these things?

5. *"Is it against the conscience of the spouse?"* If your wife is coerced into performing a sexual act that goes against what her own conscience tells her, manipulating her encourages her to sin. If either spouse does not want to participate in anal sex because of their conscience, then it should not happen. Period!

6. *"What is your motive? What is the condition of your heart?"* Previously, we asked you to do a self-check. If you want to have anal sex with your spouse, first ask yourself and respond honestly to the questions Carson poses: "Why does he or she want to do this? Is it love? Is it motivated by the desire to give? Does it fulfill the purpose of glorifying God? Will it enhance the worship experience of sex together? Or are there other motives? Is it driven by selfishness? Is it driven by the lust of the flesh? Is the spouse who desires this particular act doing so because of pornography, fantasies, regular masturbation, or other experiences which make routine sex with his or her spouse seem boring? Does he or she believe that their typical sex can no longer satisfy?" Each case is different, but answering these questions may give you some clarity as to your motives for wanting or asking for anal sex.[26]

In summary, anal sex is absolutely a deviation from God's plan for humanity, and therefore it is a sin. It is in no sense a biblically acceptable alternative to sexual intercourse for married couples.

---

1. Willard Harley, *Fall in Love, Stay in Love* (Grand Rapids, MI: Revell, 2020), 44.
2. Nancy C. Anderson, "Respect Your Husband (Even if You Don't Think He 'Deserves' It),"

CBN, accessed August 20, 2020, https://www1.cbn.com/marriage/respect-your-husband-even -if-you-dont-think-he-deserves-it.

3. Shaunti Feldhahn, "How to Respect an Imperfect Husband," Shaunti Feldhahn, June 5, 2017, https://shaunti.com/2017/06/how-to-respect-an-imperfect-husband/; emphasis in original.

4. Feldhahn, "How to Respect"; emphasis in original.

5. S. Feldhahn, (2020), meme, Pinterest, accessed September 28, 2020, https://www .pinterest.co.uk/pin/702913454314578256/.

6. Wikipedia, s.v. "Jewish Views on Marriage," updated May 4, 2020, https://en.wikipedia .org/wiki/Jewish_views_on_marriage.

7. Juli Slattery, "Understanding His Sexuality," Focus on the Family, January 1, 2009, https:// www.focusonthefamily.com/marriage/understanding-his-sexuality/.

8. Slattery, "Understanding His Sexuality."

9. Richard Tate and Rita Tate, *11 Reasons Families Succeed* (Tulsa: Hensley Publishing, 2002).

10. Shmuley Boteach, *Kosher Sex* (Jerusalem, Israel: Gefen, 2019).

11. Jill Renich, quoted in Gary Thomas, *Sacred Marriage* (Grand Rapids, MI: Zondervan, 2015), 159.

12. John Gray, *Men Are From Mars, Women Are From Venus* (New York: HarperCollins, 1994).

13. Naftali Brawer, "Why Is Sex Allowed on Shabbat?" *Jewish Chronicle*, June 8, 2012, https:// www.thejc.com/judaism/rabbi-i-have-a-problem/why-is-sex-allowed-on-shabbat-1.33812.

14. Malka Zeiger Simkovich, "Intimacy on Shabbat: Was It Always a Mitzvah?" TheTorah .com, accessed August 20, 2020, https://www.thetorah.com/article/intimacy-on-shabbat.

15. Michael W. Campbell, "Sex on the Sabbath," *Ministry*, April 2015, 14–16.

16. "What Does the Bible Say About Oral Sex?" GotQuestions.org, accessed August 6, 2020, https://www.gotquestions.org/Bible-oral-sex.html.

17. "What Does the Bible Say About Oral Sex?"

18. "Is Oral Sex a Sin?" All About . . . , accessed August 5, 2020, https://www.allaboutgod .com/is-oral-sex-a-sin.htm.

19. "Is Oral Sex a Sin?"

20. Kevin Carson, "What Does the Bible Teach About Oral Sex?" Kevin Carson, March 16, 2019, https://kevincarson.com/2019/03/16/copy-what-does-the-bible-teach-about-oral-sex/.

21. Carson, "What Does the Bible Teach About Oral Sex?"

22. "What Does the Bible Say About Oral Sex?" GotQuestions.org.

23. *Merriam-Webster*, s.v. "sodomy (n.)," accessed August 6, 2020, https://unabridged.merriam -webster.com/collegiate/sodomy.

24. Clifford Penner and Joyce Penner, *The Gift of Sex: A Guide to Sexual Fulfillment* (Nash-ville: W Publishing Group, 2003), 215, 216.

25. Douglas E. Rosenau, *A Celebration of Sex* (Nashville: Thomas Nelson, 2002), 158.

26. Kevin Carson, "What Does the Bible Teach About Anal Sex?" Kevin Carson, March 9, 2019, https://kevincarson.com/2019/03/09/what-does-the-bible-say-about-anal-sex/.

What I Need From Him

*Husbands, love your wives, just as Christ loved the church
and gave himself up for her.*

—Ephesians 5:25, NIV

We devoted the previous chapter to the five most important emotional needs of men, in general terms. However, some men may identify with one or more of the five needs we will mention in this chapter, and some women may choose some of the ones we mentioned in the previous chapter. That does not make you strange or abnormal. Each of us has different needs. So, at the conclusion of this chapter, you will look over the list of all ten emotional needs. Then you husbands will decide which of the ten best apply to you, and you wives will do the same. Understanding your own personal needs and dialoguing about them together is a good step toward a stronger, healthier relationship.

Husbands, in this chapter, we are speaking to you because we will be discussing some of the key things that your wife needs from you. Let's get started with a question for you to think about.

For discussion

Before you begin to discover the most important emotional needs of women, we would like to ask you, husbands, to make a list of what you think are the top three things your wife needs. Wives, make a list of the top three things you actually need. Don't peek at each other's list until you are finished. Then share with each other and discuss your responses. The list may change after you have read this chapter, but this exercise will help you think about this chapter and reflect on your thoughts.

1. _____
2. _____
3. _____

Now that you have shared your lists with each other, let's look at the top five things that a wife needs, according to research. Remember, it's OK if husbands share the need for some of the same items discussed in the following pages.

1. HUSBAND, LOVE YOUR WIFE

One of our favorite films as a family is *Fiddler on the Roof.* One of the songs in the musical is a dialogue between the two main characters, Tevye and his wife, Golde. After twenty-five years of marriage, Tevye asks Golde if she loves him, to which she responds:

> Do I love you?
> For twenty-five years, I've washed your clothes,
> Cooked your meals, cleaned your house, . . .
> . . . why talk about love right now?[1]

Imagine, after twenty-five years of being married, having to ask your spouse if he or she loves you! All those years have passed by for this couple, and never once have they said the words *I love you* to each other. Is it important to say those words to each other? The real question may be, Is it important to show and express love to each other?

Let's read our verse for this chapter once again: "Husbands, love your wives, just as Christ loved the church and gave himself up for her" (Ephesians 5:25, NIV). Jesus directed you, as a husband, to love your wife—snd not just to love your wife, but to love her in the same way that He loves His bride, the church. Loving your wife is more than mere words that you say (although she does like to hear them); it also extends to the loving things you do with and for her each day.

Think back over this past week. In what specific ways did you let your wife know she is special? In fact, what have you done today? You see, we often wait for special occasions, such as birthdays, anniversaries, Valentine's Day, or Christmas to give tangible expressions of our love. But showing love to your wife is something that should be done on ordinary days—in fact, on every day of the week. You can do it through words, greeting cards, gifts, hugs, kisses, and other courtesies, such as holding her hand when you walk together, opening the door of the car for her, or pulling out her chair. You do it when you create an environment that clearly and repeatedly expresses to her how much you care about her and love her.

No, we are not talking about expensive gifts. You do not need to buy a dozen roses or take her out to a fancy restaurant. Rather, it is more about the little things you do throughout the day. What will you do today that says to her, "You are a treasure to me, and I love you"? There is actually another word that women often use when referring to this need. They will say, "I wish my husband was more romantic." *Romantic.* A man's eyes will often roll when he hears that word because, truth be told, he has no idea what that word means in practical terms. Here's a tip for you, husbands: ask her. Romance means different things to different women. There is no one list that fits all women. Ask your wife what she enjoys, what makes her feel loved and special. Make a mental note of that, and then do it!

Of course, some women will say, "He should know. I shouldn't have to tell him!" But we remind them that the only one who can read our minds is God. Not even the devil can read our minds (and we praise God for that). Why not help your husband out and let him know what you consider romantic actions on his part? Don't just drop some vague hints. Be clear and specific. It makes it easier for him to understand and remember. First, you ladies need to clearly know in your own mind what you would like from your husband and then communicate it to him. At times we have talked to wives who ask their husbands to be more romantic, but when asked to be more specific about what they want, they seem confused or unsure themselves. When their husbands try to be romantic—the way they understand romance—they often miss the target because it is a moving target. Women, don't make your husbands guess. What is romantic to you?

Well, men, since you asked for some ideas, here are some we have shared in the past. It is usually the little things that mean a lot, things such as holding her hand, putting your arm around her in public, winking at her, leaving her a handwritten note in a place where she will find it during her day (such as in her lunch bag, on the bathroom mirror, or on the steering wheel of her car), sending her an unexpected text message in the middle of your workday that tells her how much you miss her, putting a piece of chocolate on her pillow, offering to make her a meal, drawing a bubble bath for her, making sure her car has enough gas so she doesn't have to go to the gas station, or taking her car in for maintenance and repairs or to the car wash (unless you do it all yourself, which is also nice). Romance can be simple acts of courtesy, kindness, and love spread throughout her day, one day at a time!

Or maybe you can write her a poem. In one of our favorite comic strips, *Pickles*, Earl approaches his wife and tells her, "I wrote you a little poem for Valentine's Day. Do you want to hear it?" Opal, in turn, asks, "Do I have to?" Earl says, "No," and goes on to read the poem he has lovingly written for her: "Roses are red, I like spaghetti, especially with meatballs, when will it be ready?" That's creativity, don't you think?

My husband has a sense of humor. He always keeps me laughing, and the unexpected is always expected around him. When it comes to showing love, he always finds ways to surprise me. He is naturally a morning person, which is the opposite of how I am. If I do not have to get up at 3:00 A.M. to catch a plane, you will find me still under my covers, enjoying my dreams. However, Claudio wakes up before the sun, even if we do not have an early morning flight to catch.

Most wives will understand when I say that many men, if left unsupervised, find ways to get into trouble. Claudio is no different! On one particular morning, he was up at his usual predawn time and, since there was no plane for me to catch, he was unsupervised. He wandered into our bathroom, took the roll of toilet paper off the holder, and unwound the roll. Somehow, he located a red marker and used it to draw red hearts all over the toilet paper and also wrote *I love you* over and over again. Then he rolled that toilet paper roll back up, replaced it in the bathroom, and waited for me to wake up and discover his love notes, scrawled all over the toilet paper. A few hours later, I was met with his surprise as I awoke, headed to the bathroom, and then reached for the toilet paper. Of course, he was hiding by the door and laughing at this point. This is just one example of the ways in which my hubby combines his humor and creativity to express his love. Needless to say, I needed him to hand me a fresh roll of toilet paper to use! After all, what wife can use toilet paper that has red hearts and love messages written all over it?

Some men believe that people are born with or without a romantic gene. Let's clear up this myth. Being romantic is not a special gene some people have; it's a learned behavior. Most of us learned it from our parents. We watched them be kind and loving toward each other. We may have witnessed our dad holding our mom's hand or kissing her or telling her he loved her. At times we thought it was funny, and at other times we thought it was embarrassing. But that's how we learned how a loving couple behaves when it comes to romance. Sadly, some people never had that example, so when they got married, they simply repeated what they witnessed growing up, which was no affection between a husband and wife. They tell us, "I'd like to be more romantic with my spouse, but I don't know how." We tell them, "It's not too late for you to learn. Learn from others." By the way, we make it clear: learn from others—not *with* others.

We tell a story that illustrates this idea. A new couple had just moved across the street from a longtime resident. She was one of those people who loved to sit at her window, watching what everybody else in her neighborhood did. She noticed that the new neighbor across the street would come home from work every day and that in his hand he always had a small gift for his wife. Some days he would bring her flowers, other days chocolates, still others a greeting card or some other small surprise. This happened every day of the week. His wife would come out of the house to greet him, and he would present the gift to her. She would smile with delight, hug him, and kiss him all the way up their driveway until they disappeared into their house. The scene was repeated without fail every single day, which was filling this neighbor lady's heart with growing jealousy.

One day, as her own husband walked in the front door from work and only wanted to plop down in his easy chair, she asked him, "Have you noticed the new neighbors across the street?"

Her husband was a bit shocked and was barely able to drop his briefcase in order to sit down to take his shoes off.

"No, honey," he responded, "I have not noticed the new neighbors across the street."

"Well, let me tell you," she told him emphatically, "every day when that man comes home from work, he has in his hand something for his wife. Some days, he brings her flowers. Other days, he brings her chocolates. Other days, he brings her a greeting card. Every day, he has some small gift for her." Then she pointed an accusing finger at her husband and yelled, "Why don't you do that?"

Confused, the man responded to his wife, "Honey, I can't do that. I hardly know that woman!" He missed the whole point. But that's why we say, "Learn from others—not *with* others."

We find it interesting that men who have an affair tend to be so much more romantic and affectionate with the other woman than they are with their own wife. If they treated their own wife like they treat the other woman, they would probably have a wonderful, loving relationship with their wife. So, again, if you don't feel like the romantic type or don't know how to show your wife love, ask her what she would like for you to do, and do it for her.

As we said earlier, sometimes it is the simple things that mean the most. We met an older couple several years ago. They came to one of our couples' retreats and sought us out during a break. They wanted to tell us about something they had been doing during their marriage of several decades together. Excitedly, the wife told us, "You know the Popsicle that has two sticks?" We affirmed that we did. She continued, "Sometimes my husband buys one of those, then we break it in half, and each of us takes one half and eats it. We've been doing that for years. It's so much fun!" Both wife and husband smiled like little children telling us their story of love and sharing. It is such a simple and inexpensive way to share love. It really is the small things you do that can mean so much!

We remember reading another story that illustrates the value of sharing as a romantic action. The lady that wrote the story said that she and her daughter were at a McDonald's restaurant waiting in line to order their food. As they waited, they noticed an older couple ahead of them. She and her daughter noticed they were poorly dressed, and when they placed their order, all they asked for was one hamburger, one pack of french fries, and one drink. When they received their order, they sat at a table where they proceeded to cut the burger in half and divide the french fries in half. The wife began to eat her half of the hamburger.

The lady and her daughter were moved as they watched that scene, thinking to themselves that this poor old couple couldn't afford to order their own burger, fries, and drink. Moved with compassion, they approached the old couple cautiously, apologized for intruding on their private meal, and said, "We noticed that you ordered only one burger, one pack of fries, and one drink. My daughter and I would be honored to buy you another burger, another pack of fries, and another drink so that you each could have your own."

The man shook his head, and shyly responded, "Oh no, thank you. It's just that we share everything."

The lady was filled with emotion. Her eyes teared up, and she was barely able to respond, "Oh, that is so sweet. But, may I ask you, how come your wife is eating, and you're not?" "Well," the old man responded, "I'm waiting for her to finish, so I can borrow her dentures." Hopefully, you read this after dinner and not before! We didn't mean to ruin your appetite.

Here's an important fact that some men don't understand—not all women like to receive flowers. Pamela is one of those who love flowers in their natural setting but would not be too impressed if I were to bring her a dozen roses. She would be much happier if I brought her a box of her favorite chocolates. But if your wife is one of those who likes flowers, bring her flowers. More important, as we stated earlier, don't just do it once a year for your wedding anniversary, her birthday, or Mother's Day and Valentine's Day. Bring her flowers on a day that is not particularly special at all. Bring her flowers just because you were thinking about her, because you wanted to brighten her day, or because you want to see her smile. Remember, your gesture means more when you do things for her on days that are not special occasions.

We knew a lady who loved flowers, and her husband would bring her flowers every single day. Needless to say, she was delighted every day as he came home with fresh flowers—until she found out her husband would go by the cemetery on his way home from work every day and get the flowers off of someone's grave to bring to his wife. Guys, come on. Don't be so cheap! If your wife likes flowers, you can find them in many places, sometimes for a reasonable cost.

If we have learned something through the years, it is that expressing love does not have to cost a lot of money. Sure, you can stop by a store and pick up a greeting card. Some of them are quite elaborate and fancy but also quite expensive. Think about it—someone got paid to draw the illustration on the card, and somebody else was paid to write the message on it. All you have to do is add a few words of your own or even simply sign it. It doesn't take much effort, which is often the message you give your wife: that she's not worth the effort. Buying a card is the easy way out (and more expensive).

At home, I (Pam) have a memory box in which I put all those special cards, small gifts, and mementos my husband has given me through the years. That memory box now resides in a dresser in one of our spare rooms. After more than forty-one years together, I have saved a lot of things. I have Valentine's Day, Mother's Day, and birthday cards along with thirty-eight anniversary cards and other small mementos of our time together. But my favorite card in that large collection is one that didn't cost my husband any money at all. He found a piece of plain-white paper, folded it in half, drew a vase with flowers, colored each flower with different crayons, and wrote a few words from his heart. He even figured out how to make a flower vase pop up when I opened the card. While it didn't cost him any money, it took a great deal of time, effort, and creativity to make that card. That is my favorite card in my large collection because he made it for me.

So, husbands, find out what your wife considers romantic actions and do those things frequently and repeatedly. You will be making deposits in her emotional Love Bank, and your account will continue to grow more each day.

FOR DISCUSSION
Husbands, have a discussion with your wife and ask her what five things she would like for you to do that she feels are romantic and show your love for her. Below, write what she reveals.

1. _____
2. _____
3. _____
4. _____
5. _____

Now that you know, there are no excuses. Make it your goal to do these things often. In the beginning, you may have to put them on your calendar so you can remember until they become a natural habit.

2. COMMUNICATE WITH HER
When we ask men to guess what a woman's number one need is, they usually shout out this one. They tell us how much she likes to talk—so, surely, that need must be on the list. Well, here it is. Yes, it is true that wives need their husbands to communicate with them. When you do not talk to your wife, she gets worried that perhaps something is wrong with your relationship. Communication is one of the ways in which she connects with you emotionally.

A difficulty that most men have in meeting this need for their wife is that men do not typically connect at the emotional level through communication. Silence is truly golden to them, and they bask in it. Therefore, most researchers who study the differences between males and females will put the need to communicate on the list for females but exclude it from the list of the males' needs.

In contrast, picture two women at the gym after they have finished their exercise. One says to the other, "Did you hear that Sue's getting a divorce?" The other one responds, "No! What happened?" And they will spend a good deal of time talking about who and what and where and why and how it all happened. That's why a friend told us the definition of eternity is two women saying goodbye. Just when it looks as if they are saying goodbye, one may say, "Please give your mom a hug from me. Oh, by the way, how is your mom?" And just like that, the conversation begins all over again. A few minutes later one will say, "I better get going, I told my husband I would meet him at 4:00 P.M.," to which the other responds, "Oh sure, did he get that job promotion he was hoping for?" And the conversation gets started once again. However, once we men say goodbye, that's the end. Psychologists and marriage experts Les and Leslie Parrott refer to the work of Deborah Tannen, who "explains that men focus most of their communication on 'report talk' (gathering information) while women focus on 'rapport talk' (building camaraderie)."[2]

According to an article by Nikelle Murphy, "Studies showed that women speak approximately 20,000 words per day, compared to men who speak about 7,000."[3] Wow! If true, that is more than double. Other researchers have argued that this finding is flawed, and the number of words is closer to equal; however, we think many men would agree with the initial finding. When I (Claudio) mention that women use twice as many words as men do, Pam is quick to remind me that the reason for that is because she has to tell me everything twice. (I'm not sure I understand what she means by that, and I wish she would explain it again.) Yes, that explains why it's doubled!

According to an article published online by the *Daily Mail*, "Studies have shown that the female love of chit-chat begins at a young age. Girls learn to speak earlier and more quickly than boys. They produce their first words and sentences earlier, have larger vocabularies and use a greater variety of sentence types than boys of the same age."[4]

Whether or not you agree as to the finding that women talk more than men, another issue that arises is the difference in *the way* we communicate. You see, women like all the details and men, on the other hand, prefer minimal facts. And trying to get all the details out of your husband is often like pulling teeth!

It's not that men don't like talking; we do it every day at work or with family or friends. It's just that men don't have the need to know every single detail about everything, particularly in other people's lives. For instance, picture two guys sitting at the gym after a workout session. One says to the other, "Hey, did you hear Dave's getting a divorce?" The other one responds, "Wow! No, I didn't know. By the way, are you watching the game tonight?" And they continue to talk about this, that, or the other. A little bit of information, the basics, is all we need. We don't need to go into all the details of what happened.

My (Claudio's) sister is a typical female and an extrovert on top of that. She tells me about her neighbors, whom I've never met, and cousins, whom I have not seen in years, and total strangers she met on the bus. I don't need to know all that information. I am not only an introvert but also a shy introvert. I don't talk to strangers, and when I do, I run out of things to say and questions to ask after the basic, "Cold today, eh?" or, "Hello."

Men need to recognize that women have the need to communicate. They want to hear about the details of your day, who you talked to, where you went, what you did, and so on. The problem is that at the end of the day—after you have used most, if not all, of your seven thousand words—you get home and your wife asks about your day, and you don't have any words left to tell her. You barely respond, "Fine." But *fine* is not enough for her. So she begins asking additional questions, which may make you very nervous and perhaps even irritated.

On the other hand, your wife has been talking all day, but she still has thousands of words in her arsenal, and she wants to tell you all about her day and needs someone to listen to her. The closest and most logical choice of a listener is you, her husband. Just as you sit down to watch the game and quietly enjoy watching your team battle against another, she wants to talk with you about her day. During the last few minutes of the game, when the destiny of your team is about to be decided, she wants to tell you about the sale at the fabric store, the news that Dave and Sue are getting a divorce, or how frustrated she is with something that happened at work. If you don't take the time to listen to her, she will be upset and possibly become frustrated, perhaps even angry.

This is a very delicate balance we need to maintain. Men need to learn to be better listeners, and women need to give men space to not talk. We tell men: When your wife needs to talk, disconnect from whatever you're doing, look her in the eye, concentrate on what she's telling you, and listen for the underlying feelings she's sharing. Don't try to fix her problems. Unless she's asking for your advice, do not offer any. Comment on what she's telling you so she knows you are paying attention to her. Don't dismiss her feelings but validate them. Follow the biblical words: "You should be quick to listen and slow to speak or to get angry" (James 1:19, CEV).

To you wives, we say: If you want your husband to listen to you, wait until he is looking you in the eyes. If he's distracted doing something else, chances are he never heard a word you said. We saw a comic strip where a wife is talking to her husband. She says to him, "Go to the store, lay down the mulch, wash and wax the car, get the kids to school, rent some videos, and finish the rest of the dishes." This is what he heard: "Go . . . lay down . . . and . . . get . . . some . . . rest."

We husbands think it's helpful if you ladies will get to the point as soon as possible. We understand you want to give us a lot of details, but we really need you to get to the bottom line as soon as possible. Someone illustrated the difference between how men and women tell stories like this:

How Men Tell Stories

How Women Tell Stories

Probably one of the biggest enemies in good communication we have today is all the technology that surrounds us. Our parents and grandparents spent a lot of time sitting on the front porch or in the living room, just talking about the events of the day, their family, their work, or whatever. Occasionally, our grandparents would turn the radio on to hear the latest news. The next generation (our parents) began to gather around the television set but for limited amounts of time. But today, we have technology constantly with us, no matter where we go. If the television is not on, we're looking at a screen of some sort, such as a laptop, tablet, or cell phone.

All you need to do to prove this point is to go to a restaurant and notice how many people are engaged in meaningful conversations around the table versus how many have their heads buried in some electronic device. Why not stay at home? Why spend money on a family meal at a restaurant if all that the family members are going to do is look at their phones or other handheld devices?

We often think of a comic strip showing a couple sitting at a coffee shop. The man is looking at his cell phone, and his lady friend tells him, "Do you mind if I strap your phone to my forehead so I can pretend you're looking at me when I talk?"

That wonderful piece of technology has taken over our lives to such a degree that it has invaded the quality time we should be spending with our spouse and with our families. If you answer the cell phone every time it rings, you are sending the message to your wife or children that whoever is calling or texting you is more important than they are. Is that the message you want to give to those closest to you? Let the phone ring. If it's important, the caller will leave a message that you can check later. For now, enjoy good communication with your wife. It is much more important to you and your marriage.

3. BE TRUSTWORTHY

We previously discussed how dishonesty was identified as one of the key things that is most destructive in a marital relationship, so it should be no surprise that honesty is one of a woman's most important needs. A wife needs to know that she can trust her husband. Trust becomes the foundation upon which all other building blocks of a healthy marriage are added. Without trust, the home crumbles.

Something in our world today has greatly eroded the sense of trust that many couples in the past have enjoyed. It is something that is most likely close to you, within your reach, at this very moment. Yes, again, it is your cell phone! You see, this little thing has been one of our greatest blessings, in that it enables us to remain in contact with friends and family, allows us to conduct business, and opens up the world in new ways. It has also enabled us to share the gospel in ways never before possible. At the same time, however, it is the number one tool that is being utilized by Satan to destroy our homes.

You see, the cell phone is the primary way in which pornography is being accessed. We need to stop pretending that porn is not affecting our homes. Here are some startling statistics from a website we recently launched:

- "There are 68 million internet search queries for pornography each day."
- "The top five porn sites in the world have a combined 17.73 billion visits per month (that's 738,750,000 per hour, 12,312,500 per minute, or 205,208 per second)."
- "[Seventy-seven percent] of Christian men ages 18–30 view porn at least monthly."
- "[Thirty percent] of pastors report they have visited a pornography site within the last 30 days."
- "The average age of exposure to porn in the U.S. is 11 years old and dropping."[5]

Those statistics are alarming. The sad truth is that we don't even need to go searching for porn, because porn will find its own way to our phones, computers, or similar electronic devices. We need to make the decision now that, when it does, we will instantly delete it and not give in to the temptation to open the file and view it. Preventing addiction to pornography is so much easier than breaking the addiction once it has taken hold of us.

Being trustworthy in today's world is not just about who you are spending time with face-to-face. You must also include all aspects of your online viewing and behavior. What videos and images are you viewing? Who are you chatting with online? What kind of text messages are you sending or receiving? What sites are you visiting? Do you erase your browser history? Do you quickly delete your messages? Is there anything you are doing online that you would not want your wife to know about?

Be honest and faithful to your marriage and your wife in all of your face-to-face interactions as well as in your online behavior. Be trustworthy because trust is the bedrock of a strong marriage. Of course, pornography consumption is but one of the areas in which honesty in marriage can be violated. When you're not completely truthful with your wife, you are also being dishonest. Honesty in marriage means that you reveal to your spouse positive and negative feelings. If you are angry, chances are your wife can see it—or at the very least sense it. When she asks you if you're upset, and you, instead, tell her you're not—even though you know you are—you're being dishonest. You may think that it's better not to say anything at the moment, or maybe you don't feel like talking about it right then and there, but you are withholding personal information, which gives your wife the clear message that you are not being honest with her.

One of the things we explain during our couples' retreats is that sometimes wives train their husbands to be dishonest. How does a wife do that? Here's an example. The wife tries on a dress and asks her husband, "Do I look fat in this dress?" In a matter of nanoseconds, his heart begins to beat rapidly and sweat begins to form on his forehead and upper lip. He wants to be truthful and honest but very cautious at the same time. Softly and carefully he begins to answer, "Well . . . hmmm . . . ah . . . I mean . . . perhaps . . ." Immediately the wife starts sobbing and says, "I can't believe you told me I'm fat." And the husband runs out of the room. Wives, I guarantee you that the next time you ask him that question, he is not going to tell you what he thinks, even if it's the truth. He's probably going to say, "Absolutely not! You look fantastic. I love that outfit on you"—even if he doesn't think so. You see, he doesn't want to hurt you because he loves you. However, you are training him to be dishonest in order not to hurt your feelings. You have to decide whether you want your husband to be honest with you all the time, even if you don't like what he has to tell you, or if you would rather have him lie to you when you don't want to hear the truth.

Now, to you guys, we say: Be honest, but be kind. Don't be rude as you answer truthfully. One of the comic strips we show to illustrate this point shows a young lady standing in front of a mirror at a clothing store as she tries on a pair of jeans. She turns around to get a better view of her backside as she asks her husband, "Be honest, do these jeans make my booty look huge?" Eagerly her husband replies, "No, not at all, sweetie. The jeans don't have anything to do with it. I'd say it's all that dairy you eat every day." The caption at the bottom of the comic reads, "And the 'quit while you're ahead' award goes to . . ." That may be the honest thing to say, but it is also very rude and unkind.

When wives ask their husbands how they look, men will go to any length to evade the question or to answer it without incriminating themselves. One of my favorite comic strips of all time is entitled "Stalemate." In this picture, an older, larger lady is standing on one side of the room, wearing a red dress, and she asks her husband, "Do I look fat?" The husband, who is tying his necktie in front of the mirror, replies, "Do I look stupid?"

No man wants to answer any question that has to do with the appearance of his wife. In another comic strip, Opal comes to her husband, Earl, who is sitting on the couch and reading the newspaper, "Do you really think my hair is getting thin?" Earl quickly dismisses her concerns by telling her, "I think your hair is fine." But that's not enough for Opal, who comes back with, "Fine? Do you mean 'fine' as in thin and wispy or 'fine' as in full and healthy?" Earl, knowing where this discussion may lead, stands up and walks away as he responds, "I mean 'fine' as in now is a fine time for me to take a walk."

What we men find interesting is the tricky way in which wives sometimes ask those questions. It feels like a trap, and there's no safe way out. Another comic strip that illustrates the difficulty men have in answering "How do I look?" shows a wife holding a blue dress and a red dress as she asks her husband, "Which dress makes me look thinner, the blue or the red?" He immediately recognizes the danger in answering directly, so he responds, "This is a setup." She assures him that's not the case: "That's not true. I want your opinion." Falling for that explanation, he innocently responds, "Fine, blue." To which she comes back with, "So, I look fat in the red dress?"

Again, husbands, be honest. Share with your wife your positive and negative feelings, events from the past, daily events and schedules, and your plans for the future. Don't leave her with a false impression; instead, answer her questions truthfully. But as you answer truthfully, do so with love and kindness. Wives, accept his honesty even if it's not what you wanted to hear. It may hurt your feelings, but in the end, it will strengthen your marriage as you build it on the solid pillar of trust.

For discussion

It may be best to have this conversation before the question comes up so that both of you will handle the situation in a positive way. Ask your wife how she would feel most comfortable for you to answer questions about her weight, the way she looks, and other questions dealing with her.

4. ENSURE YOUR FAMILY'S FINANCIAL SECURITY

As a joke of sorts, we ask the question, "What is the number one cause of divorce?" People respond with communication, finances, conflict resolution, sex, and other reasons. We then tell them that the number one cause of divorce is . . . marriage. Isn't that the truth? If no one would get married, there would be no divorce. Now, seriously, if we were to ask, "What is the number one complaint married couples have?" we could answer truthfully that it is financial difficulties. Most men find their identity and their meaning in life by being able to provide financially for their families. They want to be able to have enough money to take care of the necessities for their wife and children and to provide additional funds to have fun, to travel, and to enjoy life.

On the other hand, it gives a woman security to know that the family finances are in order. Many ladies have approached us to tell us how worried they are about their family's finances and how afraid they are that they may lose everything they have. We remember one couple in this situation. She told us they were about to lose their house because they were several months behind on their mortgage payments. The problem was that she had just found out her husband had been sending large amounts of money to his family in another country. As she told us, "He built a house for his parents, for his brothers, and for his sisters, and here we are about to lose our own home because we don't have money to make our own mortgage payments." This couple's marriage was in trouble. The two emotional needs of trustworthiness and financial security are very important for many couples. Sometimes spouses, such as this one, have committed what is known as financial infidelity. This happens when one spouse uses money without the knowledge or consent of the other.

Some women have put their careers on hold in order to stay home and take care of the children. In doing so, these women have become completely financially dependent on their husbands. While this may be an agreed-upon situation and both may do it gladly, it still puts the woman in a somewhat precarious situation. It's one thing to depend on someone for money when you're a kid living at home with Mom and Dad, but it's another thing to be dependent on someone as an adult, particularly when you have a career of your own, a college education, and marketable work skills.

When my (Claudio's) parents were married early in the twentieth century (boy, that sounds like a very long time ago), they agreed, as was the custom at the time, that my dad would work and my mom would stay home to take care of him, the kids, and the home in general. I'm amazed when I think about how my dad was able to support a family of six children on a tractor salesman's salary. But when he suddenly died at the age of fifty-five, my then forty-nine-year-old mother was left to take care of the youngest three kids still at home, and she had not worked one day during the twenty-eight years they were married. We were blessed that the house was paid for, and there was enough money in the bank to last for a while, but unexpectedly my mother found herself trying to make a living, with no recent employment experience.

An article on *Financial Samurai* provides ideas to help the stay-at-home wife be more financially secure in her future:

- *"Marry."* It may seem redundant to make this statement in a book about marriage, but sometimes couples need to be reminded that being married brings the couple many financial benefits. As the author of the article states, "Marriage brings about stability for the less wealthy spouse. . . . A spouse will also receive their deceased spouse's Social Security benefits."
- *"Establish independent financial accounts."* Include in your family budget a certain amount of discretionary money for each spouse—some of that money may be used to set up an extra independent bank account if desired. The independent account would be in addition to your joint account and offers "each spouse the freedom to spend as they choose." Again, each spouse should have a small amount of discretionary funds budgeted each month.
- *"Create a business and give ownership."* You could work together to create a new business venture on the side. As the author explains, "One way to create more equality is to give a greater percentage of ownership to the spouse who earns less or doesn't earn at all. Not only does this show good faith, but a higher ownership structure might also motivate the spouse to work hard at building the business."
- *"Contribute extra to retirement accounts."* Since you can't contribute to someone else's IRA or 401(k), perhaps "it's best to help build your spouse's after-tax investment accounts."
- *"Pay down debt."* Pay off both your credit card and/or student loan debt as soon as you get married. Obviously, it would be good to eliminate all debt as soon as you can. As in my parents' case, it was a blessing that our house had been paid off by the time my father died. Having that worry off your spouse's and your own shoulders is good for both you and your marriage.
- *"Assign a value to the stay-at-home parent."* The author notes that "no job is more important than taking care of a child." So why not assign a top salary to the stay-at-home parent? "Do an honest assessment of

the number of hours the [stay-at-home] parent works in a 24-hour period." In other words, if the wife is a stay-at-home mom, it is very detrimental to the marriage to make her feel as if she is contributing nothing to the family financially. After all, think of how much money you would need to pay someone to babysit, clean the house, cook the meals, and all the other things she does.[6]

We want to be very clear about something. We are not saying that your wife needs to live in the biggest mansion in the nicest neighborhood, wear designer shoes, or carry expensive designer bags. Wives have told us they would be content having a small house, an older model car, and clothes from a secondhand store. What matters is the knowledge that the roof over their head is secure, they will not be asked to move for failure to pay the mortgage, the basic financial needs of the home are met. They value the security of knowing there will be food on the table for the next meal, the rent or the mortgage has been paid, and the children will have warm clothes in the winter months. Perhaps not all the family's wants are fulfilled, but all of the needs are cared for—and that brings a sense of security.

Husbands, please understand. Let us reiterate once again. We are not saying that you need to work two or three jobs in order to provide for your family. No, to the contrary—we are stating that financial security is all about the basic needs of life being met. Being a workaholic or trying to amass worldly possessions will ultimately destroy your family. Paul taught young Pastor Timothy, "But if anyone does not provide for his own, and especially for those of his household, he has denied the faith and is worse than an unbeliever" (1 Timothy 5:8).

We received a slip of paper during one of our couples' retreats that illustrates this point. The note read: "My husband has a mistress, and I don't know how to compete for his love. He says he loves me, but I need more of his time! His mistress is his work." (We will talk more about finances in chapter 8.)

FOR DISCUSSION
Husbands, make a list of the top three priorities in your life. Be honest and list them in order of what gets your most focused attention—write down what is your first priority, your second, and your third.

1. _____

2. _____

3. _____

After you have made your list, share and discuss it with your wife and see if she sees your actions as being aligned with the priorities you have written. What adjustments do you need to make?

5. MAKE FAMILY A PRIORITY

Husbands, how did you do on that priority list? Where did your wife and children fall? In which position did you place your career or work? And what about technology use? You see, it's easy to make a list of where they *should* be. In fact, most of us get that correct; however, it becomes more challenging to ensure that the list truly reflects our behavior. Go ahead, take out your calendar. As you look at your appointments for the next month, you may see things such as boards or committees at work, a dental appointment, kids' soccer practice, a church board meeting, an appointment at a car garage, and the list goes on. Wait! Did you see "Date night with my wife" on that calendar? How about "Family night?" You see, if we are not intentional about scheduling these things, they will not happen automatically. They need to be put on our calendars, and those times need to be held as sacred blocks of time.

It is our belief that God should always take first place in our life. This should be reflected in our regular personal and family devotional time, Bible study, church involvement, and how we practice our faith in daily life. It's the second place that we often struggle with the most. Many of you may say that your wife takes the second slot (as she should), but when it comes to practicing this, we often fall short. The thing that most often pushes our spouse aside is our work. Having a good work ethic is admirable, and being recognized as an outstanding employee for the company is commendable; however, we should never lose sight of the fact that our marriages are the most important treasures God has entrusted us with on this earth, and they are the only thing that we can take to heaven with us!

We often say, "The best gift you can give your children is your marriage." So, on your priority list, your spouse should come even before your children. This is one of the mistakes that couples with young children often make—when their new baby is born, they turn all of their attention toward the child and away from each other.

Researcher John Gottman discovered that "after having a baby, 67 percent of couples see their marital satisfaction plummet."[7] Yes, marital bliss, according to research, takes a dive within a year after the birth of a couple's first child. So it is critical for you as a couple to recognize this danger and be intentional about nurturing your own marriage and making time for yourselves, apart from the children.

For years, we have been encouraging couples to implement a simple formula to spend a better quality and quantity of time together as a couple. We encourage you to follow this formula by spending time together as a couple—no kids, extended family, friends, or colleagues—and no technology (no TV, computer, tablets, cell phones, and the like). We encourage you to spend at least

- thirty minutes each day;
- one night each week;
- one day each month; and
- one weekend each quarter.

Make sure you don't use that time for

- dealing with conflict or problems;
- having money discussions;
- running errands; or
- shopping.

Besides doing everything in your power to maintain a strong and healthy marital relationship, family commitment also means taking care of the family circle, not allowing anybody else to disrupt the family unit. Some spouses have not learned to maintain proper boundaries with the extended family or with friends who come into their home and have no respect for those inside the family unit.

Making family a priority also means spending adequate time with the children. Since we're talking about the most important emotional needs of women, we can tell you that the average woman wants and needs her husband's support in raising their children. In many homes, that responsibility falls almost entirely on the mother's shoulders. The dad feels that since he's the one working to support the family financially, it is the mother's responsibility to take care of the children. In today's society, many women work outside the home and come home to continue the work of taking care of their husbands, their kids, and their home.

Husbands, see what you can do to help your wife with the important responsibility of raising your children. Can you help them with their homework, or at least help to see that they do it? Could you be more supportive in disciplining them? Can you assist more in the care and maintenance of the home so that all of you will have more family time together?

One of the things that I (Claudio) started doing when our daughters were small was to take them, individually, on daddy-daughter dates. Pam would always make sure they dressed pretty, and off we would go on our special dates together. It was nothing fancy or expensive, and often it was nothing more than a trip to Taco Bell or to the park; however, what mattered was that we were spending one-on-one time together. On these outings, Daddy was modeling for his daughters how a man should treat a woman as he opened the car door for them, held their little hands as they walked through the park, complimented them on how pretty they looked, and so on. Dad was showing them the practical acts of courtesy and kindness that they should expect from a man. These daddy-daughter dates became life lessons that they would carry with them as they one day made the important decision regarding whom to spend their lives with. As the girls grew, these dates became a cherished time, and we have maintained this practice of daddy-daughter dates. Today, they themselves will call to set up the next daddy-daughter date.

Husbands, if you are a daddy, showing commitment to your role as a father is one of the things that means the most to your wife. Honor that responsibility by being the father God has called you to be. It's a sacred calling and one that deserves a place of priority in your schedule.

CONCLUSION

This chapter has addressed the needs of women. In doing so, it was really speaking to the men. So let's talk to the ladies for a bit. Ladies, instead of asking what we need from our husbands, perhaps we should ask what we can give our husbands. For it is in mutually meeting each other's needs that we discover that our own needs are being met in return.

As you have read and discussed this chapter, the purpose has not been to point an accusing finger at the other but to take a hard look at ourselves in the mirror. It is easy to accuse our spouses of not meeting our needs and to put the blame on them. Marriage, however, is about mutual love. We appreciate the counsel in Romans 12:10, "Outdo one another in showing honor" (ESV). What would happen if we put our spouses before ourselves and tried to "outdo one another"?

FOR DISCUSSION

What is the next step? The preceding two chapters have provided you with a list of the ten most important emotional needs of men and women in general. Now we must put our knowledge into practice. Here are all ten of the needs, summarized in one list:

1. Respect
2. Sex
3. Self-care
4. Playtime
5. A peaceful home

6. Love
7. Communication
8. Trust
9. Financial security
10. Commitment to family

As a couple, complete the following four steps:

1. Individually, look at the list of all ten needs. Then make a list of your five most important needs.
2. Feel free to go back and read any section again if you need to be reminded about the specifics.
3. Once you have each made your list, share your list of five with your spouse.
4. Discuss how you can each make changes to meet the needs that your spouse listed.

Remember, the goal is not to throw your list in front of your spouse and demand they meet your needs. Rather, the goal is for you to learn what your spouse's most important emotional needs are and aim to meet them. Perhaps we could paraphrase the words of the apostle Paul here: "Don't act out of selfish ambition or be conceited. Instead, humbly think of your spouse as being better than yourself. Don't be concerned only about your own interests, but also be concerned about the interests of your spouse" (Philippians 2:3, 4).

---

1. Berry Gordy Jr., "Do You Love Me?" Lyrics.com, https://www.lyrics.com/lyric/875918/Zero+Mostel.

2. Les Parrott and Leslie Parrott, *Meditations on Proverbs for Couples* (Grand Rapids, MI: Zondervan, 2018), 48.

3. Nikelle Murphy, "Science Explains Why Women Talk More Than Men," Showbiz Cheat Sheet, September 20, 2015, https://www.cheatsheet.com/health-fitness/science-explains-why-women-talk-more-than-men.html/.

4. Fiona Macrae, "Sorry to Interrupt, Dear, but Women Really Do Talk More Than Men (13,000 Words a Day More to Be Precise)," *Daily Mail*, February 20, 2013, https://www.dailymail.co.uk/sciencetech/article-2281891/Women-really-talk-men-13-000-words-day-precise.html.

5. "Stats," The Truth About Love and Porn, accessed August 20, 2020, https://www.newfreedomtolove.org/.

6. Sam Dogen (Financial Samurai), "If You Love Your Spouse, You'd Make Them Financially Independent," *Financial Samurai* (blog), accessed August 20, 2020, https://www.financialsamurai.com/if-you-love-your-spouse-youd-make-them-financially-independent/.

7. Sadie Dingfelder, "Must Babies Always Breed Marital Discontent?" *Monitory on Psychology* 42, no. 9 (October 2011), https://www.apa.org/monitor/2011/10/babies#:~:text=After%20having%20a%20baby%2C%2067,14%2C%20No.

Chapter Six

Can You Hear Me Now?

My dear brothers and sisters, take note of this: Everyone should be
quick to listen, slow to speak and slow to become angry.
—James 1:19, NIV

What is the most important skill to bring into your marriage? Of course, there are many elements we bring into our relationship, but perhaps none is more important than good communication. And, when it comes to that, it is definitely more important to listen than to speak.

Communication has many parts, but we usually give undue attention to what we will say—rather than shutting up and listening. Feeling like you have been heard is priceless and will go a long way in managing conflict, even when you don't agree. One of the cartoons we show during our couples' retreat shows a couple speaking. With cell phone in hand, the wife tells her husband, "This app automatically translates what you say into what you mean!"

While we quoted American journalist Mignon McLaughlin in an earlier chapter, her words bear repeating: "We hear only half of what is said to us, understand only half of that, believe only half of that, and remember only half of that."[1] Communication becomes even more challenging as we understand the differences between the genders' communication styles.

In a *Blondie* comic strip, Blondie asks, "Dear, when did you really learn to understand what a woman means when she says something?" The center panel shows Dagwood with a deer-in-the-headlights look on his face and in total silence. On the final panel, Blondie turns to him and asks, "Dear?" Totally confused, Dagwood asks, "Well, what do you mean?" Why is it so hard to communicate? It should be a normal, natural thing to do for all of us humans; yet even though we have the ability to speak, we fall short when it comes to communicating.

BASIC CONCEPTS

Let's begin our conversation about communication by gaining an understanding of the basic concepts surrounding it. First of all, there are four basic avenues through which we communicate with others:

1. *Verbal communication.* The first, verbal communication, is absolutely necessary for healthy relationships. You must make a commitment to communicate verbally, even if it is sometimes uncomfortable or painful. Good communication makes everyone feel valued and may keep resentment and anger from building up and erupting later. People who don't talk don't know one another and won't have a way to understand one another or heal damaged relationships. When communicating, you must understand the power of words and choose your words wisely because they can either hurt or heal. In fact, the Bible states in Proverbs 18:21, "The tongue has the power of life and death, and those who love it will eat its fruit" (NIV). Successful verbal communication begins by using words that are bathed in love. Good words are honest but also caring, calming, not volatile; they are appropriate words, not harsh or demeaning. The old saying "Sticks and stones may break my bones, but words will never hurt me" is simply not true. According to Ephesians 4:29, only a certain type of communication should occur within the family: "Do not let any unwholesome talk come out of your mouths, but only what is helpful for building others up according to their needs, that it may benefit those who listen" (NIV).

2. *Nonverbal communication.* The second form of communication is nonverbal body language. We give each other nonverbal cues all the time. These may include posture, gestures, eye movement, or facial expressions. Even so, we can pick up only certain clues from a person's behavior. It's impossible to know what another is thinking simply by looking at them. For example, someone may be a deeply caring person who comes to tears easily. The tears may be misread by people who think they are troubled or hurt when the tears are really the result of great joy or compassion. We will know for sure only if the person chooses to tell us why they are crying. Nonverbal communication gives us clues, but we should never rely on it alone to determine another person's motives, feelings, or thoughts.

3. *Written communication.* The third form of communication is the act of writing, typing, or printing symbols, letters, and numbers to convey information or a message. This is helpful because it provides a record of information for reference. Early in the history of humanity, much communication was verbal. People told other people stories and passed on traditions, and these were passed from generation to generation. But at some point, oral communication and the passing on of

traditions changed to written communication and became a permanent record that we can still see and read today, hundreds or thousands of years later. Writing is commonly used to share information through books, pamphlets, blogs, letters, memos, and so on. Emails and chats are a common form of written communication in the workplace. Unfortunately, the written word also has flaws and does not always convey the feelings of the person writing. Emails and text messages can often be misunderstood by the receiver because they don't always express the emotional content or intent of the sender.

4. *Visual communication.* Visual communication is done through photographs, art, drawings, sketches, charts, and graphs to convey information or a message. We often use visuals to help during a presentation so we can provide helpful context along with whatever written and verbal information we provide. Because we all have different learning styles (visual, auditory, kinesthetic, and so on), visual communication may be more helpful for some while verbal messages may be more helpful to others.

The bottom line is that everything we do is communication. Psychotherapist, sociologist, philosopher, and author Paul Watzlawick said it in a different way: "One cannot not communicate."[2] What he was saying is that communication happens all the time, even when you don't say anything at all. Just try a simple experiment. The next time you're talking with your spouse or a friend, just stop talking midthought. You will see that it is harder than you expect to keep the silence up for more than five or ten seconds, but it will also be awkward for the person with whom you were talking. The other person will probably be very confused and concerned—or maybe even angry. Your silence communicated something. What your silence communicated is up to speculation, as perhaps it was a lack of interest, ignorance, or something completely different.

You probably have experienced something similar to this scenario: Someone walks into the office, and you already know that they are in a bad mood before you have even spoken with them. Their demeanor and facial expression communicated the message to you. They communicated without saying one word. We always communicate, even when we don't say anything. The challenge is that our nonverbals do not always communicate the reality of our thoughts and feelings.

MAIN INGREDIENTS OF HEALTHY VERBAL COMMUNICATION
Let's focus on verbal communication for a moment. Healthy verbal communication has two ingredients: (1) assertiveness and (2) active listening. Let's look at each.

1. Assertiveness

"Assertiveness is the ability to express your feelings and ask for what you want in the relationship," notes the *PREPARE/ENRICH Couple's Workbook*.[3] Being assertive does not mean that you are selfish or aggressive. If you ask people to describe someone who is assertive, they may tell you that an assertive person is forceful, overbearing, aggressive, and strong and that they speak their mind. But these descriptive words for an aggressive individual don't necessarily describe an assertive one. Assertiveness means that you would like to see more clear, open, nondefensive, and nonoffensive communication in your relationship. "Assertiveness is a valuable communication skill," the *PREPARE/ENRICH Couple's Workbook* states. "In successful couples, both individuals tend to be quite assertive. Rather than assuming their partner can read their minds, they share how they feel and ask clearly and directly for what they want."[4]

Zoe Reyes describes the characteristics of an assertive person:

- *They have confidence in themselves.* Reyes notes that assertive individuals know what their boundaries are and what they like and what they don't like.
- *They respect the opinions of others.* Reyes writes, "Assertive people feel confident about their opinions and beliefs, but don't feel it's necessary to insult or degrade another person's opinions."
- *Assertive people have the ability to validate others' feelings.* Reyes observes that "people often want to feel they are understood." An assertive person does not have to agree with the other person's feelings, but they can be aware of them, show respect, and not minimize or disregard the other person's feelings. An assertive person would not tell the other person, "You're being silly," or, "You're being stupid for feeling that way." Each person's feelings are important for them and should be respected.
- *Assertive individuals are good listeners.* Respectful listening includes "good eye contact, not interrupting when the other person is talking, and reflecting back what was just said to confirm the information was heard correctly," says Reyes.
- *Assertive people are good at problem solving and compromise.* Reyes says that compromise shows that the other person's needs have been heard and this is the attempt at providing a solution that all can be content with."[5]

Perhaps one of the best ways to be assertive is to use *I* statements and to avoid using *you* statements. Most of the time, particularly when we are angry or frustrated, we tend to point an accusing finger (both literally and figuratively) toward the other person. We also tend to make generalized statements or global accusations like "You always . . ." or "You never . . ." For instance, your spouse is late coming home or is late for an appointment you had with them, and out of frustration you may say something like, "You're always late," or, "You make me so mad." As we saw in a previous chapter, pointing that accusing finger tends to make the other person get defensive and point the finger back in your direction. Instead of starting with *you*, begin by talking about yourself and your feelings. For instance, you may say something like, "When you didn't call to tell me you'd be late, I was worried that you might have been hurt." These *I* statements simply express your feelings without placing blame or accusing the other person. By talking about yourself and your feelings, you don't point the finger at your spouse. And your feelings are *your* feelings. Your spouse can't argue with your feelings. Hopefully, they will listen to you express your feelings, validate them, and be able to talk calmly about what happened and what can be done in the future.

When you are assertive, you make a constructive request, and you are positive and respectful in your communication. You also use polite phrases such as *please* and *thank you*.[6] Here are some examples of assertive statements:

- " 'I'm feeling out of balance. While I love spending time with you, I also want to spend time with my friends. I would like us to find some time to talk about this.' "
- " 'I want to take a ski vacation next winter, but I know you like to go to the beach. I'm feeling confused about what choice we should make.' "[7]

2. Active listening

The second ingredient of healthy communication is active listening, which "is the ability to let your partner know you understand them by restating their message."[8] Simply responding with one-word phrases or nodding does not tell your spouse whether you understood or were even listening. In order to practice active listening, it is important that you listen attentively without interruption and then restate what you heard.[9] You don't simply repeat words like a parrot. Instead, acknowledge both the content and the feelings of the other person. When you restate what you heard the other person say, you let them know whether you clearly understood the message they sent. Here are a couple of examples of active listening, based on the assertive statements we considered earlier:

- " 'I heard you say you are feeling "out of balance," and enjoy the time we spend together but that you also need more time to be with your friends. You want to plan a time to talk about this.' "

- " 'If I understand what you said, you are concerned because you would prefer to go skiing next winter. But you think I would rather go to the beach. Is that correct?' "[10]

As we stated before, active listening is more than simply repeating back what the other person said, like a parrot or a voice recorder. Active listening means focusing on the other person completely. Remember, you listen with your ears, but the rest of your body sends the message that you are actively listening. You will give lots of nonverbal cues that you are indeed paying attention. Here are some of those cues, according to an article on the website SkillsYouNeed:

- *Smiling.* This is not a wide grin or an openmouthed smile like you might use after hearing a joke but a small smile, which can show your spouse that you're "paying attention to what is being said," notes the website. A modest smile can also show them you agree or are happy about the message being received. If you combine that small smile with a nod of the head, you are sending a powerful affirmation that you are hearing and understanding what they are trying to tell you.
- *Mirroring.* When you reflect or mirror facial expressions used by your spouse as they talk to you, it "can be a sign of attentive listening. These reflective expressions can help to show sympathy and empathy in more emotional situations." Obviously, these are the natural result of listening attentively, not just a conscious effort to try to mimic facial expressions.
- *Using attentive posture.* When you are listening attentively, you may find that you "lean slightly forward or sideways whilst sitting. Other signs of active listening may include a slight slant of the head or resting the head on one hand."
- *Avoiding distraction.* When listening attentively, "refrain from fidgeting, looking at a clock or watch, doodling, playing with [your] hair or picking [your] fingernails."[11]

When each of you knows what the other person feels and wants (through the use of assertiveness), and when each knows they have been heard and understood (through the use of active listening), intimacy is deepened. These two communication skills, when used together, can help you grow closer as a couple.

"ARE YOU LISTENING TO ME?"

Listening is not as easy as it sounds, because we're often distracted by other things or even by our very thoughts. Often, instead of listening attentively to what our spouse or somebody else is telling us, we are already thinking of what we're going to say next. Here are some ways you can show that you are truly listening.

1. Listen with your eyes

"Listening is something that happens as much with your eyes as with your ears," says an article on *Law Technology Today*.[12] While the article is focused on the lawyer-client relationship, the same principles apply in a marital relationship. You convey you are being attentive to your spouse by listening with both your eyes and your ears. When your spouse is talking to you, "be sure to look at him or her clearly and directly, eye to eye. Eye contact is the single, most powerful way to communicate care and interest."[13] Do not allow your eyes to wander to the dishes on the counter, the television set, your cell phone, your computer, your iPad, or anything or anyone else. When you focus your gaze on your spouse, you reinforce how important they are.

There was a commercial on television some time ago; we can't remember what the product was, but it portrayed a man sitting at the kitchen table reading the newspaper. His wife came through the kitchen door behind her husband and asked him, "Do I look fat in this dress?" Without taking his eyes off the newspaper, listening to her question, or bothering to look at her, he responded, "Absolutely!" Often, we respond without really listening first.

Is it really important that we look at someone when they are talking to us? Try this experiment described by *Law Technology Today* with your spouse just so you can demonstrate to yourself how important eye contact really is. Ask your mate to have a conversation with you. As both of you talk, ask your spouse to take three different postures at different times:

1. Facing you, looking directly at you.

2. With his or her back to you.

3. With his or her side to you, not looking at you.[14]

Make a mental note of your emotional reaction to each of the three body positions. The article describes some possible reactions:

> When your friend faces you, you may find that you are encouraged to speak and that you feel that what you say matters to your friend. When your friend turns sideways, you may experience frustration and find it difficult to continue the conversation. When your friend faces directly away from you, you are likely to feel ignored and will not want to continue the conversation.
>
> Your friend is perfectly capable of carrying on the conversation politely, respectfully, and attentively without ever looking at you. When your friend takes his or her eyes off you, however, the conversation is ruined for you. Regardless of the fact that your friend can hear you and respond appropriately, you don't feel that your friend is really listening.[15]

You can try it the other way with your spouse as the speaker and you as the listener. "After doing this exercise yourself," notes the article, "imagine how it feels to your [spouse] to be listened to without the benefit of your eye contact. Remember to always give your [spouse] the respectful consideration they deserve by supplementing your good listening skills with eye contact."[16]

2. Listen with your mind

Instead of constantly repeating phrases such as "Very good," "Yes," "For sure," or the like, it may be better to elaborate and explain why you agree with a certain point, and later you can ask questions for clarification. We say to ask questions later because you must first allow your spouse to tell their story and express their feelings. To help you listen with your mind, try to use the following techniques, as described in an article on the website SkillsYouNeed:

- *Remembering.* Trying to remember some of "the details, ideas and concepts" proves that you are paying attention, and it will likely encourage your spouse to continue talking.
- *Questioning.* You "can demonstrate that [you] have been paying attention by asking relevant questions and/or making statements that build or help to clarify what [your spouse] has said." Relevant questions also "reinforce that [you] have an interest in what [your spouse] has been saying."
- *Reflection.* "Reflecting is closely repeating or paraphrasing what the speaker has said in order to show comprehension. Reflection is a powerful skill that can reinforce the message [your spouse is trying to share]," and it demonstrates that you are not simply hearing the sound of their voice but are truly trying to understand their message and their feelings.
- *Clarification.* Sometimes it is important that you ask questions, not to get more information but to make sure you understand the message. It assures your spouse that the correct message has been received. "Clarification usually involves asking open questions which enable [your spouse] to expand on certain points as necessary." You could ask them something like, "I'm not sure I'm clear on what you meant by that. Could you please elaborate a little bit more?" Or you may say, "Can you tell me a little bit more about . . . ?"
- *Summarization.* Stating a summary of what your spouse has said "involves taking the main points of the received message and reiterating them in a logical and clear way, giving [your spouse] the chance to correct if necessary."[17]

TWO EARS, ONE MOUTH

Did you ever pause to consider the fact that God gave you two ears and one mouth? Is there a lesson in that for us? Some philosophers have surmised that it was because God wanted us to listen twice as much as we talk. Yet we tend to do the opposite. We talk more then we listen. According to James 1:19, "Everyone should be quick to listen, slow to speak and slow to become angry" (NIV).

A wonderful Chinese character, or pictograph, describes the effective listener. The symbol is a composite of four individual word characters: *ears* (we listen with our ears); *eyes* (we listen with our eyes); *heart* (we must listen with empathy);

and *king* (we listen and then have the power of a king to act on what we have heard with effectiveness). Individually, each symbol carries its own definition and use; but when placed together, the symbols become the single Chinese word meaning *listen*.

EAR

YOU

EYES

UNDIVIDED ATTENTION

HEART

Successful communicators have learned that we cannot really hear someone without listening to them. Effective listening is unselfish. It focuses on what our spouse feels and needs rather than on our needs. The goal is to understand what our spouse is saying and why they are saying it. Look for the meaning behind the words, and, if you are finding that difficult to do, ask for clarification.

MEN VERSUS WOMEN

Perhaps one of the biggest communication challenges comes from the fact that men and women communicate differently. As we stated in a previous chapter, women connect at the emotional level through communication, whereas men use communication as a gathering of facts and information. Because men are content with the basic facts, we don't feel a need to know all of the details. But when we share only the basic facts with our wives, we must understand that it is usually insufficient. Part of the problem, though, is that we can only tell our wives as much as we know, and no matter how many questions our wives may ask, we can't tell them any more than what we know. Here is an actual conversation that took place in our home:

CLAUDIO: Hey, I just got a text message that Mark was in a car accident.

PAMELA: Oh no, was Kathy [his wife] with him?

CLAUDIO: I don't know. All the text message says is that Mark was in a car accident.

PAMELA: Were the kids in the car too?

CLAUDIO: I don't know. All the text message says is that Mark was in a car accident.

PAMELA: How badly is he hurt?

CLAUDIO: I don't know. All the text message says is that Mark was in a car accident.

PAMELA: What hospital is he in?

CLAUDIO: I don't know. All the text message says is that Mark was in a car accident.

At that point, Pam grabbed her own phone and contacted the sender of the text message to find out the answer to all those questions. I (Claudio) figured I'd get some or all of that information at some point in time. I simply wanted to tell her what I knew at that moment. Pam, on the other hand, wanted to know everything possible, right then and there.

When the tables are turned, and I (Claudio) ask for some information, all I want is the bottom line, and Pam wants to give me the whole spiel. I left one morning and reminded her that the plumber was coming to check the leaky pipe under the sink. (While I am not totally mechanically disinclined, there are many things I prefer to leave to the pros.) When I got back that afternoon, I asked Pam, "Did the plumber come?"

"Yes," she told me.

"Well, what did he say?" I asked.

She proceeded to tell me, "He rang the doorbell, and when I answered the door, he said, 'Hello, Mrs. Consuegra. I'm Mike, the plumber. How are you?' I said, 'Well, I'm fine, thank you. And how are you?' 'Oh, I'm all right, I suppose, although it is blazing hot out here. Man, oh man! It's hotter than a blister bug in a pepper patch. It's so hot you could fry an egg on the hood of that car.' 'Really?' I asked him. 'Is it hotter than Georgia asphalt?' Oh, he laughed and said, 'Ma'am, it's so hot the ice cream truck melted.' "

She was telling me every detail, every word both of them said, and I was still waiting patiently for the answer to my question. After what seemed like three hours, which was probably longer than it took him to fix the pipe, she said to me, "And he said it was $350."

That's it—that's what I had asked! Why did it take her so long to tell me that? All I wanted was the bottom line, as I couldn't care less about all the other details of the plumber's visit to the house.

On the other hand, when your wife is telling you about a problem she's dealing with, she's not asking for your advice (unless she clearly says so). Because men are fixers, you may want to fix whatever is bothering your wife, but that's not what she is asking from you. She's asking you to listen, to understand, to commiserate, and to sympathize with her predicament.

I remember the day my wife came home from school to tell me that one of her students had been acting out, and she had had to call his parents in, and they had blamed her for the incident. Well, I responded like most men—by giving her suggestions as to how she could have handled it. She stopped talking to me and said, "You just don't understand."

But I learned, and the next time something similar happened, I stopped what I was doing and listened carefully to what she was telling me. Every so often, I would reflect, "Oh my, that had to be upsetting!" She'd say, "You bet it was," and then she would tell me a little more. Then I would ask, "You mean to tell me she said that?" And she would say, "Can you believe it?" Then she'd tell me a little more. After a while, she had calmed down and was smiling more, and then she said, "Thank you for being so understanding." She wasn't asking for my advice. She was asking me for emotional support through active, attentive listening. Give that a try next time, and you may be surprised at the results.

WAYS *NOT* TO LISTEN

Often, instead of listening, we act and speak out of turn. We play a role that is good in the appropriate settings but not if we're trying to maintain good, healthy communication with our spouse. Here are three roles *not* to play when communicating:

1. *Don't play the judge.* The judge is the person who believes they are always right. Their mind is already made up, so they see no benefit in listening to others. This person is usually negative and critical. They voice their opinion instead of listening. Psalm 115:6 refers to this type of person: "They have ears, but they can't hear" (CEB). As you are speaking, the judge is ready to lower their gavel and hand down the sentence before you are even finished.

2. *Don't play the counselor.* The counselor listens only long enough to make a quick assessment and move on. This person is preoccupied with evaluating and offering advice that is usually not requested. They only listen long enough to dictate to you what should be done. Proverbs 18:13 refers to this person: "To answer before listening—that is folly and shame" (NIV). If your spouse wants your counsel, he or she will ask for it. Making statements such as "You should have . . ." or "You could have . . ." is not truly listening to their feelings.

3. *Don't play the inquisitor.* This person believes the way to listen is to constantly shoot questions at the other person, something which can be tiresome and counterproductive. The inquisitor is prone to interrupt and is easily distracted. Asking questions in order to clarify understanding is important, but the inquisitor overdoes this tactic. The

questions are so many that you cannot even relay the story or your feelings. The tiny details in the story become more important to the inquisitor than listening to you.

Many women are guilty of the third tactic because it is their attempt to get all of the details. Pamela admits that she has a tendency to be the inquisitor type. Often, when I'm trying to tell her something, she will interrupt me multiple times to ask for more details or for clarification. I remember the day I came home from the hospital after visiting one of my elders and his wife, who had just had a baby. I walked through the door of our house, went to the living room where my wife was reading, and told her, "I just came from the hospital from visiting so-and-so. They had a baby." Immediately the interrogation began: How long was the baby? How much did the baby weigh? Was it a boy or a girl? Who did the baby look like? What were they going to name the baby? How long was she in labor? When would she get to go home? Were there any complications? What color hair did the baby have? What color eyes did the baby have? And on and on and on went the interrogation. I have to confess that I didn't have an answer to most of her questions. But I had a very valid reason for that. You see, when I was a theology student preparing for the pastoral ministry, our teacher taught us that hospital visits should be very brief. No one goes to the hospital to get rest, and no one gets rest while at the hospital. The doctors come in, talk to you, ask you questions, and poke you here and there. The nurses come in to take your temperature, your blood pressure, check on any bandages you may have, and straighten out the bed a little. The cleaning person comes in and goes out. The person that brings you your meal comes in and later comes back to remove the tray. There is the phlebotomist, the respiratory therapist, the orderly, the physical therapist, the speech-language pathologist, and on and on. Sometimes the door to your room feels like a revolving door. Family and friends come to see you, and then in comes the pastor. Now, most people are happy to see the pastor—but they are tired too. So, my teacher told us, make your pastoral visits brief, ask a couple of questions to check on their well-being, have prayer, and then tell them when they're home, you will visit them when they are more rested.

So when I went to the hospital to visit the elder and his wife and their new-born baby, it was late at night, and I was aware of what my teacher had told me. I walked into the room, and the elder's wife was very apologetic: "Oh, pastor, hello. I'm sorry my hair looks awful [as she was trying to straighten it a bit]. Please come in [as she fixed her gown and the sheets on her bed]." And then they brought the baby in, and the baby was crying, and the nurses told the mother she needed to start nursing the baby. So I just had a quick prayer, told them my wife and I would visit them at home, and then left them to enjoy their newborn baby. That's why I didn't have all the answers to those questions my wife asked. I didn't stop to look at the baby's hair color, I didn't open the baby's eyes to see what color they were, and I didn't check to see who the baby looked like.

But I am a good and fast learner, so the next time I went to the hospital to check on a newborn baby and his parents, I came home and told my wife, "I just came from the hospital from visiting so-and-so. They just had a baby. Here's the phone number for her room. Why don't you give her a call?" Because I know that if I ask a thousand questions, Pam will ask five hundred more for which I have no answers.

Often what happens, though, is that men don't like the interrogation process and will clam up. This, in turn, frustrates their wives to no end, so they either continue to question their husbands, which drives the couple further apart, or they will begin to wonder why their husbands are not talking to them and will worry that their husbands don't love them anymore.

WAYS TO LISTEN

Instead of judging, counseling, and asking a ton of questions, focus on these objectives:

1. *Listen for the underlying feelings.* By far, the most effective listener is the person who not only listens to the words being said but also tries to understand the feelings of the person who is speaking. Put yourself in their shoes by asking yourself, *What kinds of feelings are being expressed? What feelings are they experiencing?*
2. *Look for nonverbal cues.* The good listener pays close attention to nonverbal cues such as body language and facial expressions.
3. *Listen without judging.* The good listener is not judgmental of what is being said or how it is being expressed. Remember, you are not the judge or the jury in the other person's story.
4. *Understanding is more important than responding.* The good listener's desire is to first understand and then respond accordingly.

THE DANCE OF COMMUNICATION

We love watching pair skating competitions during the Winter Olympics. We enjoy how the skaters move together in such synchrony with the music, gliding across the ice, turning, and jumping as if held by the strings of a professional puppet artist. Good communication is like a well-choreographed dance. We want to share with you a few suggestions to help you choreograph your own dance of good, healthy communication.

The Ungame

Quite a few years ago, we became acquainted with what we consider to be the best board game ever invented. It is called The Ungame.[18] We have no connection with the manufacturer, so this is not a commercial ad to get royalties. It is our recommendation from personal experience. The Ungame was designed to help you learn good communication while simultaneously enjoying time with your family or friends. We like games with simple rules. Some games have so many rules that it takes a long time just to understand them. But The Ungame has only one basic rule: whoever has the turn speaks, and everybody else listens. You can't interrupt the person that has a turn; you must wait for your own turn. When it's your turn, you can share as many of your thoughts, ideas, and feelings as you feel comfortable. All participating players can develop a deeper understanding of others and of themselves.

To play, you roll the dice and move in any direction you wish. Players take turns rolling and moving. When your piece lands on a space, you do what that space says. Usually, you will draw a card or answer the question on the board. There are no winners or losers, and the only objective of the game is to spend time in good communication (players determine the length of time before playing). You practice the skill of listening (when it's not your turn) and of speaking and expressing your feelings (when it is your turn). The game encourages connecting with the other players on a deeper level. Every player who plays the game correctly emerges a winner.

The game comes with several sets of cards. One of them is like an icebreaker and has simple questions about everyday life. For instance, a question may ask something like, "How many lightbulbs are in your house?" If it's your turn, you can count in your mind how many there are and conclude that there are fifteen. Maybe your spouse or one of your children start to say that there are more or fewer but remember, it is not their turn. They will have to wait until it is their turn, and then they can say whatever they wish.

Another set of cards deals with spiritual understanding. For instance, one of the cards may read, "What does baptism mean to you?" The point is not to establish a theological explanation of what baptism is but to express what you believe it is. When it is another's turn, they may choose to use their turn to ask you to clarify or explain further, or they may state what their personal beliefs of baptism are.

There's another set of cards for couples and a set of cards for families. The company also sells sets of cards separately, but we think it's more fun to play with the board and not just by reading the cards alone. We found the board game on Amazon for fewer than twenty-five dollars. Also, check out all the different card sets you can purchase to go along with the board game. We think that spending that much is a great investment with fantastic returns for you and your spouse, your family, and your friends.

Good communication begins with U

We have stated before that good communication has two components— assertiveness and active listening. We have also stated several times that it is better to begin a conversation by using *I* statements rather than *you* statements. We have found that some people have a difficult time knowing how to make *I* statements in such a way that they don't sound like *you* statements. One technique we have used and explained to others is what we call the Talking U. We developed this method to help people express themselves in a personal, positive way instead of a negative, accusatory way.

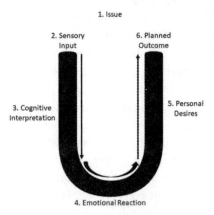

The graphic depicts the Talking U. Let's imagine that you want to tell your spouse about an incident that is causing you to have negative feelings. You could let it fester inside until it poisons your relationship; instead, you want to practice assertive communication. Here are the six steps you can take to work your way around the Talking U:

1. *The issue.* Even if there are many issues that you would like to add to the list, you must resist that urge and stick with the one issue that you are dealing with at the moment. Don't get historical; that is, don't bring up everything you can think of from the past. Don't get sidetracked, don't go on tangents—instead, stick to one topic.
2. *Sensory input.* Begin by stating what you experienced through your senses. For instance, you could say something like, "When I heard you tell me that . . ." or "Yesterday, when I saw . . ." You are simply stating

what you saw or heard or smelled or physically felt or tasted. This is the shallowest level of a conversation. You are just stating a fact, something that your senses perceived.

3. *Cognitive interpretation.* Often, what we experience at the sensory level doesn't just stay there. The brain interprets that sensory input and, without trying, you begin to think about what it means. Think of an unkind action. For example, you came home expecting a warm, home-cooked meal to find that there was nothing to eat because your wife went out shopping and was not yet back. The sensory input is that you see there is no meal ready. You may even go as far as to say that you didn't smell the delicious aroma of a good meal, or you didn't hear her working as the meal was being prepared. You may even identify the sensation you felt (physical hunger) when you walked through the door. That is all part of the sensory input. But then the brain interprets that sensory input in many ways. For instance, you could reason, *Maybe she ran out to get something to fix dinner. She may have gotten caught in traffic. She forgot I told her I would come home early tonight.* Keep in mind that this interpretation may or may not be accurate. However, cognitive interpretation does not have to involve a negative situation. We typically interpret positive actions too. For instance, when your husband brings you flowers, you first see them, perhaps smell them, and maybe even touch the delicate petals (that's the sensory input). Immediately your brain interprets that action. It may interpret it from the aesthetic point of view (*They are beautiful*), as a thoughtful action on his part (*How nice that he thought of me*), or as a generous act (*How generous that he spent money to buy me flowers*). The brain interprets all of the sensory data.

4. *Emotional reaction.* Usually, the actions of another person toward us don't stay at the sensory level or even at the cognitive level; rather, they go on to affect us at the emotional level. They go deep inside us. We may even point to our heart to indicate that something is affecting us emotionally. Let's refer to the examples in the preceding point:

   a. In the first example, when you came home expecting a warm, delicious, home-cooked meal but your wife was not home, your senses told you she was not there, there was no warm meal waiting for you, that you couldn't smell anything good, much less taste it. Your brain interprets that as concern, confusion, questioning, and so on. Your mind reacts emotionally with fear (*I hope nothing has happened to her*), frustration or anger (*I can't believe she would just go out and not care that I'm hungry*), or perhaps disappointment or sadness (*She doesn't love me enough to have a warm meal waiting for me when I get home*).

  b. In the second example, when your husband brings you flowers, you receive the sensory message, and your brain interprets that as beautiful flowers, a kind action, wonderful scents, and so on. But then your heart reacts emotionally with love, gratitude, joy, and similar feelings.

A lot of people express their cognitive interpretation or their emotional reaction by pointing the finger (i.e., using *you* statements). "You don't care about me," "You'd rather enjoy your shopping than take care of your husband." Talking through the U helps you start with an *I* statement, talk about your cognitive interpretation of the event, and then share your emotional reaction. For instance, "When I came home, I saw that you were not here and a warm meal was not ready for me. I thought that perhaps you had gone out to get some missing ingredients or that perhaps something might have happened to you. I was concerned for your safety." You're not pointing an accusing finger, and therefore your wife doesn't have to assume a defensive attitude. Making such a statement may be sufficient, but it would be best to continue on the other side of the Talking U.

5. *Personal desires.* Once you have stated the issue at hand, what you thought, and what you felt, the next step on this communication journey is to ask for what you would like to see done differently in the future. For instance, you may say, "The next time you go out, could you please let me know so I won't worry?" Or perhaps you may make a request like, "If you are going to be delayed, please give me a call to let me know you're on your way."

6. *Planned outcome.* The final step in the Talking U is to make a decision together as to how you both plan to handle the situation next time. For instance, your wife may ask you, "The next time you know you will be coming home earlier, please text me in advance so I can have a meal ready for you." Or you could say, "In the future, please let me know that you're not home, and I can pick something up for dinner."

As you can see, the issue (remember, only one issue) starts at the sensory level, moves to the cognitive level, and then goes deeper to the emotional level; but instead of staying there, it moves back up to the level where you state your desires and, ultimately, goes to the level of planned outcome, where you make calm, rational plans for the future.

The success of the Talking U is dependent on the listener as well. The next technique, I Have the Floor, is a very simple yet useful way to maneuver through the otherwise troubled waters of communication and even conflict management.

I Have the Floor

Scott Stanley, researcher and professor at the University of Denver, and his colleagues, Howard Markman and Susan Blumberg, developed the Speaker Listener Technique, sometimes called, I Have the Floor.[19] You can do it yourself or buy the premade cards they sell. If you make the cards yourself, simply get a small piece of floor tile as a visual reminder of what to do. Whoever has the piece of floor tile is the speaker for the moment, and the other person is the listener.

Following are the rules *both of you* must agree on in order to use the technique effectively:

1. *"The Speaker has the floor."* Whoever has the piece of tile is the Speaker. The Speaker holds the floor while the Listener paraphrases; this ensures each person knows their role during the conversation.
2. *"Share the floor."* The authors write that "you share the floor over the course of a conversation." If you're the Speaker, you can't keep the floor to yourself all the time. The Speaker has the tile to begin the conversation and may say a few things. If you want the Listener to paraphrase what you said, you need to make sure to keep what you say concise. Be sure to give control of the floor over to your spouse periodically.
3. *"No problem solving."* The authors caution readers, "When using this technique, you are going to focus on having good discussions, not on trying to come to solutions." This is an opportunity to practice sharing your thoughts and feelings (if you're the Speaker) and to work on paying careful attention to the Speaker and paraphrasing (if you're the Listener). You must consciously avoid coming to solutions prematurely.[20]

Markman, Stanley, and Blumberg go on to describe rules that *the Speaker* must adhere to:

1. *"Speak for yourself."* Don't mind-read. Don't try to read your spouse's mind. Instead, "talk about *your* thoughts, feelings, and concerns, not your perceptions of the Listener's point of view or motives. Try to use 'I' statements, and talk about your own point of view."
2. *"Don't go on and on."* Because you will both have chances to say what

you need to say, don't try to get it all in at once. The authors note that "it's very important that you keep what you say in manageable pieces" to help the Listener actively listen. "If you are in the habit of giving monologues, remember that having the floor protects you from interruption," the authors go on to say. In other words, it is to your benefit to pause and let your spouse paraphrase to be sure they understood you. A good rule of thumb is to keep your statements to just a sentence or two, particularly when you're both learning the technique. If you speak for a long time, it makes it more difficult for your spouse to understand everything and paraphrase it back to you. When they don't do it to your satisfaction, you will be frustrated that they didn't capture everything to your satisfaction, and they will be frustrated they can't seem to do it right.

3. *"Stop and let the Listener paraphrase."* Once you have made your statement (maybe just a sentence or two), "stop and allow the Listener to paraphrase what you just said. If the paraphrase was not quite accurate, you should politely try and restate what you meant to say." Your goal is to help your spouse hear and understand your point of view.[21]

Finally, Markman, Stanley, and Blumberg list rules that *the Listener* needs to observe:

1. *"Paraphrase what you hear."* To paraphrase, "briefly repeat back what you heard the Speaker say, using your own words if you like." Don't try to provide an interpretation of what you think they said or meant. Instead, show your spouse that you are listening by restating what you heard them say. If your paraphrase is not quite right (which often happens, especially when you first try this technique), your spouse should gently clarify the point being made. "If you truly don't understand a phrase or example," the authors write, "you may ask the Speaker to clarify."

2. *"Don't rebut."* Focus on the Speaker's message. The authors acknowledge that "this may be the hardest part of being a good Listener." Focus on your spouse's message. Do not offer your opinion or thoughts. If what your spouse says upsets you, withhold any response you may want to make so that you can continue to pay attention to what your spouse is saying. Wait until you have the floor to state your response. As the Listener, "your job is to speak only in the service of understanding your partner. Any words or gestures to show your opinion are not allowed, including making faces!" Your main goal is to understand. It does not

mean you have to agree or accept whatever your spouse says. Again, you can express disagreement when it's your turn to have the floor.[22]

Please keep in mind that, according to the authors, "The Speaker is always the one who determines if the Listener's paraphrase was on target. Only the Speaker knows what the intended message is. If the paraphrase was not on target, it is very important that the Speaker gently clarify or restate the point—not respond angrily or critically."[23]

On the other hand, when you are in the Listener role, "be sincere in your effort to show you are listening carefully and respectfully. Even when you disagree with the point your partner is making, your goal is to show respect for—and validation of—his or her perspective. That means waiting for your turn and not making faces or looking angry."[24] The goal is to show respect and honor each other. As Markman, Stanley, and Blumberg put it: "You can disagree completely with your mate about something and still show respect."[25] And the Bible tells us, "Respect everyone, and love the family of believers" (1 Peter 2:17, NLT). So, when practicing communication with your mate, respectfully wait until you have the floor to share your side of the issue.

Here are a couple more points. It is important to stay on the topic you intend to discuss. There are many things you may need or want to talk about, but when it comes to other important issues, it is best to deal with each one separately. Also, learn and practice this technique on some of the less controversial topics first. Don't try to problem solve prematurely. Focus on having a good discussion where you can get the issues on the table.

You may be thinking, *This is technique fake and superficial.* Yes, it sure looks like that, but that's one of the reasons it is so effective. When couples face conflict, it is more natural to get angry and speak in hurtful and harmful ways than it is to listen to understand. Again, Scripture's advice is to "be quick to listen and slow to speak or to get angry" (James 1:19, CEV). In fact, James goes on to say that "if you think you are being religious, but can't control your tongue, you are fooling yourself, and everything you do is useless" (verse 26, CEV).

The I Have the Floor technique will help you keep a tight rein on your tongue. That's why it works so well. When you use it, you are making the choice to limit the defensive responses that come naturally; instead, you are making a loving effort to understand your spouse. Don't fool yourself by thinking it's so simple that it's easy. The simple structure can make it easier; however, successfully mastering the art of communication takes dedication and commitment. And your marriage is worth any effort it takes.

CONCLUSION

Communication is both a science and an art that will always require practice in order for us to get better at it. Don't give up if you find it takes intentional effort. The more you utilize the techniques described in this chapter, the quicker healthy communication will become second nature to you. However, even with the best communicators, conflicts are bound to happen. So stay tuned—we will discuss conflict management in the next chapter.

1. "Mignon McLaughlin," Wikiquote, updated on May 13, 2019, https://en.wikiquote.org/wiki/Mignon_McLaughlin.

2. Harald Sack, "You Cannot Not Communicate—Paul Watzlawick," *SciHi Blog*, July 25, 2018, http://scihi.org/communication-paul-watzlawick/.

3. PREPARE/ENRICH, *PREPARE/ENRICH Couple's Workbook* (Minneapolis, MN: Life Innovations, 2008), 3, http://heldtogether.net/files/files/uploads/2015/08/Customized-Couples-Workbook.pdf.

4. PREPARE/ENRICH, *Couple's Workbook*, 3.

5. Zoe Reyes, "5 Characteristics of an Assertive Person," The Peak Counseling Group, September 7, 2015, https://thepeakcounselinggroup.org/5-characteristics-of-an-assertive-person/.

6. PREPARE/ENRICH, *Couple's Workbook*, 3.

7. PREPARE/ENRICH, 3.

8. PREPARE/ENRICH, 3.

9. PREPARE/ENRICH, 3.

10. PREPARE/ENRICH, 3.

11. "Active Listening," SkillsYouNeed, accessed August 9, 2020, https://www.skillsyouneed.com/ips/active-listening.html.

12. Law Technology Today, "Eye Contact Is a Powerful Listening Tool," *Law Technology Today* (blog), September 9, 2015, https://www.lawtechnologytoday.org/2015/09/eye-contact-is-a-powerful-listening-tool/.

13. Law Technology Today, "Eye Contact."

14. Law Technology Today, "Eye Contact."

15. Law Technology Today, "Eye Contact."

16. Law Technology Today, "Eye Contact."

17. "Active Listening."

18. The Ungame may be available at Amazon.com, https://www.amazon.com/TaliCor-4101221-The-Ungame/dp/B000QX9Y9O/ref=sr_1_1?crid=2V0WI5NG5RI2D&dchild=1&keywords=the+ungame&qid=1588100935&sprefix=the+Ungame%2Caps%2C131&sr=8-1.

19. Howard J. Markman, Scott M. Stanley, and Susan L. Blumberg, *Fighting for Your Marriage* (San Francisco: Josey-Bass, 2010).

20. Markman, Stanley, and Blumberg, *Fighting*, 112, 113.

21. Markman, Stanley, and Blumberg, 113, 114; emphasis in original.

22. Markman, Stanley, and Blumberg, 114.

23. Markman, Stanley, and Blumberg, 115.

24. Markman, Stanley, and Blumberg, 115.

25. Markman, Stanley, and Blumberg, 115.

Chapter Seven

Managing Anger and Conflict

Live in harmony with one another.
—Romans 12:16, NIV

When two ideas, personalities, or actions collide, conflict takes place. Conflict happens to everyone, everywhere at some point; and it's so potent that when we try to avoid it, the conflict only becomes worse. As strange as it may seem, a life void of conflict is not healthy. Just remember this important principle: not all conflict is bad! Conflict is normal, and, sooner or later, you will experience it in one form or another. The greatest challenge will be in how you handle that conflict.

We don't mean to convey that constant arguing, shouting, or physical disputes are a normal or acceptable way of living. On the contrary, such situations are a symptom of deeper problems. Toxic relationships tend to create an unhealthy atmosphere, and we can become so accustomed to it that it seems like a normal way of living. For too many couples, verbal and physical abuse, constant arguing, and screaming seem normal. Often, it is because that's all they know.

Make no mistake; some situations deserve and demand professional help. In cases of abuse, we do not recommend that it be tolerated. It is not acceptable and is no way for a daughter or son of God to be treated. Seek help immediately, and if needed, remove yourself and your children from an abusive situation. You may find more resources on abuse on our website at enditnownorthamerica.org. In this chapter, however, we want to focus on the conflict that happens in couples and families that can generally be managed by understanding and applying a few basic principles.

ANGER'S DESTRUCTIVE FIRE

In a previous chapter, we talked about those two battling forces or sides of our personality that fight for control in our relationship: the side that is unselfish and wants to give and the side that is selfish and wants to take. One side wants to make our spouse happy, even if it makes us unhappy. The other side wants us to be happy, even if it makes our spouse unhappy. It's that battle that produces conflict in a relationship. Often, that conflict becomes outwardly obvious through anger and, if not managed correctly, could lead to the demise of the relationship. So before we talk about managing conflict, we need to understand the role of anger in conflict.

"Anger is one of the basic human emotions, as elemental as happiness, sadness, anxiety, or disgust," notes *Psychology Today*. These emotions are tied to the basic need for survival, says *Psychology Today*: "Anger is related to the 'fight, flight, or freeze' response of the sympathetic nervous system; it prepares humans to fight. But fighting doesn't necessarily mean throwing punches; it might motivate communities to combat injustice by changing laws or enforcing new behavioral norms."[1] In other words, anger can propel us to act in ways that are beneficial.

ROLE OF ANGER IN RELATIONSHIPS

Sometimes we think of anger as a bad thing. But anger is a normal, natural emotion, and it may be very positive and constructive. God designed our body to flee, fight, or freeze in the event of an emergency. You may be interested to know that the Bible tells us twice to "be angry." We need to read these passages to make sure we don't misunderstand them. Here they are:

- "Be angry, and do not sin. Meditate within your heart on your bed, and be still" (Psalm 4:4).
- " 'Be angry, and do not sin': do not let the sun go down on your wrath" (Ephesians 4:26).

Both of these texts tell us to be angry, so anger must not be a bad thing. But both texts also tell us that while it is normal to be angry, we should not let anger lead to sin. You might think that being angry is normal as long as you don't express it. In actuality, repressed anger can be more damaging to you and possibly to your relationship, as we will see later. On the other hand, expressed anger can and should be a normal part of our life. The Bible speaks of several instances of appropriately expressed anger. Here are some examples:

- *Jesus chastising Peter.* "But He turned and said to Peter, 'Get behind Me, Satan! You are an offense to Me, for you are not mindful of the things of God, but the things of men' " (Matthew 16:23).
- *Jesus cursing the fig tree.* "And seeing a fig tree by the road, He came to it and found nothing on it but leaves, and said to it, 'Let no fruit grow on you ever again.' Immediately the fig tree withered away" (Matthew 21:19).
- *Jesus driving the money changers out of the temple.* "And He said to

those who sold doves, 'Take these things away! Do not make My Father's house a house of merchandise' " (John 2:16).

Unfortunately, there are also many examples of uncontrolled anger in the Bible. Following are just two of those instances:

- *Moses striking the rock.* "Then Moses lifted his hand and struck the rock twice with his rod; and water came out abundantly, and the congregation and their animals drank" (Numbers 20:11).
- *Paul's argument with Barnabas.* "Then the contention became so sharp that they parted from one another. And so Barnabas took Mark and sailed to Cyprus" (Acts 15:39; read the entire episode in Acts 15:36–41).

While there may be many reasons a person becomes angry, the root cause can be generalized into three categories: hurt, conditioned response, and instinctive protection. Let's look at each of the reasons.

HURT

A major source of anger is hurt. Whether we have been hurt physically or psychologically (including hurt inflicted verbally), it often makes us angry. When someone hurts us, it usually triggers the need to repay in kind or get even. *Maxine* is a comic strip about a very bitter, angry old woman who says what she thinks, most of the time in a negative way. Often, what she says is funny because it resembles what we sometimes think or what we wish we could say. In one of the *Maxine* comics, she says, "Never go to bed angry . . . stay up and plot your revenge." Often, that is what people do. When they are hurt by their spouse, they would rather be angry all night, thinking of how they will win the argument the next day or how they will retaliate rather than thinking of a way to come to a good resolution.

CONDITIONED RESPONSE

A conditioned response is similar to a bad habit. When we get angry often, we can become addicted to our anger in the same way that we could become addicted to a chemical substance. When you become habituated to anger, it keeps you from acting in your best interest or in the best interest of others. We may have been responding in a like manner for so long (perhaps since childhood) that it's second nature. The reason why anger, as a conditioned response, is so hard to control is that, by the time we're adults, it has become a habit, the product of entrenched conditioned responses.

A conditioned response, or a trigger, occurs with a repeated association of A with B: when A, the trigger, occurs, B results automatically. You most likely have read of Pavlov's famous experiments with dogs. He trained dogs to associate the sound of a bell with food. Whenever he sounded the bell, he would give the dogs food. The dogs learned that when the bell rang, they would get fed, so whenever the bell rang, the dogs would begin to salivate. We may think that conditioning only works with dogs, but it also works with people. The moment your phone rings or vibrates, you reach for it. In the case of anger, when something triggers a threat to you, your habitual response of anger kicks in.

INSTINCTIVE PROTECTION

But anger can also be a very positive, healthy response. God wired it into our system as instinctive protection. It gives us the power and courage to overcome a life-threatening situation. It is anger that gives us the strength to defend ourselves and puts the body into a fight, flight, or freeze mode.

Anger follows a somewhat predictable path or pattern, which we describe as the A of Anger.

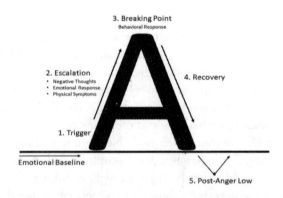

We use this graphic to explain how the anger response usually follows a pattern or cycle. The emotional baseline is what we normally experience in everyday life, when nothing threatens us, when we are calm, cool, and collected.

1. Trigger

"The trigger phase happens when we perceive a threat or loss," says Rebecca Jasper.[2] The trigger phase begins the moment we are attacked, hurt, violated, or invalidated. At that moment, the mind and body prepare to react. Suddenly, "there is a subtle change from an individual's normal/adaptive state into this stressed state."[3] What triggers anger may vary from person to person. For instance, a husband doesn't pick up the clothes from the cleaners as his wife had asked him to do. The wife had sent a dress to be cleaned for a business trip the next day. She had asked her husband to go by the cleaners and pick up the dress, telling him how important that dress was for her trip. For whatever reason, the husband doesn't pick up the clothes from the cleaners, and when he gets home, the wife asks him if he stopped by the cleaners. He simply tells her he forgot. That is the trigger for his wife.

2. Escalation

In this phase, the anger response progressively appears. "Our body prepares for a crisis after perceiving the trigger," explains Jasper. Several dynamics are taking place all at once:

- *Negative thoughts.* As we explained in the previous chapter, when the trigger takes place, we interpret it in a negative way. In the earlier example, the wife may interpret her husband's actions by thinking, *He is very forgetful and careless, and he never does what I ask him to do).* Sometimes these thoughts are irrational and negative.
- *Emotional response.* As much as positive thoughts lead to positive feelings, so negative thoughts lead to negative feelings: "For as he thinks in his heart, so is he" (Proverbs 23:7). If the thoughts are irrational, the feelings will be too. For instance, the wife in the example may think, *He is forgetful; that's because he doesn't love me*, or, *He never listens to me; therefore, I'm not important in his life*, or, *How can he be so careless? He must not care about me!*
- *Physical symptoms.* As those thoughts and feelings begin to brew in your mind, your body automatically responds with several physical symptoms. Your heart begins to race, your breath accelerates, you begin to sweat, your blood pressure goes up, and perhaps you clench your fists or begin to shake.

Once the escalation phase is reached, there is less of a chance of calming down as this is the phase where the body prepares for a fight, flight, or to freeze. This is the moment when the prevention rule works best:

> The start of an argument
> is like a water leak—
> so stop it before
> real trouble breaks out (Proverbs 17:14, CEV).

If you have learned to control your anger in healthy ways, you can derail the escalation before it causes any damage. We'll talk more about this in the next few pages.

If we consider the example of the forgotten dress, at this point, the wife senses her irritation due to shaking, and her blood pressure is rising. She thinks to herself, *Doesn't he know how important this meeting is and that I want to look my best?* She is hurt that he would be so careless.

3. Breaking Point

The escalation phase is progressive, and it is here, in the breaking-point phase, that anger reaches its peak. In this phase, our body is on high alert and fully prepared to react to the trigger. Because the rushing blood has quickly carried fight-or-flight hormones throughout the body, logic and rationality are limited as the anger instinct takes over. In extreme cases, during the breaking point phase, a person may be a danger to themselves or other people.

In this phase, escalation reaches its boiling point, and you express it by fighting, arguing, yelling, criticizing, stomping out, shutting down, or ceasing to speak to your spouse altogether. When anger is externalized through words, you may carelessly say things that hurt your spouse or make them defensive (remember the story of David and Michal). Just a few words, loaded with anger, can cause irreparable damage: "Even so the tongue is a little member and boasts great things. See how great a forest a little fire kindles" (James 3:5).

Continuing with our illustration, when the wife reaches her breaking point, she yells at her husband, telling him he's an idiot who never listens to her. She may be so angry that she tells him that she hates him and that when she returns from her business trip, she wants a divorce. He, in turn, feels attacked and defensive, so he retaliates with a few choice words of his own. He may even tell her to do as she pleases, and he'll be happy to sign the divorce papers. This example may sound a little exaggerated, but believe us, we have heard such things from people seeking our help and guidance. A molehill can quickly become an insurmountable mountain when unmanaged anger is in control.

4. Recovery

The recovery phase happens when the energy created by anger has been spent (or has, at least, subsided), and there is a steady return to a person's normal emotional baseline. In this stage, little by little, the person's reasoning and awareness return. As a few minutes pass, perhaps you both have stopped arguing or gone to different sides of the house. Perhaps you begin to practice some calming techniques, such as deep breathing, prayer, and biblical meditation. Your heart rate slows down, your blood pressure returns to normal, and, in general, you feel more relaxed. If that is the case, you may now begin to think more calmly and rationally about the whole event. The transition from the recovery phase to the post-anger low is delicate, as the anger may be retriggered. It's important to use those techniques to calm down during this phase in order to move on.

5. Post-Anger Low

The post-anger low marks a return to a person's normal, adaptive ways, their emotional baseline. Physically, their vital signs—such as heart rate, blood pressure, and temperature—return to normal so that the body can recover equilibrium. Once that happens, the person gets full use of their faculties, and they are better able to assess what just took place. As a result, during this stage, they may experience embarrassment, guilt, regret, and even a certain amount of depression until they return to their emotional baseline and until a new trigger starts the entire cycle all over again.

When the anger begins to subside for the couple in our example, the wife recognizes that it's not that big of a deal—she has other outfits that would be just as appropriate—and perhaps she was a little too harsh on her husband. She feels bad that she overreacted, yelled at him, and threatened to divorce him. He, too, feels bad that he let his wife down by not picking up the clothes from the cleaners and that instead of apologizing and offering to make things better, he became defensive, raised his voice, and expressed a willingness to proceed with her threat of divorce. They both may feel embarrassed that they acted in such a way, guilty for what they did, and sorry for the words they spoke, and they may wonder how something so small got out of hand so quickly.

MANAGING ANGER

Once we can identify the phases of anger, know what triggers it, and understand why it happens, we can learn how to manage it. No two people manage anger in the same way. In general terms, there are five ways we may choose to react when the trigger happens. The first three options are unhealthy, damaging to us and our relationship, and tend to perpetuate the anger cycle. On the other hand, the last two choices usually interrupt the anger cycle before it reaches the breaking point, leading to effective, healthy management of anger. Following are the five possible ways to handle anger, according to an article appearing on the website of New Hope LI, a Christian counseling center:

1. *"Suppressing anger."* From the time we were small, our parents told us that being angry was not good, even though, we often saw it in them. Sometimes they were angry when they punished us for being angry, which left us in a quandary. Is it good to be angry? Are there times anger is acceptable? So we may have grown up equating anger

with sin or with negative consequences. As a result, we may have learned to suppress anger. Regardless, however, we knew it was there, under the surface, ready to explode at any moment. And it often did at the worst and most unexpected moments. Anger usually festered deep down inside us until one day something triggered it, and before we could control it, it erupted in bitterness toward others, in depression, or in health problems, such as ulcers and heart attacks.

2. *"Open aggression."* Another way we could choose to deal with our anger is through open aggression. When we do this, says New Hope LI, we express our "anger at the expense of someone else." Whether or not we realize it, in effect, we are saying, "I am the one who matters here, and nobody else does. My feelings are important; yours are not. I am looking out for number one, and I don't care who I hurt. The only thing that matters is that I express my anger." Some therapists and counselors recommend open aggression as a healthy expression of self. While they may not encourage physical aggression toward another person (but perhaps hitting a pillow or a punching bag), it may lead to the other unhealthy expressions of aggression toward the spouse. Instead of punching their spouse, a person may yell and humiliate their spouse in order to get their anger out. They may even excuse themselves by saying that they are simply getting things off their chest. While it is normal to want to be heard, anger expressed in this manner is exactly what the Bible tells us we should not do: "Be angry, and do not sin" (Psalm 4:4). This explosive behavior shows emotional immaturity.

3. *"Passive aggression."* As opposed to openly aggressive people, passive-aggressive people operate somewhat quietly and secretly in an attempt "to preserve worth, draw attention to unmet needs, or preserve convictions at the expense of another person." This usually happens, notes the article, because they don't consider themselves "competent to bring their anger out in the open." They're afraid that if they express their anger openly, they may leave themselves open to retaliation—a counterattack—or they may look bad to others. It is not unusual for passive-aggressive people to deny being angry because they believe that if they express it outwardly, it would be sinful or disgraceful. They express it indirectly by being unkind or rude—but with a smile on their face as if to say, "Oops, I didn't mean it." According to New Hope LI, passive aggression "is caused by the need to have control with the least amount of vulnerability." In healthy relationships, no one is trying to keep score about who is right and wrong, but the passive-aggressive

person is out to win without openly competing in the contest. Just as the openly aggressive person is engaged in a battle for superiority, the passive-aggressive one is competing for the same thing—but in a sly and dishonest manner.

4. *"Assertive conflict management."* As we have already discussed, assertiveness does not mean that you are abrasive, harsh, or forceful, nor does it mean that you have to be rude or cause harm. Being assertive simply means that you communicate your views, feelings, needs, likes, dislikes, and convictions firmly and fairly, but with consideration and respect for your spouse's views, feelings, needs, and convictions. You can see assertiveness at work in the husband and wife who are able to talk about their differences without sarcasm, blame, or bringing up old offenses.

5. *"Dropping anger."* When you choose to drop your anger, you are not suppressing or denying it. When you drop your anger, you are very aware that hatred, bitterness, and grudges are options you could take, but instead, you choose the better option of a less complicated, more peaceful life—one without bitterness and resentment. In our previous example, for instance, the wife comes to recognize that her husband's forgetting the dress was a simple mishap and not an intentional act. He did not mean any harm to her, so she can drop the anger after the trigger and before the breaking point, which would be ideal. Or she may drop the anger even after the breaking point and apologize for losing control of her emotions. While it would be best if she dropped the anger before the breaking point, even if she drops it after the breaking point and chooses not to bring it up again, not to be resentful, and to extend forgiveness, the cycle can be broken before the marriage is irreparably damaged.[4]

BREAKING THE ANGER CYCLE

If you recognize that you have anger that you have not been able to control, and it is causing serious harm to your relationship, psychologist Len McMillan offers three suggestions to help you break the cycle of anger in your life:

1. *Make yourself accountable to a trusted friend.* Let that person know you are struggling with anger. Ask them to help you in your struggle.
2. *Live in the present.* Learn to forgive today. Don't worry about forgiving tomorrow. You don't have the ability to decide your emotions for tomorrow or next week. You can only choose your emotional response for today.
3. *Write out your feelings.* Keep a journal or write them in a letter. Read

your writings with the attitude that you will choose to let go of your anger and frustration.[5]

As you begin the process of learning how to manage your anger, it is important you agree to certain basic conditions:

1. *Do not hurt yourself.* Whenever you suppress anger, you are causing injury to yourself, either physically or psychologically.
2. *Do not hurt other people.* Any violent expression of anger can be dangerous. Abuse and crimes of passion are often triggered by anger.
3. *Do not break or hurt things.* In other words, do not use objects as a substitute for your anger. Refrain from kicking the door or punching the wall.

MANAGING THE BATTLE WITH CONFLICT

Do you ever think that home seems more like a battlefield than a place that you look forward to being after a long day? While conflict is normal, unresolved issues or the inability to manage the conflict is something that must be addressed, or it will become a festering wound that could destroy your marriage. The Bible tells us, "A simple meal with love is better than a feast where there is hatred" (Proverbs 15:17, CEV). It reiterates:

> A dry crust of bread eaten
> in peace and quiet
> is better than a feast eaten
> where everyone argues (Proverbs 17:1, CEV).

Instead of fighting *with* our spouse, perhaps we should instead try to fight *for* our marriage! This one word changes it all. Don't fight *with* your spouse. Instead, imagine what could happen if you fought *for* the relationship. Maybe we should be fighting for our marriages and fighting to manage the conflicts that so often divide us.

When it comes to conflict, we have four possible choices as to how it may end. Think about your marriage relationship and ask yourself if one of these options is your preferred choice:

1. *"I win; you lose."* It's always nice when we're the one who wins. In some marriages, one of the spouses not only enjoys this but demands it. They are angry, selfish, and controlling, so their spouse has no choice but to submit and lose.
2. *"You win; I lose."* Some spouses choose this response because they don't

like confrontation and conflict. They fight to maintain peace at all costs, even if that means that they have no choice in any matter.

3. *"We both lose, and no one wins."* While this is not a choice either partner wants, it is often the result of choosing one of the preceding options. We might think we need to win in order to have control and be happy, but in the end, we may lose our spouse, our family, and our happiness. Or we might think keeping our mouth shut and simply going along with everything our spouse wants is the way to go, but the result will be frustration, anger, and depression.

4. *"We both win, and no one loses."* The best option is when we manage conflict in such a way that we both feel like winners. It is not an individual win but a bigger win for our marriage.

All too often, spouses leave a situation, and both parties feel like losers. No one is happy, the situation is not manageable, and anger remains. Your goal should be that you both walk away from a conflict feeling like winners. You may not have gotten everything you wanted, but you now feel like the situation is manageable and something you can live with. Let's get some tools to help everyone win.

CONFLICT MANAGEMENT VERSUS CONFLICT RESOLUTION

Did you happen to notice that in the title of this chapter we used the word *management* instead of *resolution*? What is the difference? *Conflict management* and *conflict resolution* are terms that are often used synonymously. If your goal is to resolve conflict, you may be frustrated that, through the years, you have not been able to solve all of the conflicts in your relationship. Even though you still have a good marriage, you may be frustrated that it is not free from conflict. The idea of managing conflict implies that the conflict exists, but it is controlled in such a way that it is not a major problem. Remember, every couple has conflict, so the goal is not to resolve all conflict, because that will probably never happen; rather, we need to learn to manage it in such a way that it will not affect our relationship negatively.

Marni Feuerman of The Gottman Institute notes the following:

> Dr. John Gottman's research proves that 69% of problems in a relationship are unsolvable. These may be things like personality traits your partner has that rub you the wrong way, or long-standing issues around spending and saving money. [Gottman's] research findings emphasize the idea that couples must learn to manage conflict rather

than try to avoid or attempt to eliminate it.

Trying to solve unsolvable problems is counterproductive, and no couple will ever completely eliminate them.[6]

Did you catch the fact that, according to research, 69 percent of issues are unsolvable? It's no wonder that we often get frustrated when we try to resolve instead of manage our conflict.

CALM, COOL, AND COLLECTED

How important is it to cool down? Well, it is imperative that we calm down before we attempt to have a discussion. Anger prevents healthy communication from occurring, and many decisions are made and many words are spoken in the heat of battle that cannot be reversed.

How long does it take to calm down? As we were researching this question, we came upon an interesting fact. Think about your car for a moment. If it overheats, how long does it take to cool down? According to a car insurance company, "It typically takes at least 30 minutes for a hot engine to cool down."[7] We laughed as we read that about a car because humans definitely have a great deal in common with cars when it comes to cooling down.

According to *Psychology Today*, we need to take ample time to calm ourselves:

> The body takes about 20 minutes to return to normal after a full fight/ flight response. In other words, angry people need time to calm down before they can think clearly again. Angry people will not completely comprehend any explanations, solutions, or problem solving options until their body returns to normal again. Allowing for this refractory period is a critical part of any anger management strategy. The important thing to remember is that you must remain calm in the face of anger. If you remain calm, your cortex will send a signal to your limbic system to dampen the fight/flight response allowing you to develop well thought out survival strategies. When the fight/flight mechanism is fully engaged, it takes about 20 minutes to regain the ability to fully process information again.[8]

So the first strategy for managing conflict is to take the necessary time—at least twenty minutes—to calm down. Again, it takes at least thirty minutes for a car and at least twenty minutes for a human. In either case, the takeaway is that cooling down takes time, and trying to deal with an overheated situation immediately may prove futile.

STEPS TO MANAGING CONFLICT

What are the rules of engagement as you approach this process of managing conflict? First, you need to agree to some rules:

- "Never threaten divorce."
- "Never confront in public."
- "Never nag."
- "Never verbally attack."
- "Never resurrect the past."[9]

At the same time, agree to do the following:

- "Always ask permission to address the conflict."
- "Always invite God to be part of your discussion."
- "Always admit when you're wrong."
- "Always listen."
- "Always keep your arguments out of the bedroom."
- "Always stick to the subject."
- "Always deal with disagreements as soon as possible."
- "Always decide on a plan."[10]

For more than three decades, we have been training pastors and counselors in the use of PREPARE/ENRICH, the premarital preparation and marriage enrichment tool for couples. One of the core exercises in the program is the Ten Steps to guide you on the process of learning how to manage couple conflict.[11] The following paragraphs give a brief description of the Ten Steps.

1. Decide on a place and time

In order to prevent someone from feeling compelled to give an account of themselves on the spot and to avoid an indefinite delay for resolving conflict, setting a time and place for discussion is a must. Feel free to say, "Hey, I need time to process this," or, "I am too frustrated to give a good response at the moment," and then ask for a time to resume the discussion. This lets your spouse know you care about them and that you aren't running away from conflict, even if you aren't currently able to discuss it. You both need to agree on a specific time and place when you can discuss the issue in private and give it the dedicated time it deserves.

2. Define the issue

Define the problem, and don't be vague. What is it that you need to manage?

Notice that it is *one* issue. Do not try to deal with multiple problems. If you do, you will accomplish nothing.

3. Acknowledge that you're each part of the problem

Every issue has two sides, and even when someone is right, they may not express their point in the right way. Take a moment to list the ways you have contributed to the conflict. Your spouse will do the same. Please note that you are not to list the ways your spouse is part of the problem but, rather, what *your own* contribution is. You will see why this step is so important later. You both must own the issue and accept responsibility for the part you played. On one occasion, a wife said to us, "But I didn't say anything." We told her that was her part of the problem. As we wrote before, good listening involves responding by paraphrasing what was heard. To say nothing does not help the situation.

4. Perform a historical analysis

If this is an old conflict, list past attempts that have been made to manage the issue. If something has not worked in the past, it probably won't be successful now. List these efforts in order to avoid repeating the same mistake. A wife once asked her husband, "I support recycling bottles, cans, and paper, but what good does it do to keep recycling old arguments?" Some words often repeated remind us that "insanity is doing the same thing over and over again and expecting a different result."[12] It is indeed insane to continue to do the same thing and yet expect different results. If you have been trying the same solutions to fix the same problems and nothing has changed, it is time to try something different.

5. Brainstorm new solutions

In this step, you pool your brainpower to come up with as many potential new solutions as possible. Don't stop to evaluate each possibility because if you do, it will shut down the brainstorming process. Just list as many potential solutions that you can think of as a couple and write them all down. Don't move on from this step until you are completely out of ideas. Some solutions you come up with may be good and reasonable while others may be absolutely crazy and ridiculous, but the point of this exercise is to continue coming up with as many ideas as possible. Sometimes, in the midst of sharing some impractical and ridiculous solutions, you may actually come up with a great one that you've never considered before. That's the value of brainstorming.

We remember working with a couple facing marital difficulties. As we talked with them, they told us that the main issue they had been dealing with had to do with finances. At this point, we asked them to tell us all the possible solutions that came to mind, and we would write them down. The husband began, "I could get a second job, a part-time job." His wife then said, "I could get an additional part-time job too." We were writing down all of the ideas they were telling us. He then said, "We could sell the house and buy a smaller house." She then said, "We could sell one of the cars and just have one instead of two." He then said, "We could sell the kids." The wife looked at him like he was crazy and was about to say something, but we stopped her and told them to continue. They gave us about fifteen possible solutions until they couldn't come up with any more.

6. Evaluate each solution on your brainstorming list

Now, look at each possibility that you have come up with and weigh the pros and cons. Discuss each, and decide together if a solution has any chance of success. If not, then cross it off the list. On the other hand, if a possibility could offer resolution, then keep it. Continue this until you have gone through each item and are left with a list of possibilities.

As we spoke with our couple, we began to read the items on the list they had brainstormed. The first item was the husband's: "I could get a second job, a part-time job." His wife responded, "I suppose you could, but then we would never see you at home. I don't like that option." So we scratched it off the list. The second item was the wife's: "I could get an additional part-time job too." This time the husband said, "That would create the same issue. We would never see you at home, and we need you at home." So we scratched that off the list too.

We continued with the third item: "We could sell the house and buy a smaller house." The wife responded to that item by saying that while that was a possibility, the family was growing, and going to a smaller house would be very uncomfortable, but they both agreed to leave that on the list as a possibility.

The next item was, "We could sell one of the cars and just have one instead of two." This time the husband responded that while that would be a possibility it would mean that he would have to drive his wife to her job, which was on the south end of the city, then drop the kids off at their school, which was closer to their home on the eastern side of the city, and then drive to his work on the north side, and then do the reverse route in the evening. "And what happens if one of the kids gets sick and we need to take them to the doctor?" asked the wife. So they determined that it was not a good solution. "What about selling the kids?" we asked. The husband quickly responded, with a smile on his face, "Nah, who's going to want to buy those snot-faced rascals?"

The bottom line is that from the list of about fifteen ideas, they narrowed it down to just five, the ones with the greatest possibilities of success in dealing with their financial challenge.

7. Agree on an attempt

The brainstorming list has now been narrowed down to a small list of possibilities. In this step, you will decide on one that you both agree has the most potential to manage the issue.

8. Acknowledge that you're each part of the solution

In step 3, you both agreed that you were each part of the problem. This was an important step because now you will each decide how you can be a part of the solution. After all, if you both own the problem, then you both must be part of the solution. Discuss how each of you will approach the solution. You have identified the problem, you have decided on one potential solution, and now you must be specific about the steps you will each take to contribute to the solution. The more specific each of you is, the better.

9. Check on your progress

This step is simply setting up another meeting after the solution has been tried to check in with each other to see how things are going and to determine whether it has worked or if you need to try another solution. Don't be discouraged if you need to keep trying. It's part of the healthy process. Just go back to the brainstorming step and try another solution if either of you feels the issue has not been managed in a satisfactory way.

10. Reward each other

The successful managing of conflict and saving of a marriage deserves celebration. This step is a way of acknowledging and thanking your spouse for the part they played in moving forward. Plan a date together, or do something meaningful to reinforce the value of going through the process of conflict management together.

This may seem a bit exhaustive, and, certainly, not all conflicts warrant this much attention or the need to go through all of the steps. One of the main benefits to this process is that it forces us to slow down in the heat of the moment so we can think about the issue in a calm and careful way instead of aggressively trying to win—an approach that will inevitably make us both lose.

ADMIT WHEN YOU NEED HELP, AND SEEK IT

We have been talking about anger and conflict management, but there are times and situations where practicing everything we have shared does not seem to change the marriage for the better. In that case, don't wait until it is too late. Seek professional help immediately. Of course, you are not going to seek help unless you first get to the point where you admit that you need it. Too many people have the mistaken belief that seeking help is a sign of weakness. In reality, seeking help when it is needed is not a sign of weakness but a sign of strength! Here are some signs that you may need outside intervention:

1. *You go over the same issues again and again with no resolution or closure.* A constant cycle of repeating the same arguments about the same problem is a clear sign that you need outside help. Every attempt at reasonable conversation fails and ends with shouting, disregard, or someone walking out of the room with no closure or resolution.

2. *Physical and/or emotional abuse are occurring.* We have made it very clear that physical, emotional, or verbal abuse should not be tolerated under any circumstances. Abuse is a clear sign that intervention is needed immediately. The sad reality is that without professional help, the chances that the abuse will end are minimal. Instead, the chances that the abuse will escalate are almost certain, and, in many cases, it ends only with the death of the victim.

3. *You pretend to respect a certain family member.* This is an indication of a serious problem. One dysfunctional family member can rule the rest of the family, usually by fear.

4. *You fear saying certain things.* When there is fear, and you don't feel comfortable sharing your feelings and thoughts without being demeaned, criticized, bullied, or threatened, something is terribly wrong. A professional counselor or mediator can be very helpful in these situations.

5. *You deny, excuse, or ignore serious problems such as drug or alcohol abuse.* Substance abuse is an indication of problems greater than simple emotional distress or fatigue. A key issue is when family members excuse the behavior by saying, "I can stop anytime; I'm not addicted." This is the height of denial and a key indicator that help is needed.

6. *Someone in the family has suicidal thoughts.* You may hear words such as, "You would be better off without me. I should never have been born. It would be best if I died." These kinds of negative thoughts reveal a need for professional help. All of us have things we regret or are sorry about; however, when it becomes a daily obsession, there should be deeper consideration as to its reason and impact.

7. *No one admits there's a problem, yet everyone knows it exists.* Some people think that it is an admission of failure to admit that there's a problem. This avoidance can be fatal to a marriage or family. Everyone else who is looking in sees clearly that there is an issue and may even tell you, but the people who have the problem usually meet those words with denial.

8. *You ignore or excuse signs of bad behavior in a family member.* Such bad

behaviors as bullying, giving orders, pulling rank, verbal abuse, arrogance, and indifference to the feelings of others are signs that should not be overlooked, excused, or allowed to continue. Intervention is called for.[13]

There are two things to keep in mind when seeking outside help:

1. *Find a skilled, godly counselor.* Yes, seek biblically based counseling. This is so important. Make certain the individual or agency that is giving counsel is grounded in the Word of God. I (Claudio) have a counseling psychology degree from a state university. I know and understand the strengths of psychology, but I also know its weaknesses and have concerns about some theories and practices common among secular psychologists. Far too many don't base their practice, counsel, or beliefs on the Word of God and may even expose their clients to dangerous practices. So far as it is possible, seek a counselor that has spiritual beliefs well-grounded in the Bible.

2. *Do not go to family members, friends, or colleagues.* Why? Because all too often, the individuals that make up those groups are biased. Family members may be especially biased, as they usually do not see things as well as someone who can be more objective in looking at all sides of the issue. You need a neutral party. Also, once the issue has been resolved, it may be harder for your family members to forgive your spouse and restore the relationship that has been broken by the knowledge you gave them. Remember the first principle: seek outside biblically based counseling.

CONCLUSION
Managing your anger and your couple conflicts takes dedicated time and effort as well as lots of giving and taking. But in the end, you will discover that you have grown closer through the process. Don't give up easily. Seek outside help if needed. Most important, bathe the process in prayer and ask God to lead as you endeavor to work through the things that may divide you.

---

1. "Anger," *Psychology Today*, accessed August 3, 2020, https://www.psychologytoday.com/us/basics/anger#:~:text=Anger%20is%20one%20of%20the,it%20prepares%20humans%20to%20fight.

2. Rebecca Jasper, "Understanding Anger," Balancing Change Mindfully, November 14, 2016, http://balancingchangemindfully.com/understanding-anger/#:~:text=The%20trigger%20phase%20happens%20when,or%20from%20our%20thought%20processes.

3. Jasper, "Understanding Anger."

4. "How Do You Deal With Your Anger?" New Hope LI, accessed August 11, 2020, http://www.newhopeli.com/how-do-i-deal-with-your-anger/.

5. Len McMillan, *Adventist Family Ministries Training Curriculum*, 4th ed. (Lincoln, NE: AdventSource, 2012).

6. Marni Feuerman, "Managing Vs. Resolving Conflict in Relationships: The Blueprints for Success," The Gottman Institute, November 9, 2017, https://www.gottman.com/blog/managing-vs-resolving-conflict-relationships-blueprints-success/.

7. The Allstate Blog Team, "What to Do When Your Car's Engine Overheats," *The Allstate Blog*, April 16, 2019, https://blog.esurance.com/what-to-do-if-your-car-overheats/.

8. Jack Schafer, "Controlling Angry People," *Psychology Today*, January 5, 2011, https://www.psychologytoday.com/us/blog/let-their-words-do-the-talking/201101/controlling-angry-people.

9. Howard Dayton, "Chapter 2—Two Parts and Three T's," Money and Marriage Small Group Pilot Study, accessed August 12, 2020, https://compassebooks.org/learn_lessons/3937-money-marriage-pilot?client_subdomain=compass&sample=true&section_id=28606.

10. Dayton, "Chapter 2."

11. PREPARE/ENRICH, "Conflict Resolution: Ten Steps for Resolving Conflict," *WORKBOOK for COUPLES*, PREPARE/ENRICH, 28, accessed September 29, 2020, https://www.prepare-enrich.com/prepare_enrich_content/training/section_07.pdf.

12. Betsy Pickle, "Al-Anon Helps Family, Friends to Orderly Lives," *Knoxville News-Sentinel*, October 11, 1981, quoted in Garson O'Toole, "Insanity Is Doing the Same Thing Over and Over Again and Expecting Different Results," Quote Investigator, updated July 31, 2019, https://quoteinvestigator.com/2017/03/23/same/.

13. This list has been adapted from Claudio Consuegra and Pamela Consuegra, "Help for Those Who Need It," *Love for a Lifetime* (blog), November 12, 2012, https://claudiooutlook.wordpress.com/page/64/?app-download=android.

Chapter Eight

It Makes Cents

*"Do not store up for yourselves treasures on earth, where moths
and vermin destroy, and where thieves break in and steal."*
—Matthew 6:19, NIV

What would you say if someone were to ask, "How important is money to you?" In a post on the blog *Sara's Musings*, the author describes the findings of a book entitled *The Day America Told the Truth*. The authors of the book discovered in their research some disturbing trends. Americans were asked, "What would you give up in order to get $10 million?"

- 25 percent said they would abandon their family.
- 25 percent said they would abandon God and the church.
- 16 percent said they would leave their spouse.[1]

Wow! Money is so important to some people that they would actually abandon their families and faith over it. The apostle Paul was correct when he wrote, "For the love of money is the root of all kinds of evil. And some people, craving money, have wandered from the true faith and pierced themselves with many sorrows" (1 Timothy 6:10, NLT). We are used to reading those words but don't always pay attention to the context, so let's look at the entire section to better understand what Paul was talking about:

> Yet true godliness with contentment is itself great wealth. After all, we brought nothing with us when we came into the world, and we can't take anything with us when we leave it. So if we have enough food and clothing, let us be content.
>   But people who long to be rich fall into temptation and are trapped by many foolish and harmful desires that plunge them into ruin and destruction. For the love of money is the root of all kinds of evil. And

some people, craving money, have wandered from the true faith and pierced themselves with many sorrows (1 Timothy 6:6–10, NLT).

Paul is describing people teaching error in Ephesus and how greedy they were. Like many today, their goal was to get numerous possessions and become as wealthy as possible by any means, including teaching false doctrines. That desire to be rich, warned Paul, was driving them to temptations and "foolish and harmful desires" that eventually would destroy them. Now, that's the negative part of that passage, but we want to make sure we don't miss the positive part found in verses 7 and 8.

First, Paul states a very important principle for us today in verse 7: "Godliness with contentment is itself great wealth" (NLT). True wealth is not measured in dollars and cents, but in a reflection of our relationship with our Father in Heaven. That's what godliness is: God-like-ness. True wealth happens as we are daily made into the image of God while being content in whatever circumstances we find ourselves. To explain further:

> Paul here defines the most priceless possession man can own. Men and women have searched the world for peace of mind and an untroubled heart. Billions of dollars are being spent annually as man endeavors to find contentment in amusement, travel, liquor, and the satisfaction of physical passion. Yet, the object of their quest eludes them because man must still live with his conscience and face the question of his eternal destiny. However, the gift of God is not only eternal life; it also brings an untroubled mind, one that has learned to trust a loving God amid all the uncertainties of life.[2]

Second, Paul emphasizes that any riches we may be able to accumulate will have to be left behind because "we brought nothing with us when we came into the world, and we can't take anything with us when we leave it" (verse 7, NLT). As someone stated, "You have never seen a hearse pulling a U-Haul trailer." Even if you are buried with everything you own or your most prized possession, it won't do you any good. Ten years later, someone could unearth your "treasures" only to discover they are corroded, damaged, rusted, and moth-eaten. They would no longer bear any resemblance to the prized treasure that was buried.

We're reminded of the story of a very wealthy man who died. His final will and testament stated his desire to be buried with all his money. After his funeral, friends of the man's widow asked her if she had done as her husband had stipulated in his will. She told them that indeed she had. Flabbergasted, her friends asked, "You really put all his money in the casket with him?" To which she calmly responded, "I did. I wrote a check for the full amount and put it in his jacket pocket." She demonstrated the principle of our passage. You can't take anything with you when you leave this life.

A similar story, with a more spiritual slant, tells of a very wealthy man who was approached by the angel of death who told him he would die that evening. Horrified, the man asked the angel if he could take some of his possessions to heaven with him. The angel told him he could take nothing. The man insisted and asked if he could just take one suitcase. Finally, the angel agreed, and that evening he came to take the man and his suitcase to heaven. When they arrived in heaven, Saint Peter asked him what he had in his suitcase. The man opened it to reveal that it was full of pure gold. Saint Peter then asked him, "Gold? Why did you bring pavement with you?" If in heaven the streets are made of gold, why take any with us? Now, understand that this story is a joke intended to illustrate a spiritual principle: we can't take anything of earthly value to heaven. The founder of Apple, Steve Jobs, said, "Being the richest man in the cemetery doesn't matter to me. Going to bed at night saying we've done something wonderful, that's what matters to me."[3]

Even during the most trying circumstances—in jail, stoned by the people of the city, almost drowned, rejected by his own religious friends—Paul continued to express, "I have learned in whatever state I am, to be content" (Philippians 4:11). Again he wrote, "And having food and clothing, with these we shall be content" (1 Timothy 6:8). And one more time he reiterated, "Be content with such things as you have" (Hebrews 13:5).

There's nothing wrong with wanting to improve your quality of life, but at some point, we need to realize that simply having more is not what will make us happy. One of the richest men on earth, John D. Rockefeller, was supposedly asked, "How much money is enough?" To which he responded, "Just a little bit more." According to Byron Moore, writing for the *Shreveport Times*, "At the peak of his wealth, Rockefeller had a net worth of about 1% of the entire US economy. He owned 90% of all the oil and gas industry of his time. Compared to today's rich guys, Rockefeller makes Bill Gates and Warren Buffett look like paupers. And yet he still wanted 'just a little bit more.' "[4]

That's why Paul writes that it is better to be content no matter how much or how little you have. If you choose to pursue happiness through wealth, chances are you will never be truly satisfied. On the other hand, if you pursue godliness (or God-like-ness), then every day is full of satisfaction. It's true; you really can't love both God and money (Matthew 6:24).

Again, we want to emphasize that there's nothing wrong with the desire to improve your life and earn more money. It is good to have some material goals for yourself and for your family. In fact, if you, husbands, would like to make more money, we want to tell you the secret: kiss your wife every morning when you leave for work. Wait a minute! What does that have to do with wanting to make more money? Well, you see, a psychological study conducted in Germany by Dr. Arthur Szabo "found that men who kissed their wives before going to work in the morning lived an average of five years longer than husbands who didn't kiss."[5] Not only that, but the good-morning kissers had fewer car accidents on the way to work than did the nonkissers. In addition, the kissing husbands used less sick time than their peers, and—get this—they earned 20 to 35 percent more money than those who left without kissing their wives. What was the reason for this? The study's results are quoted in *Psychology Today*:

> Husbands who leave home in the morning without kissing their wives do so either because the couple has had a spat, or because they have grown apart. In either case, the husband begins the day with a negative attitude. He tends to be moody and depressed. He is disinterested in his work and surroundings. While a great many men feign indifference to their wives nearly all of them are deceiving themselves. Even if a man has ceased to love his wife, he is still influenced by her attitude toward him. Our research proves this and conclusively so. A husband who kisses his wife every morning before he goes to the office begins the day with a positive attitude. His feeling of harmony is reflected physiologically as well as mentally.[6]

So do you want to make more money? There's nothing wrong with that—as long as your motivation is not simply to have "just a little bit more." If you want to make more money, what if you start by kissing your wife every morning? You will feel better, will have fewer sick days, will have fewer car accidents on the way to work (hopefully none), and will earn more money. But the best result is not just more money—you will have a positive attitude toward your wife, and your wife will be happier as well. Who could ask for anything more? As Paul stated, "Don't be jealous or proud, but be humble and consider others more important than yourselves. Care about them as much as you care about yourselves" (Philippians 2:3, 4, CEV).

THE NUMBER ONE COMPLAINT IN MARRIAGE

As we wrote in an article on our blog, "A familiar phrase from wedding ceremonies, ' 'Til death us do part,' has tragically become, ' 'Til debt us do part!' "[7] If you find that you and your mate are arguing about money, you are not alone. An article on financial expert Dave Ramsey's website notes, "When you put together couples and money, you're bound to get a few spats."[8] In fact, the article shares that "money is the number one issue married couples fight about. . . . When it comes to marital problems, money fights are the second leading cause of divorce, behind infidelity."[9]

Wow! Based on those startling statistics, it is clear that we need to address this issue before it destroys our homes. Let's look at some of the common mistakes couples make that lead them down the path to marital ruin.

COMMON FINANCIAL MISTAKES

There are common mistakes that couples who find themselves in financial difficulties have made. In the following quotations, you will find some of those mistakes; but more importantly, you will discover ways to work on correcting the mistake:

1. *They keep separate bank accounts.* "Some couples think the best way to avoid money arguments is to keep separate checking accounts. His paycheck goes in one account, hers goes into another, and they each pay bills separately. No harm, no foul, *right?* Wrong. This lays the groundwork for [financial] problems" as time goes on.

   How to work on it: "Marriage is a partnership." Both parties need to be involved in financial decisions. "Separating the money and splitting the bills is a bad idea that only leads to more money and relationship problems down the road. Don't keep separate accounts. Put all of your money together and begin to look at it as a whole."

2. *They disagree about their lifestyle.* "Let's say you're perfectly content shopping at Goodwill when you need to update your [closet], but your spouse loves to buy name-brand items at full price. If you have an income that doesn't support expensive taste, that's going to be a problem."

   How to work on it: Marriage is all about compromise. If one of you is attached to name-brand items, "consider shopping at an outlet mall to snag those brands at affordable prices. . . .

   . . .The bottom line is: Your lifestyle needs to line up with your actual income—not what you wish it was."

3. *They let personality differences come between them.* "Everyone's money mindset is different, and opposites tend to attract. Chances are, one of you loves working with numbers (the nerd)" and managing the finances "and the other one would rather not be tied down by what the numbers show (the free spirit). One of you might be the saver and the other is more inclined to spend."

   While that can cause some marital problems, it isn't the real issue.

"The source of the problem is [that] one of you neglects to hear the other's input." Or one of you bows out from participating in the financial dealings altogether.

How to work on it: "Listen up, financial nerds. Don't keep the money details all to yourself." And stop acting like a know-it-all while "using your 'knowledge' to boss around your free-spirit spouse." And "if you're the more carefree spouse, don't just nod your head and say, 'That looks great, [dear].' You have a vote in the budget meetings! Give feedback, criticism and encouragement."

4. *They let salary differences divide them.* "For most couples, one of them probably makes more money than the other. Rarely will you both be making the exact same salary. But whether the amount comes to $50 or $50,000 more a year, the same problem can arise.

"Instead of seeing the full pot as 'our money,' you might think you have leverage over your spouse. . . . Sometimes the spouse bringing in the most money can feel entitled to the most say. *Don't even go there.* That's just asking for more money and relationship troubles."

How to work on it: "It's not *yours* or *mine*—it's *ours*. There's no reason to hold a higher income over the other's head. *You're on the same team.* Start acting like it."

5. *They commit financial unfaithfulness.* Being unfaithful to your spouse doesn't always involve an affair. Sometimes it's when you're unfaithful to a shared financial goal by opening a side bank account or stashing away cash. That's deceitful. The same applies if you have a credit card your spouse knows nothing about."

How to work on it: "Be open and honest about any side checking or savings accounts or secret credit cards you have. It's time to own up to the truth and clear the air. Then, work toward establishing financial trust again. Recommit to your shared financial goals and remember *why* you're doing it. You're in this together!"

6. *They let their expectations get the best of them.* One of the biggest dividers between couples and money is when they have unmet expectations. "The quickest way to feel unfulfilled and unsatisfied with your spouse is when you expect things to go a certain way, only to find out reality is a *bit* different.

If you've always thought you have to immediately buy a house after getting married, you might feel let down when you celebrate your first anniversary in the apartment you're renting. Don't let your unrealistic expectations pave the way for money and marriage problems" and discord!

How to work on it: "There is no rule stating married couples [must] buy a home, start a family, or go on a trip to Paris during their first year of marriage. If those things aren't feasible for you right now, stop worrying. Get your money in order *now* so that *later* you can make your dreams a reality.

7. *They let the kids run the show.* "Your kids are begging you for the latest video game. You think about how well they've behaved lately and figure, why not? But your spouse is upset because it isn't in the budget. *Hello, impending money argument!* Whether it's buying them toys, giving them an allowance, or just paying for their sports equipment, kids have a way of bringing out the way couples view money differently."

How to work on it: "Talk about it, and make a plan. Decide together how to budget for the things your children need. But what about all of their pesky *wants*? Discuss the possibility of establishing chores and a commission (or allowance) for the work they do. This can help them establish a great work ethic, all while teaching them how important it is to wait for the things you want in life!"[10]

Clearly, "the love of money" is not our focus; rather, we should concentrate on the principles of good stewardship. Perhaps you have heard it said that money can't buy you love. It's true. Money cannot buy us love. However, we can't deny the fact that having good financial health and stability in the home is very important.

God is very interested in the issue of finances as well. In fact, it's so important to Him that in the Bible, there are more than five hundred verses about prayer and about five hundred verses that discuss faith; but there are more than two thousand references to money and possessions! Of the thirty-eight parables in the Bible, sixteen of them—almost half—are about money.

STEWARDSHIP

What is stewardship? According to the dictionary, *stewardship* refers to "the office, duties, and obligations of a steward" or the "the conducting, supervising, or managing of something," including "the careful and responsible management of something entrusted to one's care."[11]

How do you view everything under your care? What do you think about everything you have? Do you think you own the things you have when, in reality, they're all gifts on loan from God? Understanding that we have all we have because God has entrusted it to our care forces us to look at our possessions through different lenses.

You see, nothing *really* belongs to us. All that we have belongs to God. We are the stewards. As we once wrote, "Our house, cars, clothing, children, and jobs were all gifts from a loving Father, and we are simply stewards [or caretakers] of those gifts. A steward knows that his [or her] responsibility is to care for the possessions [in the best interest] of the owner. He never sees them as his own. God gives to us not so we can possess, keep, and hoard [material goods], but so that we can be vessels and pipelines of His blessing to others."[12]

Stewardship, in the truest sense, means that we faithfully take care of all the gifts God has entrusted to us. That means our time, talents, and treasures (i.e., our finances). Solomon wisely counseled:

> Be sensible and store up
>> precious treasures—
>> don't waste them
>> like a fool (Proverbs 21:20, CEV).

As individuals, as couples, and as families, we need to decide and define what stewardship means to us.

COUPLE OR FAMILY STEWARDSHIP EXERCISE

As you think of what stewardship means to you, try the following exercise:

1. Individually, make a list of the things you own, the things that you consider yours.
2. Now, put your list together with those of your family members to compile one family list.
3. Cross off all of the items on the list that truly belong to God.
4. When you have done that, circle what you have left.

If you have done this sincerely and honestly, you know that there's nothing left on the list that really belongs to you. Truthfully, all of our possessions should be seen as gifts from Him (even our television sets, our cars, our cell phones, and so on). Now, if there's nothing that belongs to you because everything belongs to God, what does that tell you? Understanding this concept should give you so much comfort and freedom. Consider two possible responses to this idea: (1) "Because everything belongs to God, if I lose everything, I have not lost anything that's mine"; (2) "Because everything belongs to God, I don't have to worry about any of those things." Also, remember the words of Jesus:

> "That is why I tell you not to worry about everyday life—whether you have enough food and drink, or enough clothes to wear. Isn't life more

than food, and your body more than clothing? Look at the birds. They don't plant or harvest or store food in barns, for your heavenly Father feeds them. And aren't you far more valuable to him than they are? Can all your worries add a single moment to your life?

"And why worry about your clothing? Look at the lilies of the field and how they grow. They don't work or make their clothing, yet Solomon in all his glory was not dressed as beautifully as they are. And if God cares so wonderfully for wildflowers that are here today and thrown into the fire tomorrow, he will certainly care for you. Why do you have so little faith?

"So don't worry about these things, saying, 'What will we eat? What will we drink? What will we wear?' These things dominate the thoughts of unbelievers, but your heavenly Father already knows all your needs. Seek the Kingdom of God above all else, and live righteously, and he will give you everything you need.

"So don't worry about tomorrow, for tomorrow will bring its own worries. Today's trouble is enough for today" (Matthew 6:25–34, NLT).

Jesus tells us not to worry about anything. God takes care of all our needs. He also reminds us, "For I know the plans I have for you, declares the LORD, plans for welfare and not for evil, to give you a future and a hope" (Jeremiah 29:11, ESV). However, God also wants us to work today, save, and plan for the future. Twice, in Proverbs, He uses the ant as an example for us to follow:

- Go to the ant, you sluggard!
  Consider her ways and be wise,
  Which, having no captain,
  Overseer or ruler,
  Provides her supplies in the summer,
  And gathers her food in the harvest" (Proverbs 6:6–8).

- "The ants are a people not strong, yet they prepare their food in the summer" (Proverbs 30:25).

The lesson for us from these two passages is that we need to work to provide for our family today and save to provide for our family in the future. The best way to fulfill these two goals is to develop and maintain a good budget, as we will see next.

BUDGETING

Why is budgeting so important? For one thing, it is a way for you to prioritize financial goals. A household budget is important because it helps you identify the areas where you spend so that you can take necessary steps to curtail unnecessary purchases. Are you still not convinced that budgeting is worth the effort? Well, here are some more reasons why budgeting is crucial to the financial wellness of your family, according to Amy Bell, writing for Investopedia:

1. *"It helps you keep your eye on the prize."* Bell writes, "A budget helps you figure out your long-term goals and work towards them. If you just drift aimlessly through life, tossing your money at every pretty, shiny object that happens to catch your eye, how will you ever save up enough money to buy a car, take that trip to Aruba, or put a down payment on a house?" In addition, Bell notes that a budget helps you "map out your goals, save your money, keep track of your progress, and make your dreams a reality."

2. *"It helps ensure you don't spend money you don't have."* For too many consumers, the idea is, "Let's spend money we don't have; we can use credit cards." But "before the age of plastic," Bell says, "people tended to know if they were living within their means. At the end of the month, if they had enough money left to pay the bills and sock some away in savings, they were on track. These days, people who overuse and abuse credit cards don't always realize they're overspending until they're drowning in debt. However, if you create and stick to a budget, you'll never find yourself in this precarious position. You'll know exactly how much money you earn, how much you can afford to spend each month and how much you need to save."

3. *"It helps lead to a happier retirement."* Bell provides this counsel: "Let's say you spend your money responsibly, follow your budget to a T, and never carry credit card debt. Good for you! But aren't you forgetting something? As important as it is to spend your money wisely today, saving is also critical for your future." A budget can help you do that, she notes. Even if you set aside only a small amount each month to contribute to your retirement fund, you'll eventually see this grow into a tidy sum. "Although you may have to sacrifice a little now," Bell reassures us, "it will be worth it down the road." There are too many people who are unable to retire because they did not plan properly when they were younger.

4. *"It helps you prepare for emergencies."* Bell acknowledges that the unforeseen happens, writing, "Life is filled with unexpected surprises, some better than others. When you get laid off, become sick or injured, . . . or have a death in the family, it can lead to some serious financial turmoil." But how much should we put away for emergencies? Bell writes, "Your budget should include an emergency fund that consists of at least three to six months' worth of living expenses. This extra money will ensure that you don't spiral into the depths of debt after a life crisis. Of course, it will take time to save up three to six months' worth of living expenses. Don't try to dump the majority of your paycheck into your emergency fund right away. Build it into your budget, set realistic goals and start small." Little by little, that emergency fund will grow.

5. *"It helps shed light on bad spending habits."* Bell says that "building a budget forces you to take a close look at your spending habits. You may notice that you're spending money on things you don't really need. Do you honestly watch all 500 channels on your costly extended cable plan? Do you really need 30 pairs of black shoes? Budgeting allows you to rethink your spending habits and refocus your financial goals."

6. *"It's better than counting sheep."* Finally, Bell goes on to tell us that we may even get more rest if we budget properly: "Following a budget will also help you catch more shut-eye. How many nights have you tossed and turned worrying about how you were going to pay the bills? People who lose sleep over financial issues are allowing their money to control them. Take back the control. When you budget your money wisely, you'll never lose sleep over financial issues again."[13]

Budgeting is simply *planning on paper (or in an app) how and when to spend and save your money.* Budgeting allows you to determine in advance what your priorities are and how you will use your financial resources. On the other hand, the lack of a plan can lead to financial ruin, family conflict, and even the breakup of your marriage.

STEPS TO DEVELOP YOUR BUDGET

Of course, it's one thing to agree that it is important to have a budget and another to actually create one. Here are the simple steps you can take to develop an initial budget for your family:

1. Record your income and spending for thirty to sixty days. This step takes the most time, but it's difficult to move on until you know how

much money is coming in and where it is currently going.

2. Complete the first draft of your spending plan. Review what you learned in step 1. Did you find unnecessary spending you can eliminate?

3. Adjust your spending plan to make sure you're not spending more money than you are bringing in.

4. Select your system. It could be a simple spreadsheet (we have included a sample on page 199), an electronic one in Microsoft Excel or a similar program, an online budgeting tool, or one you create yourself.

5. Record and review. As you receive money (income) and spend money (expenditures), record and keep track of everything. Only spend what you have money for in your budget.

We recommend you sit down as a couple to develop your budget together. But we also recommend that you sit down and pay the bills together. There are several reasons for this:

- Neither must carry the burden alone for taking care of the finances.
- When both spouses are fully aware of their finances, they are more conscientious about how they spend money.
- Because of the feeling that whoever controls the money has the power, if you develop the budget together and pay the bills together, neither of you will feel that the other has control over the finances.
- Neither spouse is keeping financial secrets or committing financial infidelity.

If both of you work outside the home, it may be wise to develop a budget using just one income or an amount lower than your combined income. Why? This allows for that extra income to go into savings and creates a nice fund for unexpected emergencies, such as a job furlough, illness, and other unforeseen events. This tactic is not possible in all cases; but if it's possible for you, begin to build up that emergency savings fund that we discussed earlier. Following is a simple budget sheet you may use, or you may make your own. You can be as detailed or as general as you wish. This is only a sample.

Budget Worksheet

Monthly income (gross)		
	Total for spouse 1:	
	Total for spouse 2:	
	Total for couple:	

Monthly expenses		Actual	Budget
Donations	Tithes		
	Offerings		
Housing	Mortgage/rent		
	Municipal services		
Loan/debts	Auto		
	Personal		
	Credit cards		
Auto	Gas		
	Repairs/maintenance		
Insurance	Medical		
	Auto		
	Home/health		
Clothing			
Personal expenses			
Home expenses			
Utilities	Heat		
	Gas		
	Electricity		
	Cable/satellite		
	Internet		
Other expenses	Savings account		
	Cell phone(s)		
	Cleaners/laundry		
	Gifts		
	Entertainment		
	Childcare		
	Other		
His spending money			
Her spending money			
	Total income		
	Total expenses		
	Excess or deficit		

IDENTIFY AND DECIDE ON YOUR FINANCIAL GOALS

Once you have completed your budget and kept at it for a couple of months, have a conversation with your spouse and decide on the following.

Short-term goals (six months to a year):

1. _____
2. _____
3. _____

Long-term goals (one to five years):

1. _____
2. _____
3. _____

Once you have created a budget and are sticking to it, this step helps you establish future goals, both short-term and long-term. You can revise the list of goals periodically, but it is always good to have an initial goal in mind—something to aim for.

STEPS TO FINANCIAL WELLNESS

Some couples find themselves deep in trouble—bill collectors calling them regularly, a very low credit score, their cars or house in urgent need of repairs, and so on. They find themselves in this endless downward spiral and seem unable to find a way out. Here are some steps to put you on the path to financial wellness:

1. *Develop a budget.* As discussed earlier, this is key to being financially healthy. Many couples today do not have a budget. They just go from paycheck to paycheck and dole out the cash with no thought of actual budgeting.
2. *Keep accurate spending records.* The culprit in most family's finance problems is not any big-ticket item. Rather, it is the steady spending on little purchases that no one tracks. Many use their debit card or hit the ATM all weekend long and end up broke on Monday, with no idea where the money went. The absence of an accurate spending record keeps some couples from making good financial decisions.
3. *Pay your bills.* When we purchase various items, we are also making a commitment to pay the price. This is a matter of integrity and honesty.

Pay what you owe. Not paying your bills damages your credit history and, in the long run, will cost you more with higher interest rates.

4. *Change your lifestyle.* There is an important understanding which must be clarified about living in the cycle of debt: We can either live within our means by spending no more than we make each month, or we can live above our means. Living above our means will catch up with us eventually. Living within our means may mean that we have to give up some things right now, but in the long run, we will be better able to reach our financial goals.

5. *Seek help if needed.* If you do not know how to set up a family budget or if your debts are so high that you can't make ends meet, please seek financial counseling. Good financial health is just as important as good physical health. There are free financial and credit counseling agencies that can help.

OVERCOMING DEBT WITH A SNOWBALL

This is one of the most accurate of Bible maxims: "The poor are ruled by the rich, and those who borrow are slaves of moneylenders" (Proverbs 22:7, CEV). You may think that you are in control of your finances because the credit card companies continue to increase your credit limit, you get many credit card offers, and you faithfully pay the minimum amount every month. But the reality is that as long as we have any debt, we are slaves to the institutions we owe.

According to recent statistics, "More than 189 million Americans have credit cards. The average cardholder in the United States has at least four credit cards. On average, each household with a credit card carries $8,398 in credit card debt."[14]

Further research reveals that more than 41 percent "of all households carry some sort of credit card debt" and that "households with the lowest net worth (zero or negative) hold an average of $10,308 in credit card debt."[15] How can individuals or families get out of this sinkhole?

Let's say that you are reading this chapter and thinking it's too late. Perhaps you already have a mountain of debt that seems too big to climb. Don't despair. Have you ever considered that paying off debt is similar to rolling a snowball? Let's think about this. Did you ever roll snowballs in order to build a snowman when you were a child? You likely started with a small, compact snowball that you could easily roll through across the ground. As you continued to roll that small snowball, it picked up more snow, and, little by little, it grew into a ball large enough to serve as the base for your snowman. "It's a great technique for building snowballs," says Dave Ramsey's website, "and it's an even better method for paying off your non-mortgage debt."[16]

Ramsey's website goes on to explain that "the snowball method is a debt reduction strategy where you pay off debt in the order of smallest to largest, gaining momentum as you knock out each balance. When the smallest debt is paid in full, you roll the money you were paying on that debt into the next smallest balance."[17] Here's how it works:

Step 1: List your debts from smallest to largest regardless of interest rate.
Step 2: Make minimum payments on all your debts except the smallest.
Step 3: Pay as much as possible on your smallest debt.
Step 4: Repeat until each debt is paid in full.[18]

Let's give you an example using an imaginary couple, although, from personal experience, we can tell you this is not too far from reality. Joe and Mary listed their debts as follows, from the greatest amount to the least:

Item	Balance	Monthly or minimum payment
1. Mortgage	$356,000	$1,500
2. Joe's car payment	$16,000	$350
3. Mary's car payment	$7,000	$280
4. Joe's student loan	$6,000	$250
5. Mary's student loan	$5,000	$250
6. Credit card	$5,000	$65
7. Store credit card	$3,500	$45
8. Gas credit card	$1,500	$25
Total	**$400,000**	**$2,765**

Joe and Mary need to keep making the minimum monthly payments on the first seven debts listed. But for the eighth debt—the gas credit card—instead of the minimum payment of $25, they need to pay $100. *The caveat to this plan is that Joe and Mary can't continue to charge or to add to the balance.* If Joe and Mary pay $100 rather than the minimum $25, it will take them only fifteen to seventeen months to pay off that debt, instead of eight to ten years. Once the gas credit card is paid, Joe and Mary will look at their new balance-owed sheet, take the $100 they were paying to that gas credit card, and apply it to the next lowest balance. In this case, it's Mary's student loan. The new payment schedule will something look like this:

Item	Balance	Monthly or minimum payment
1. Mortgage	$354,000	$1,500
2. Joe's car payment	$11,100	$350
3. Mary's car payment	$2,240	$280
4. Joe's student loan	$2,000	$250
5. Mary's student loan	$1,000	$250 + $100 = $350
6. Credit card	$4,950	$65
7. Store credit card	$3,000	$45
Total	**$378,290**	**$2,840**

Mary's student loan will take about three months to pay off. Now add that $350 to the next lowest balance—in this case, Joe's student loan—and the couple will be paying $600 toward a balance of about $2,000. That means they will be able to pay it off in about four months.

Add the $600 to the next lowest balance—Mary's car payment—so that the total payment will be $880. Joe and Mary should be able to pay that car off in about three months. Once again, add the $880 to the next low balance. In this case, it's the store credit card for a total payment of $925. Depending on the interest rate, it will take them five to six months to pay that store credit card. Then they will add that $925 payment to the credit card payment, and their monthly payment will be $990, giving them about four to five months to pay it off. Joe and Mary are almost there.

Next, Joe and Mary apply the $990 credit card payment to Joe's car payment for a total of $1,340, and in about eight months, they will have only one debt remaining—the mortgage. Finally, Joe and Mary add the $1,340 to the monthly mortgage of $1,500 for a total payment of $2,840, and they will be able to pay that mortgage off a lot faster than the thirty-year loan they signed. Every penny more than the regular mortgage payment will go toward the principal, which will lower the amount of interest Joe and Mary pay, and therefore more of the mortgage payment will go toward the principal every month.

We know this technique to be successful for many other couples, but we also know it to be true in our own life. Right now, we have no debts—the house and cars are paid, we carry no balance on any credit card, and have money in savings for home improvements and emergencies. We were able to do it even though at one time, we had more than $60,000 in debt—plus a mortgage.

We were able to do it, and we know you can too. You may have to buy less expensive cars and keep them longer, change your lifestyle, and make some sacrifices, but the ultimate payoff is worth it.

DRAWING YOUR FINANCIAL ROAD MAP

Paying off your debt is just one of the steps toward your ultimate financial goals. Think of it as a journey with a destination and several signposts along the way. It would look something like this:

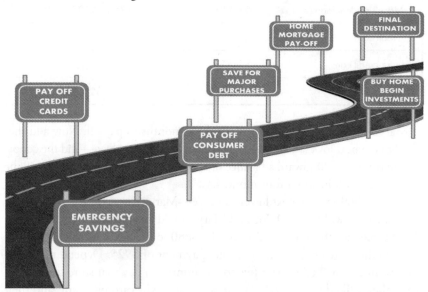

1. *Develop a budget.* We cannot say this enough. The first step in this journey, the one that will always help you reach that goal, is to develop a budget and stick faithfully to it.

2. *Save for emergencies.* The next step is to save as much as you can for emergencies. Your car may need new tires, the hot water heater may need to be replaced, or you may get laid off. Suddenly you start to panic. However, if you have an emergency savings fund, you will have a cushion to help you through these temporary setbacks.

3. *Eliminate credit card debt.* Earlier, we referred to one method to help

you pay off your credit cards: the debt snowball method. Once your credit cards are paid off, cut up as many as possible, leaving only one or two. You really don't need to have six, ten, or more credit cards. It's a recipe for financial disaster.

4. *Pay off consumer debt.* Consumer debt may include student loans, car payments, or other debts for large purchases (furniture, appliances, and so on).

5. *Save for major purchases.* Save to buy and replace appliances, furniture, cars, and other expensive items. We will talk more about buying cars a little later.

6. *Buy a home and begin investing.* If you have been saving toward the down payment on your house, it would be a great financial step to buy one and stop putting money in your landlord's pocket. If you already own a home, perhaps you can begin to put money toward some investments. Be cautious, though. Unless you have the time and you are financially savvy, you should seek the guidance of a financial adviser who can tell you where to invest and what to stay away from. Your investments may include a second or seasonal home, not just bonds or things of that nature.

7. *Pay off your mortgage.* Once you have no other debts, you can concentrate on paying off your mortgage before you retire. You don't want to carry a mortgage payment into your retirement.

8. *Reach your final destination.* All of your debts are paid, and you have money in savings. With that money, you may be able to help your children or grandchildren, you can make donations to the church or to worthy student funds, or you can enjoy some of the money going on vacations, traveling, and pursuing other interests. Ultimately, when you pass away, you can leave your children funds they can use for themselves or their own children. You could also contribute funds to further God's cause so that many others will come to know Him and be ready for the soon return of Jesus.

PAYING OFF YOUR VEHICLES

It seems as though one consumer debt that follows us throughout our life is the car loan. We have learned a very valuable lesson: don't mention anything about the car loan being paid off in front of the car, or it will begin to fall apart. I don't know how it works, but it seems that the moment you send in the final payment and begin to taste the freedom from that loan, the car suddenly needs a new transmission, the engine is not working well, and all kinds of other problems begin to appear. Keep your mouth shut and don't say anything about having paid off that car loan in front of the car!

So what can you do to get to the point where you don't have a car loan anymore? Here are some things we have learned through the years:

- *Don't watch car commercials.* Somehow those cars look so pretty and have so many neat features that your car feels antiquated. Suddenly your car does not drive comfortably anymore. It feels too tight, too small, and too unsafe. Your car does not have all those crucial features, such as a phone charger, roadside assistance, or GPS. You compare your car with all of the other cars in the commercials, and you come to the conclusion that you "need" a new car. Don't fall for this trick. That built-in GPS? Well, it is nice, but you have to pay a monthly service charge for it. Those gorgeous wheels? They're not part of the package. And the worst part is that you will not only walk out of the dealership with a new car but also with a new car loan for the next four to six years.

- *Decide to keep your car at least three years longer than your car loan.* Once you finish paying your car loan, remember to keep your mouth shut—don't say anything in front of the car. Just keep making the car payments—not to the bank or a loan company but to yourself. In other words, keep putting that amount of money into a savings account. In three to five years, you will have enough money for a sizable down payment, or possibly enough money to buy a car outright—no loan, no strings attached.

- *Decide ahead of time the maximum purchase amount for a car or car payment you are willing to make and don't budge.* If you have saved $30,000, look for cars that you can purchase for that amount. Don't be tempted by salespeople to buy a bigger, nicer, fancier car that costs more than the amount you have; otherwise, you will walk out with a nicer car—and a car loan. Decide what your budget will allow and don't go over it. We have never had a car payment higher than $200 a month. It is an arbitrary number, but that's what we have stuck by to this day. I (Claudio) confess that on my last car, we bent the rule by $8. We thought that was close enough, and in the end, we paid off the car three years sooner than the term of the loan.

- *Purchase a used car.* You may not be in a financial situation to afford a brand-new car. Perhaps you're skilled at auto repair and maintenance, and you can get a used car that you can work on for a lot less than you would pay for a new car. Some dealerships sell used cars with warranties and yet at a reduced price. The goal is to be debt-free, so do what you can to reach that goal—and the sooner, the better.

CONCLUSION

Financial wellness is not something that happens automatically. It takes intentionality, time, and planning. Achieving and maintaining financial well-being is important for you as a couple and for your entire family.

One of the most important benefits of being financially stable is that it can help reduce family stress. Unfortunately, financial stress is an unrelenting predicament in many families. The truth is that this need not be the case. With effort and planning, this stressor can not only be decreased—but it also can be eliminated.

Don't be a part of the statistics showing that financial difficulties have contributed to the breakup of your home. Instead, practice good stewardship and utilize the principles we have discussed. The use of a simple budget can greatly reduce financial stress and put you on the path to eliminating debt.

1. Sara Devine, "What Would You Do for $10 Million?" *Sara's Musings* (blog), November 1, 2012, https://sarasmusings.wordpress.com/2012/11/01/what-would-you-do-for-10-million/.

2. F. D. Nichol, ed. *The Seventh-day Adventist Bible Commentary*, vol. 7, *Philippians to Revelation* (Washington, DC: Review and Herald®, 1980), 317.

3. "Monday Motivation: Words of Wisdom to Get Your Week Started," *Telegraph*, October 16, 2016, https://www.telegraph.co.uk/men/thinking-man/monday-motivation-words-of-wisdom-to-get-your-week-started/steve-jobs-being-the-richest-man-in-the-cemetery-doesnt-matter-t/.

4. Byron Moore, "How Much Money Is Enough?" *Shreveport Times*, December 10, 2017, https://www.shreveporttimes.com/story/news/local/blogs/2017/12/10/how-much-money-enough/930449001/.

5. Linda Bloom and Charlie Bloom, "Kissing Adds Years to Your Life," *Psychology Today*, July 16, 2019, https://www.psychologytoday.com/us/blog/stronger-the-broken-places/201907/kissing-adds-years-your-life.

6. Bloom and Bloom, "Kissing."

7. Claudio Consuegra and Pamela Consuegra, "Facing the Economic Giants," *Love for a Lifetime* (blog), April 3, 2009, https://claudiooutlook.wordpress.com/2009/04/03/facing-the-economic-giants/.

8. "The Truth About Money and Relationships," Dave Ramsey, accessed August 13, 2020, https://www.daveramsey.com/blog/the-truth-about-money-and-relationships.

9. "Money and Relationships."

10. "Money and Relationships."

11. *Merriam-Webster*, s.v. "stewardship (*n.*)," https://www.merriam-webster.com/dictionary/stewardship, accessed August 16, 2020.

12. Consuegra and Consuegra, "Facing the Economic Giants."

13. Amy Bell, "6 Reasons Why You Need a Budget," Investopedia, updated January 28, 2020, https://www.investopedia.com/financial-edge/1109/6-reasons-why-you-need-a-budget.aspx#:~:text=Building%20a%20budget%20forces%20you,things%20you%20don't%20need.&text=Budgeting%20allows%20you%20to%20rethink,re%2Dfocus%20your%20financial%20goals.

14. Bill Fay, "Key Figures Behind America's Consumer Debt," Debt.org, accessed August 16, 2020, https://www.debt.org/faqs/americans-in-debt/.

15. Joe Resendiz, "Average Credit Card Debt in America," ValuePenguin, updated June 17, 2020, https://www.valuepenguin.com/average-credit-card-debt.

16. "How the Debt Snowball Method Works," Dave Ramsey, accessed August 14, 2020, https://www.daveramsey.com/blog/how-the-debt-snowball-method-works.

17. "Snowball Method Works."

18. "Snowball Method Works."

Chapter Nine

Set Yourself Free

Bear with each other and forgive one another if any of you has a
grievance against someone. Forgive as the Lord forgave you.
—Colossians 3:13, NIV

The movie *Love Story* was released in 1970 to the acclaim of the public and critics alike. If you never saw it, we'll give you a short synopsis. Oliver Barrett IV is a Harvard law student who meets and falls in love with Jennifer Cavalleri, a music student at another less prestigious college. Oliver and Jenny marry, and Oliver's father disowns them both. However, Oliver and Jenny lean on each other, trusting their love to carry them through. During a strong disagreement, they go their separate ways. But when they come together again, Oliver apologizes, and Jenny makes a pronouncement that became a mantra for a whole generation: "Love means never having to say you're sorry." Sadly, Jenny is found to have a terminal disease and dies. Oliver's dad finds out she's in the hospital and goes to see her but arrives too late. Oliver and his father meet in the lobby of the hospital. When Oliver's father expresses his regret, Oliver is the one that repeats those words to his dad: "Love means never having to say you're sorry."

Audiences, men and women, boys and girls, cried through this tragedy and learned that true love means you will never do anything to hurt the person you love, so you don't have to tell them you are sorry. While the idea may sound good in print or on the screen, offering a sincere apology and extending forgiveness do not show a lack of love. On the contrary, both actions are expressions of true love. As good as our marriage may be, there are times when, for whatever reason, we say or do something that hurts our spouse. It may be a careless word, a selfish action, a thoughtless deed, or even a hateful and harmful act. When that time comes, the injured spouse—the victim of such actions or words, the recipient of the other person's selfishness—can choose to be angry, resentful, or despondent; or they may choose to forgive.

So while it sounded good in *Love Story*, it is a myth that you should never have to say you are sorry. It is true that when you love someone, you should try your best to never hurt them. However, we are human. Sooner or later, all couples face conflict, and all couples get to the point where forgiveness needs to be sought and extended. Love means saying, "I'm sorry." Love means extending forgiveness.

APOLOGIZE IN THE CORRECT LANGUAGE

Before we talk about forgiveness, we need to discuss apology—seeking that forgiveness. One of our favorite comic strips, *The Lockhorns*, portrays a couple whom we describe as a couple that loves to hate each other. Leroy tells a friend, "Loretta said we should make up, so I made up an apology." We don't think Leroy understands what an apology looks like!

Think about this letter of apology a husband sent to his wife. Evidently, they had a disagreement about the Christmas lights. She wanted him to hang the Christmas lights on the outside of the house, but he delayed getting it done. The disagreement became a heated argument until she walked out the door and left her husband boiling with anger. After he calmed down, the husband decided to surprise his wife upon her return home and hang the Christmas lights as she had asked him to do. But he decided to take it a step farther; he wrote her a letter of apology. Here's the text of the letter, according to Jim Daly of Focus on the Family:

> Hi Sweetheart,
> I'm sorry about getting into an argument about putting up the Christmas lights. I guess that sometimes I feel like you push me too hard when you want something. I realize that I was wrong, and I am apologizing for being such a hard-headed guy. All I want is for you to be happy and be able to enjoy the holiday season. Nothing brightens the Christmas spirit like Christmas lights!
> I took the time to hang the lights for you today and now am off to the hockey rink. Again, I am very sorry for the way I acted yesterday.
> I'll be home later.
> Love you . . .[1]

We want you to notice some of the elements of a sincere apology in the husband's letter. For instance, he accepted responsibility by saying that he was wrong and that he was hardheaded. He used the words, "I am apologizing." And he also took corrective actions by hanging the Christmas lights.

Well, during our couples' retreats, we show the text of the letter, and then we reveal the photo of a jumbled mess of Christmas lights hanging from two hooks over the garage door. It's obvious that hanging the lights took no effort or love on the husband's part. If anything, it looks as though he did it that way to spite her even more.

You can imagine the shock and anger on the wife's face when she returned home, saw her husband's "loving" act of hanging the Christmas lights, and read his letter in which he expressed so much sorrow for having had the argument and his deep desire to make things better between them by hanging the Christmas lights. So she decided to write him a letter in response. Here's the text of her letter:

> Hi Honey,
> Thank you for that heartfelt apology. I don't often get an apology from you, and I truly appreciate it.
> I, too, felt bad about our argument and want to apologize. I realize that I can sometimes be a little pushy. I will try to respect your feelings from now on.
> Thank you for taking the time to hang the Christmas lights for me. It really means a lot.
> In the spirit of love and forgiveness, I washed your truck for you, and now I am off to the mall.
> I love you too![2]

The wife also took time to express her feelings in a calm way, apologized, and told her husband of her desire to make things better between them. We then reveal the photo of her heartfelt response—her husband's truck at the bottom of their swimming pool. That's what she meant by, "I washed your truck." I guess you could say she did a thorough job.

While the letters may sound conciliatory, the true spirit behind them was revealed in the spouses' actions more loudly than in their words. Gary Chapman, in his best-selling *The Five Love Languages*, explains that each of us has a certain language of love, and when our spouse speaks that language, they touch our hearts. Similarly, in *The Five Languages of Apology*, Chapman, along with coauthor Jennifer Thomas, describes how we each have our own language of apology. Discovering your mate's language of love and speaking it regularly is the best way to keep love alive in your marriage. In like manner, if you want your apology to be heard and accepted by your spouse, you need to speak their language of apology, because we all receive the sincerest apology when our primary language is spoken. Let's talk about the five languages of apology:

1. *"Expressing regret."* This is the most basic and yet most important expression of an apology that many need to hear. In fact, for most

people, if they don't hear the words, "I'm sorry," it is not really an apology. Many of us feel that in order to truly forgive, we need to see that the other person truly regrets what they have done. From the time our children are small, we want them to learn to express their sorrow for the bad actions they have taken. We encourage them by prompting, "Say you're sorry." Of course, they may learn to say the words, but it takes them longer to understand that being sorry isn't simply expressing the words but truly feeling bad for what they have done. For some people, when they hear those truly heartfelt, sincere words from the other person, they feel it more deeply than others.

2. *"Accepting responsibility."* We speak this language of apology when we say something like, "It was my fault," "I was wrong," or, "I shouldn't have done that." Often, a person will say, "I'm sorry," as if to say, "Let's get this over with and move on." But the one who has been hurt may need to hear that the offender accepts some sort of responsibility. For them, you can't just simply avoid or ignore what took place. They're not really looking for good reasons or explanations for why you did what you did. They simply want to hear you accept responsibility for the fact that your actions caused them pain.

For some people, it is very difficult, or nearly impossible, for them to accept responsibility. In *The Lockhorns*, Loretta tells her friend, "Leroy does say 'I love you,' but usually, it's to avoid saying 'I was wrong.' " While saying "I love you" is good, and expressing regret is nice, some people need to know their spouse realizes what they have done and how much it hurt them. The point is not to try to add guilt or make them feel bad, or worse, for what they have done. What matters to some spouses is to know that their spouse knows and understands what they have done, understands the hurt they have caused, and accepts responsibility. If they do that, their spouse would be much more comfortable extending forgiveness.

Accepting responsibility may surprise your spouse. In another *The Lockhorns* comic strip, Loretta is on the floor, passed out, and standing next to her is her husband, Leroy. Leroy shrugs his shoulders as he tells Loretta, "All I said was, 'I'm wrong.' " Maybe this is your spouse's language of apology; try it and see what their reaction is.

3. *"Making restitution."* For some people, just hearing that their spouse is sorry and that they accept responsibility is not good enough. Sometimes they may need restitution in order to know that the apology is sincere. Perhaps an example will help us understand better. If your child takes a toy away from another child, is it enough for them to

just say they're sorry? Or should they return the toy to the other child? The Bible has many passages in which God teaches restitution. Here are just a few:

- "If any of you commit a crime against someone, you have sinned against me. You must confess your guilt and pay the victim in full for whatever damage has been done, plus a fine of twenty percent" (Numbers 5:6, 7, CEV).
- "The LORD told Moses what the people must do when they commit other sins against the LORD: You have sinned if you rob or cheat someone, if you keep back money or valuables left in your care, or if you find something and claim not to have it. When this happens, you must return what doesn't belong to you and pay the owner a fine of twenty percent" (Leviticus 6:1–5, CEV).
- "Suppose a neighbor asks you to keep some silver or other valuables, and they are stolen from your house. If the thief is caught, the thief must repay double" (Exodus 22:7, CEV).

Perhaps the best-known illustration of restitution in the New Testament is the story of Zacchaeus (Luke 19:1–10). As Jesus was going through Jericho, Zacchaeus, who was a tax collector and a very short man, climbed a sycamore tree so he could see Jesus. As Jesus was walking by the tree, He stopped, looked up at Zacchaeus, and told him to come down because He wanted to go to Zacchaeus's house. The people who knew the chief publican to be a wicked and oppressive man began to murmur about Jesus associating with this rich sinner (verse 7). But something amazing happened in Zacchaeus's heart:

> Then Zacchaeus stood and said to the Lord, "Look, Lord, I give half of my goods to the poor; and if I have taken anything from anyone by false accusation, I restore fourfold."
>
> And Jesus said to him, "Today salvation has come to this house, because he also is a son of Abraham; for the Son of Man has come to seek and to save that which was lost" (verses 8–10).

From what Zacchaeus said, we know that he had been guilty of defrauding people; but he was also remorseful over his past actions and was committed to making restitution. On the other hand, from

Jesus' response, we learn that Zacchaeus was saved that day, and his sin was forgiven. We also see that both his public confession and his relinquishing all of his ill-gotten gains were the evidence of his salvation. Paul explained it this way: "For with the heart one believes unto righteousness, and with the mouth confession is made unto salvation" (Romans 10:10).

In the case of your spouse or a family member, restitution may not mean returning a physical object that was taken away or stolen; but it may mean reassuring the other person that they are loved and respected. Thus, restitution may also be made when you ask your spouse, "What can I do to make it better?" Of course, the answer to that question needs to be followed up by actions from you.

4. *"Genuinely repenting."* The common understanding of the word *repentance* is making a U-turn, a complete turnaround, experiencing a change of heart and mind. Without expressing a desire or a commitment to repent, an apology does not seem to be truly sincere. You can verbalize your repentance by assuring your spouse, "I won't do it again," or at the very least, "I will try to not do it again."

Many times we have heard, in a tone of utter exasperation, "But my spouse has told me that a thousand times and yet they keep doing it!" Of course, our first reaction is to say, "Why are you keeping track of all those times? When you keep track, have you actually forgiven?"

Think about this. Peter, who often played the part of the spokesperson for the band of disciples, came to Jesus and asked, "Lord, how often should I forgive someone who sins against me? Seven times?" (Matthew 18:21, NLT). The Judaism of the time taught that forgiving a person three times demonstrated that one had a true spirit of forgiveness. Some rabbis explained that a fourth time was not required. But Peter's question took it even further than three or four times.

Perhaps Peter was intended to impress Jesus and show Him how good a disciple he was, so he suggested the number seven, the perfect number. Maybe he thought Jesus would respond by saying, "Wow, Peter! You are awesome! You know that the rabbis only require a person to forgive up to three times, but here you come and suggest up to seven times? I'm impressed! Just for that, I'm going to invite you to sit on My right hand in My kingdom."

Jesus, on the other hand, was not particularly impressed by Peter's question or his generous offer: " 'No, not seven times,' Jesus replied, 'but seventy times seven' " (Matthew 18:22, NLT). Now, think about that for a moment. Simple math will tell us: 70 x 7 = 490. So does that mean that Jesus expects us to forgive the same person up to 490 times and no more? Does that mean that when your spouse fails you again, you can say to them, "Now, I have already forgiven you 489 times, so you only have one chance left, and after that, I don't have to forgive you!" Is that what Jesus meant? Or did He mean to say, "Peter, why are you keeping track? You see, Peter, if you keep track of the number of times you forgive someone, you have not really forgiven them even once."

We love the way several versions of the Bible render 1 Corinthians 13:5. In talking about the virtues of love, the New King James Version says it, "thinks no evil." Other versions chose to render those words like this:

- "It keeps no record of being wronged" (NLT).
- "It doesn't keep a record of wrongs that others do" (CEV).
- "It is not irritable or resentful" (ESV).
- It "does not take into account a wrong suffered" (NASB).
- It "doesn't keep score of the sins of others" (*The Message*).
- "It does not hold grudges and will hardly even notice when others do it wrong" (TLB).

No matter how many translations, versions, or paraphrases of the Bible we read, the point is that when you love someone, you don't keep track of every time they fail you. Rather, you choose to forgive. Jesus wasn't telling us we need to give people 490 opportunities, and then we're done with them. Imagine if God did that! We would all be sunk! So if your spouse has failed you or betrayed you again, and again they tell you, "I won't do it again," don't dismiss those words as empty and useless. Maybe they mean them, even if they have not found a way to keep them.

We have two dear friends who are a true delight. When we first met them, she told us her husband had left her for other women at least thirteen times (that she remembered). But she kept forgiving him, trusting him, and taking him back. When they studied the Bible and saw and experienced God's love and His forgiveness, they were both transformed—the Bible describes that as a "new birth." More than twenty years later, they are both very much in love with God and with each other, are very active in their church, and are committed to ministry through teaching others, sharing their transformation, and helping prepare others for baptism. Since they were baptized, he has been faithful to his God and to his wife. It may have taken him at least thirteen times of telling his wife, "I won't do it again," but he finally discovered he needed God's power to keep his promise.

Now, here's a word of caution. When it comes to abuse, if your spouse tells you they won't do it again, you may choose to forgive them, but that does not mean that you should continue to put up with abuse. If they are truly sincere and repentant, they will also be willing to do all in their power, through counseling, group work, accountability partners, anger management, and other methods, to make sure they never hurt you again. If they're not willing to do that, then the injured spouse should pack their bags and leave before they are hurt or perhaps even killed. It is that serious!

5. *"Requesting forgiveness."* The final language of apology may be the most difficult for some because when you ask your spouse to forgive you, you are admitting failure, you are relinquishing control of the fate of your relationship, you are humbling yourself and submitting to your spouse's judgment, and therefore, you are accepting the possibility that your plea will be rejected. But as hard as it may be, asking, "Will you forgive me?" has proved to be just what many need to begin the healing and renewal of their marriage.[3]

Chapman doesn't suggest that you use all five languages at the same time ("I'm sorry. It's my fault. What can I do to make it right? I won't do it again. Will you forgive me?"). Rather, he suggests that you figure out which language your spouse understands—which is most meaningful to them—and use it whenever you hurt them or fail them. You could use it in combination with some of the others, but be sure to use the one that means the most to your mate.

THE HEALING BALM OF FORGIVENESS

For many, forgiveness is like a healing balm to a hurting relationship. The scars may be felt or even visible for a long time—perhaps for the rest of your life—yet forgiveness has restored the relationship. In some ways, forgiveness is like a glue that mends broken hearts. Having said that, there is so much incorrect information about what forgiveness is and what it is not; thus, we want to take some time to explore the misconceptions before defining what forgiveness is and what steps one should take to forgive their offending spouse.

What forgiveness is *not*

We have so many misunderstandings about forgiveness that prevent us from experiencing the true freedom and healing forgiving can bring us. Let's set the record straight. Forgiveness is *not* the following:

1. *Approval.* Forgiving someone does not mean that you approve of their actions. God didn't approve of the decisions and actions of Adam and Eve in the Garden of Eden; yet He forgave them. In fact, in His act of forgiving them, God also explained to them His plan for their salvation and the salvation of all humanity. And Jesus forgave the woman who was caught in adultery, but He didn't approve of her lifestyle. Instead, He told her to "go and sin no more" (John 8:11). Forgiving someone does not mean that you approve of their actions. If your child has stolen from you, you can forgive them, but that does not mean that you approve of them taking from you.

2. *Excusing or justifying.* Forgiveness is not excusing, justifying, or covering for the sins of someone else. In *Total Forgiveness*, R. T. Kendall writes, "We do not point to circumstances in an attempt to explain away their behavior."[4] Moses did not excuse the behavior of the children of Israel. Instead, he appealed to God's mercy: "Forgive the iniquity of this people according to the greatness of your steadfast love, just as you have pardoned this people, from Egypt even until now" (Numbers 14:19, NRSV). Evil cannot be justified. Kendall goes on to explain:

   > God will never call something that is evil "right," and He does not require us to do so.
   >
   > In Moses's prayer for the Israelite people, he did not offer a hint of justification for their behavior. Instead he pointed out to God that the Egyptians would not think very highly of God's power or name if they saw Him obliterate His own people. While we are required to forgive, we should never attempt to make what is wrong look like it is right.[5]

   If your spouse has abused you, you can't excuse their behavior by saying something like, "I must have said or done something that made them lose them temper," or, "They were drunk and didn't realize what they were doing."

3. *Pardoning.* According to Kendall, "a pardon is a legal transaction that releases an offender from the consequences of their action, such as a penalty or a sentence. This is why we do not ask that the guilty rapist be exempt from punishment. He needs to pay his debt to society, and

society must be protected from him."[6] When forgiving, you are not called to release the offender from the natural consequences of their own actions.

A 1997 story appearing in the *Los Angeles Times* recounts the horrific experience of Mary Vincent, who suffered a wrong at the hands of Lawrence Singleton that would be difficult to forgive:

> In 1978, Singleton, then a 50-year-old ex-merchant mariner, picked up Vincent, then a 15-year-old hitchhiker running from Las Vegas and her parents' divorce, and raped her. He hacked off her forearms with five swings of a hatchet and stuffed her, unconscious, to die in a concrete culvert near Sacramento.
>
> A court document described the indescribable: "The next morning, two individuals found Mary Vincent wandering nude . . . she was holding up her arms so that the muscles and blood would not fall out."
>
> Under the lenient laws of that time, Singleton received concurrent sentences totaling 14 years for rape, attempted murder and sex offenses—the maximum allowed. Singleton, to the anguish of activists and the anger of communities where he was headed, served just eight years and four months.[7]

After his release, Singleton killed Roxanne Hayes, a thirty-one-year-old prostitute and mother of three. He died in 2001. Mary Vincent would do well to forgive Singleton for her own well-being. However, he did not deserve a pardon from her or anyone else. Forgiving a person and granting a pardon are two totally different things that should never be confused.

4. *Reconciliation.* Forgiveness is not always accompanied by reconciliation. "Reconciliation requires the participation of two people," says Kendall. "The person you forgive may not want to see or talk to you. Or they may have passed away since the time of the offense. Moreover, you may not want to maintain a close relationship with the person you forgave." For example, if someone sexually molests your child, you should not put your child in a position to be alone with them ever again. In a case like this, in order to safeguard your child, reconciliation should not happen. In other words, forgiveness may or may not be accompanied by reconciliation.

Sometimes people put victims of abuse in danger by telling them they need to forgive and return to their abuser's side. When we confuse reconciliation and forgiveness in instances such as abuse, we may be putting a life at risk. We agree that victims of abuse, for their own benefit, need to forgive the abuser—but in no way, shape, or form would we suggest that reconciliation must take place. Sometimes that may be possible after the abuser receives intensive treatment and very strict boundaries are set, but it must not be required of the victim.

5. *Denying or practicing willful blindness.* "Denying that an offense took place, or repression (suppressing what we really feel inside), is almost always unconscious," Kendall notes. "Some people, for various reasons, live in denial; that is, they refuse to admit or come to terms with the reality of a bad situation. It is sometimes painful to face the facts, and at times denial seems to be the easy way out." However, Kendall goes on to explain, "repression almost always has negative consequences for our psychological well-being."[8] For example, "many victims of child abuse repress the memory of the event. The conscious mind cannot accept that a parent, a trusted friend, or a relative would do such a thing, so the victim often lives in denial. Rape victims often experience the same phenomenon." But it's important to differentiate repression and willful blindness: "Some people . . . feel that to forgive is to be willfully and consciously blind to the sin that was committed." However, Kendall says, "willful blindness is slightly different from repression. Blindness is a conscious choice to pretend that a sin did not take place; repression is usually unconscious or involuntary."[9]

Some people think that forgiving the offender shows that the forgiving person is weak. But the opposite is true. A sign of strength and maturity is when we make the decision to forgive someone who has hurt us. Mahatma Gandhi said, "The weak can never forgive. Forgiveness is the attribute of the strong."[10]

6. *Forgetting.* We have all heard the saying "Forgive and forget." But to literally forget may not be realistic or possible. Kendall sheds light on this idea:

> It is usually impossible to forget meaningful events in our lives, whether positive or negative. . . .
> Love doesn't erase our memories. It is actually a demonstration of greater grace when we are fully aware of what occurred—and we still choose to forgive.[11]

The pain and even some of the details of an injury suffered at the hands of another may fade with time, but the event will probably remain with us for the rest of our lives. Only a brain injury or a mental disease will erase our memories completely. What often happens when we hear the saying "Forgive and forget" is that we feel guilty every time we remember the event and believe we have not really forgiven. Forgiving and forgetting are not one and the same.

7. *Pretending it doesn't matter.* Kendall states, "We cannot truly forgive until we see clearly the offense we are forgiving and understand its seriousness." But, he notes, "some people may think that in order to forgive they must dismiss a wrong or pass it off as inconsequential or insignificant. . . . The greater victory for the one who does the forgiving is to face up to the seriousness—even the wickedness—of what happened and still forgive." Kendall goes on to acknowledge that "it is ridiculous to think that we should have to keep a stiff upper lip when we have been injured by a spouse's infidelity . . . or betrayed . . . or molested . . . or unjustly criticized."[12] It does matter!

What forgiveness *is*

Now that we understand what forgiveness is *not*, we can move forward in our journey to understand what forgiveness *is*. Forgiveness is the following:

1. *A decision and not a feeling.* We wrote in an earlier chapter that love is not a feeling but a decision. When we say that love is a decision, we mean that love is shown through words and actions. Forgiveness is also a decision and not a feeling. As we will see, you can decide to forgive even when you don't feel like it. In some cases, the decision to forgive may come first (it usually does), while the feelings may take much longer.

2. *Being aware of the wrong and still forgiving it.* "Forgiveness is achieved only when we acknowledge what was done without denial or covering up," writes R. T. Kendall in *Total Forgiveness*.[13] Forgiveness can be painful as it doesn't erase what the offender did. You look the evil in the face but still decide to forgive.

3. *Keeping no record of wrong.* The Bible says that love "keeps no record of wrongs" (1 Corinthians 13:5, NIV). "Why do we keep track of the times we are offended?" asks Kendall. He then answers his own question: "To use them. To prove what happened. To wave them before someone who doubts what actually happened." However, "when we develop a lifestyle of total forgiveness, we learn to erase the wrong rather than file it away in our mental computer."[14]

4. *Refusing to punish the offender.* Forgiveness involves "giving up the natural desire to see [the offender] 'get what's coming to them,' " says Kendall. "It is refusing to cave in to the fear that the person or those people won't get . . . the punishment or rebuke we think they deserve."[15] It's hard to "kiss revenge good-bye," as Kendall puts it.[16] Vindication is best left to God. Indeed, Kendall asserts, "He doesn't want [or need] our help. So when we refuse to be instruments of punishment, God likes that; it sets Him free to decide what should be done." Kendall says we must examine ourselves and ask, " 'How much of what I am about to say or do is an attempt to punish?' If punishment is our motive, we are about to grieve the Holy Spirit, however much right may be on our side."[17]

5. *Choosing not to gossip.* "Anyone who truly forgives . . . does not gossip about his or her offender," Kendall writes.[18] If the situation demands that you tell someone or report inappropriate behavior, make sure that the person is trustworthy or in a position of authority. Yes, some situations (such as abuse) demand that you speak up, but all too often, we speak about things that need not be told. Use discretion! We love the story of Clara Barton, founder of the American Red Cross. When a friend reminded Barton of a malicious deed someone else had done to her years earlier, she seemed to have no recollection of the incident. Her friend asked incredulously, "Don't you remember this happening to you?"

Barton responded, "No. I distinctly remember forgetting that."[19] She had made the decision to forgive the offense and put it aside, and she would not be a part of gossiping about it years later.

6. *Mercy and grace.* We use these the words *mercy* and *grace* interchangeably to talk about what God has done for us, but they are not the same: "Mercy is not getting what we do deserve (justice); grace is getting what we don't deserve (total forgiveness)."[20] Think about it. We don't deserve salvation. The prophet Isaiah wrote, "We are all infected and impure with sin. When we display our righteous deeds, they are nothing but filthy rags" (Isaiah 64:6, NLT). But God extends His grace toward us and gives it to us. He gives us what we don't deserve. "But God showed how much he loved us by having Christ die for us, even though we were sinful" (Romans 5:8, CEV). Mercy, on the other hand, is not getting what we deserve. Because we are sinners, all we deserve is death. As Paul puts it, "For the wages of sin is death, but the free gift of God is eternal life through Christ Jesus our Lord" (Romans 6:23, NLT). God doesn't give us what we deserve (death);

instead, He gives us what we don't deserve (salvation and eternal life).

When we show mercy, we are withholding justice from those who have injured us. We are not giving them what they have coming. Grace, on the other hand, "is shown by what you *don't* say, even if what you could say would be true."[21]

FORGIVENESS IS A CHOICE

There is one item in the preceding list on what forgiveness is that bears repeating, underlining, and highlighting once again. Forgiveness is a decision and not a feeling! This one thing is perhaps the most misunderstood of all. You can still make the decision to forgive even when you don't feel like it.

Corrie ten Boom's entire family was arrested and taken to a concentration camp for harboring Jews during World War II. She alone survived and later related a powerful story that shows how forgiveness is not a feeling but rather a decision—an act influenced by the Holy Spirit:

It was in a church in Munich that I saw him, a balding heavyset man in a gray overcoat, a brown felt hat clutched between his hands. . . .

It was 1947 and I had come from Holland to defeated Germany with the message that God forgives. . . .

. . . One moment I saw the overcoat and the brown hat; the next, a blue uniform and a visored cap with its skull and crossbones. . . .

. . . This man had been a guard at Ravensbrück concentration camp where we were sent.

Now he was in front of me, hand thrust out: "A fine message, *fräulein*! How good it is to know that, as you say, all our sins are at the bottom of the sea!"

And I, who had spoken so glibly of forgiveness, fumbled in my pocketbook rather than take that hand. He would not remember me, of course—how could he remember one prisoner among those thousands of women?

But I remembered him and the leather crop swinging from his belt. It was the first time since my release that I had seen him, and my blood seemed to freeze.

"You mentioned Ravensbrück in your talk," he was saying. "I was a guard there." No, he did not remember me.

"But since that time," he went on, "I have become a Christian. I know that God has forgiven me for the cruel things I did there, but I would like to hear it from your lips as well. *Fräulein*"—again the hand came out—"will you forgive me?"

And I stood there—I whose sins had every day to be forgiven—could not. . . .

"Jesus, help me!" I prayed silently. "I can lift my hand. I can do that much. You supply the feeling."

And so woodenly, mechanically, I thrust my hand into the one stretched out to me. And as I did, an incredible thing took place. The current started in my shoulder, raced down my arm, sprang into our joined hands. And then this healing warmth seemed to flood my whole being, bringing tears to my eyes.

"I forgive you, brother!" I cried. "With all my heart!"

For a long moment we grasped each other's hands, the former guard and the former prisoner. I had never known God's love so intensely as I did then.[22]

There is no doubt that Corrie ten Boom did not realize how big a burden she was carrying until she laid it down. Finally, she was free! She chose to reach out her hand and grasp the former guard's. In doing so, the spirit of forgiveness washed over her. She was now able to truly experience the kind of forgiveness and love God had for her.

TYPES OF FORGIVENESS

Perhaps one of the reasons we struggle with forgiveness is that we don't understand one crucial distinction. According to research, there are two types of forgiveness:

1. *Decisional.* This type of forgiveness is deciding to forgive a personal offense and let go of angry and resentful thoughts and feelings toward the person who has wronged you.
2. *Emotional.* This type of forgiveness is replacing the negative emotions with healthier feelings such as compassion, sympathy, and empathy.[23]

Each of us may decide to forgive, regardless of feelings or circumstances. On the other hand, we may not all experience that emotional forgiveness that comes to the point of feeling compassion and sympathy for the person who has wronged us. It is important to understand the difference because we often think that we have not forgiven if the emotions do not come as well, and that is a misunderstanding. In other words, forgiveness always involves making a decision (decisional forgiveness), but it may or may not come with replacing negative emotions with positive ones (emotional forgiveness).

THE IMPACT OF AN UNFORGIVING SPIRIT

When you think that forgiving someone is impossible, stop and consider the alternative. Not forgiving has dire consequences that will impact you for the rest of your life and, perhaps, for eternity. Consider these words from Johns Hopkins: "Whether it's a simple spat with your spouse or long-held resentment toward a family member or friend, unresolved conflict can go deeper than you may realize—it may be affecting your physical health. The good news: Studies have found that the act of forgiveness can reap huge rewards for your health, lowering the risk of a heart attack; improving cholesterol levels and sleep; and reducing pain, blood pressure, and levels of anxiety, depression and stress. And research points to an increase in the forgiveness-health connection as you age."[24]

It has also been said that those who fail to forgive will also be unable to truly love. The great civil rights leader, Dr. Martin Luther King Jr., is quoted as stating, "We must develop and maintain the capacity to forgive. He who is devoid of the power to forgive is devoid of the power to love. There is some good in the worst of us and some evil in the best of us. When we discover this, we are less prone to hate our enemies."[25] Perhaps we have been unable to experience love the way God intended because we have not forgiven.

JOURNEY TO FORGIVENESS

We like to think of forgiveness, not as an act, an event, or a moment in time—but, rather, as a journey. A journey is a process that takes time in order to reach your desired location. There may be obstacles along the way, and you may reach your destination much later than you had planned. The same is true of forgiveness. Work through the process; expect it to take time (depending on the offense); and, as you would on a physical journey, ask God to go with you. If you have something that is keeping you from experiencing true love in your marriage the way God intended, we invite you to take these steps along your journey to forgiveness:

1. *Set a time and a place.* Set aside a time and a place that is unhurried and private to discuss the issue. Agree to meet as a couple. As you await the meeting, pray for a forgiving spirit even if you don't feel forgiving.
2. *Name it.* Be very specific and name the issue. What was the event that caused the pain? And remember, don't bring out a long list. You are discussing *one* specific issue.
3. *Explore the pain.* Don't try to whitewash the situation but fully explore the pain. Talk about the feelings you experienced and why the event was so hurtful to you. Name the feelings so that your mate can

understand why you were hurt. Why did this matter? If you are the one guilty of causing the injury, listen for your spouse's expression of feelings, try to "walk in their shoes," and try to understand how and why they are feeling that way.

4. *Ask for forgiveness.* If you are the one that caused the pain, practice the language of apology that your spouse accepts best, and then ask for forgiveness. Use the words, "Will you forgive me?" Remember that forgiveness is a choice, so asking the question acknowledges that and gives them a choice to make.

5. *Agree to forgive.* If you are the one who was hurt, are you now ready to choose to forgive? If so, state it clearly. Say, "I choose to forgive you," or simply, "I forgive you."

6. *Make a commitment.* Commit to your spouse to try to never repeat the actions that caused them pain. Understand that you may fail at times, but you will make an honest effort to refrain from causing the hurt again. How will you do that? Talk about steps you can take to make sure the situation will not be repeated.

7. *Understand that forgiveness may take time.* Yes, sometimes forgiveness takes time, so don't be discouraged. Your spouse may need time to work through the pain in order to let it go and offer forgiveness.

Lewis B. Smedes began his book on forgiveness with a beautiful fable known as "The Magic Eyes." It goes like this:

> In the village of Faken in innermost Friesland there lived a long thin baker named Fouke, a righteous man, with a long thin chin and a long thin nose. Fouke was so upright that he seemed to spray righteousness from his thin lips over everyone who came near him; so, people preferred to stay away.
>
> Fouke's wife, Hilda, was short and round, her arms were round, her bosom was round, her rump was round. Hilda did not keep people at bay with righteousness; her soft roundness seemed to invite them instead to come close to her in order to share the warm cheer of her open heart. Hilda respected her righteous husband, and loved him too, as much as he allowed her; but her heart ached for something more from him than his worthy righteousness.
>
> And there, in the bed of her need, lay the seed of sadness. One morning, having worked since dawn to knead his dough for the ovens, Fouke came home and found a stranger in his bedroom lying on Hilda's round bosom. Hilda's adultery soon became the talk of the

tavern and the scandal of the Faken congregation. Everyone assumed that Fouke would cast Hilda out of his house, so righteous was he. But he surprised everyone by keeping Hilda as his wife, saying he forgave her as the Good Book said he should.

In his heart of hearts, however, Fouke could not forgive Hilda for bringing shame to his name. Whenever he thought about her, his feelings toward her were angry and hard; he despised her as if she were a common whore. When it came right down to it, he hated her for betraying him after he had been so good and so faithful a husband to her.

He only pretended to forgive Hilda so that he could punish her with his righteous mercy. But Fouke's fakery did not sit well in heaven. So, each time that Fouke would feel his secret hate toward Hilda, an angel came to him and dropped a small pebble, hardly the size of a shirt button, into Fouke's heart. Each time a pebble dropped; Fouke would feel a stab of pain like the pain he felt the moment he came on Hilda feeding her hungry heart from a stranger's larder. Thus he hated her the more; his hate brought him pain and his pain made him hate.

The pebbles multiplied. And Fouke's heart grew very heavy with the weight of them, so heavy that the top half of his body bent forward so far that he had to strain his neck upward in order to see straight ahead. Weary with hurt, Fouke began to wish he were dead.

The angel who dropped the pebbles into his heart came to Fouke one night and told him how he could be healed of his hurt. There was one remedy, he said, only one, for the hurt of a wounded heart. Fouke would need the miracle of the magic eyes. He would need eyes that could look back to the beginning of his hurt and see his Hilda, not as a wife who betrayed him, but as a weak woman who needed him. Only a new way of looking at things through the magic eyes could heal the hurt flowing from the wounds of yesterday.

Fouke protested. "Nothing can change the past," he said. "Hilda is guilty, a fact that not even an angel can change." "Yes, poor hurting man, you are right," the angel said. "You cannot change the past, you can only heal the hurt that comes to you from the past. And you can heal it only with the vision of the magic eyes."

"And how can I get your magic eyes?" pouted Fouke. "Only ask, desiring as you ask, and they will be given you. And each time you see Hilda through your new eyes, one pebble will be lifted from your aching heart."

Fouke could not ask at once, for he had grown to love his hatred.

But the pain of his heart finally drove him to want and to ask for the magic eyes that the angel had promised. So, he asked. And the angel gave.

Soon Hilda began to change in front of Fouke's eyes, wonderfully and mysteriously. He began to see her as a needy woman who loved him instead of a wicked woman who betrayed him.

The angel kept his promise; he lifted the pebbles from Fouke's heart, one by one, though it took a long time to take them all away. Fouke gradually felt his heart grow lighter; he began to walk straight again, and somehow his nose and his chin seemed less thin and sharp than before. He invited Hilda to come into his heart again, and she came, and together they began again a journey into their second season of humble joy.[26]

CONCLUSION

When faced with the decision to forgive, consider these two key things:

1. *Jesus forgives us over and over again.* He does not count the number of times, nor does He remind us of our sinfulness. Instead, He reminds us of His love for us.
2. *An unforgiving spirit will affect* you *negatively.* Choosing not to forgive will hurt you physically, emotionally, and spiritually. As poet Maya Angelou reminds us, "It's one of the greatest gifts you give yourself, to forgive. Forgive everybody."[27] For your own sake, forgive.

We will leave you with the words of pastor and author Max Lucado:

You will never forgive anyone more than God has already forgiven you.

Is it still hard to consider the thought of forgiving the one who hurt you? If so, go one more time to the upper room. Watch Jesus as he goes from disciple to disciple. Can you see him? Can you hear the water splash? Can you hear him shuffle on the floor to the next person? Keep that image in mind. John 13:12 says, "When he had finished washing their feet . . . " Please note—Jesus *finished* washing their feet. That means he left no one out.

Why is that important? Because that means he washed the feet of Judas. Jesus washed the feet of his betrayer. That's not to say it was easy for Jesus. That's not to say it's easy for you. But that is to say, God will never call you to do what he hasn't already done![28]

1. Jim Daly with Paul Batura, "Husband and Wife Apology Letters," *Daly Focus* (blog), May 29, 2012, https://jimdaly.focusonthefamily.com/husband-and-wife-apology-letters/.

2. Daly with Batura, "Apology Letters."

3. Adapted from Gary Chapman and Jennifer Thomas, *The Five Languages of Apology* (Chicago: Northfield, 2006). At the time of this writing, the most current edition of the book (2013) is entitled *When Sorry Isn't Enough*.

4. R. T. Kendall, *Total Forgiveness*, revised and updated ed. (Lake Mary, FL: Charisma, 2007), 24.

5. Kendall, *Total Forgiveness*, 25.

6. Kendall, 25.

7. Paul Dean, "Mary Vincent Speaks Out: 'He Destroyed Everything About Me,' " *Los Angeles Times*, February 25, 1997, https://www.latimes.com/archives/la-xpm-1997-02-25-ls-32048 -story.html#:~:text=In%201978%2C%20Singleton%2C%20then%20a,a%20concrete%20 culvert%20near%20Sacramento.

8. Kendall, *Total Forgiveness*, 26.

9. Kendall, 27, 28.

10. *Oxford Essential Quotations*, s.v. "Mahatma Gandhi," Oxford Reference, https://www .oxfordreference.com/view/10.1093/acref/9780191843730.001.0001/q-oro-ed5-00004716, accessed August 16, 2020.

11. Kendall, *Total Forgiveness*, 29.

12. Kendall, 30, 31.

13. Kendall, 32.

14. Kendall, 32, 33.

15. Kendall, 33, 34.

16. Kendall, 32.

17. Kendall, 34.

18. Kendall, 35.

19. "Clara Barton," Bible.org, accessed August 16, 2020, https://bible.org/illustration /clara-barton.

20. Kendall, *Total Forgiveness*, 160.

21. Kendall, 39; emphasis in original.

22. Corrie ten Boom, "Guideposts Classics: Corrie ten Boom on Forgiveness," *Guideposts*, November 1972, posted on *Guideposts* July 24, 2014, https://www.guideposts.org/better-living /positive-living/guideposts-classics-corrie-ten-boom-on-forgiveness; emphasis in original.

23. Everett L. Worthington Jr. et al., "Forgiveness, Health, and Well-Being: A Review of Evidence for Emotional Versus Decisional Forgiveness, Dispositional Forgivingness, and Reduced Unforgiveness," *Journal of Behavioral Medicine* 30, no. 4 (August 2007): 291–302, https://doi .org/10.1007/s10865-007-9105-8.

24. "Forgiveness: Your Health Depends on It," Johns Hopkins Medicine, accessed August 16, 2020, https://www.hopkinsmedicine.org/health/wellness-and-prevention/forgiveness-your -health-depends-on-it.

25. "Editorial: 'It Is a Dream Deeply Rooted in the American Dream," *Las Vegas Review-Journal*, January 19, 2020, https://www.reviewjournal.com/opinion/editorials/editorial-it-is-a -dream-deeply-rooted-in-the-american-dream-1939269/.

26. Lewis B. Smedes, *Forgive and Forget: Healing the Hurts We Don't Deserve* (San Francisco: Harper Collins, 1984), XVII–XIX.

27. Maya Angelou, interview by Oprah Winfrey, "Oprah Talks to Maya Angelou," Oprah.com, accessed August 16, 2020, https://www.oprah.com/omagazine/maya-angelou -interviewed-by-oprah-in-2013/5.

28. Max Lucado, "It's Important to Forgive," Max Lucado, accessed August 16, 2020, https://maxlucado.com/listen/its-important-to-forgive/; emphasis in original.

Chapter Ten

"Change My Heart, O God"

Therefore, if anyone is in Christ, the new creation has come:
The old has gone, the new is here!
—2 Corinthians 5:17, NIV

An article appearing on the website For Your Marriage notes wryly: "They say that when a man marries a woman, he thinks, 'She's the one I've been waiting for. She'll never change.' . . . She always does. And a woman looks at her man, and thinks, 'He just needs a little work; after we're married, I'll help him change'—and he never does."[1] Change seems natural and easy at times. But, at other times, it seems we dig in our heels and resist change at all costs.

Actually, marriage changes us all. Being married to the right person helps us change for the better. As we look back at our earliest years of marriage, we all probably recognize that we have, indeed, changed some. Perhaps we are more mellow, more patient, less selfish, less self-centered. Those are good, positive changes.

But the sad reality is that some people have moved in the opposite direction. Whether or not they wish to recognize it, they have become more selfish, more self-centered, less patient, and much more irritable. It is often at this time that couples come to us or go to a counselor to see if there's any hope for their relationship. In fact, they come to us as their last option. We wish they had come sooner as earlier intervention is always best. At the same time, it is never too late for God, if one is open to His leading.

We remember a couples' retreat we had several years ago. During one of the breaks, an older lady approached us, wanting to talk. She began, "My husband and I have been married for forty-two years."

We were so excited that we interrupted her, "Forty-two years? That's wonderful. Praise God! What a great example you are leaving others, especially your children."

She waved for us to stop and continued, "No, no, we have been married forty-two years, but I just can't stand my husband."

Again, we interrupted, "Forty-two years! Do you know how many couples can say that? When so many marriages break up after just a few years, you two have managed to stay together for forty-two years. That is wonderful!"

She again waved for us to stop. "No, no, don't you understand? My husband and I have been having problems for many years, and I just don't know what else to do."

When people ask us these types of questions during a retreat, it is not really possible to give them that silver bullet—that one word of advice that will completely change and revolutionize their situation overnight. It's important to note that some situations, like this one that had lingered for forty-two years, may need extensive counseling. We simply told her, "You have been married for forty-two years, and you tell us that for many of those years you and your husband have been having marital problems. In addition, your husband is not here to tell his side of the story. What we recommend is that you both go to a good marriage counselor who will guide you through a process toward healing."

She immediately said, "But we're going to a marriage counselor already."

We now understood. She was not really asking for our advice but rather for ammunition against her husband or their marriage counselor. With that understanding, we continued, "We're glad you're going to a marriage counselor. Continue to go, follow their directions, and pray for healing for your relationship. Look for ways to stay together because by doing so, you will be giving your children and grandchildren a great example and a great blessing."

Through the years, people who have come to us have told us that they no longer love their spouse. Following the lead of Hollywood movies, they say, "I love them, I'm just not *in* love with them."

We think we know what they mean by that. We think they mean that while they still care about their spouse, they don't seem to have romantic feelings toward them. When we hear that, we tell them, "Well, fake it!"

Of course, with their eyes wide open in utter surprise, they ask us, "Fake it? Do you mean I should fake loving them? Isn't that hypocritical?" We tell them that it would be hypocritical if love was a feeling. But if love is a decision, and that decision is shown through actions, then it is not hypocritical. What do we mean by that?

My (Claudio's) master's degree is in counseling psychology with an emphasis in marriage and family therapy, and the area of training that I use most often is referred to as cognitive behavioral therapy (CBT). According to the National Alliance on Mental Illness, "Cognitive behavioral therapy (CBT) focuses on exploring relationships among a person's thoughts, feelings and behaviors. During CBT a therapist will actively work with a person to uncover unhealthy patterns of thought and how they may be causing self-destructive behaviors and beliefs."[2] To put it in simple terms, if I can help you change the way you think, I can help you change the way you act.

We have used a form of CBT in other settings, such as overcoming the smoking habit. In 1964, a physician, J. Wayne McFarland, and a pastor and psychologist, Elam Folkenberg, developed a program to help people break the habit of smoking. The Five-Day Plan to Quit Smoking, as the program is known, is one of the oldest and most effective smoking-cessation programs to date. More than twenty million around the world have participated in the program, which has received recognition from the World Health Organization, the American Cancer Society, the American Lung Association, and the American Heart Association.[3]

An important ingredient of the plan to stop smoking is CBT. When a person enters the program, we suggest a number of techniques to try instead of reaching for that cigarette. We suggest, when you have the craving, repeat to yourself, "I choose not to smoke for one minute." You are not making promises, because if you did smoke, you would tell yourself you are powerless to quit because you can't even keep that promise. At the same time, you don't say, "I choose to never smoke again." While that's a good decision to make, you may feel as if it is impossible. But if you say, "I choose"—not *promise*—"to not smoke for one minute"—not *for the rest of my life*—surely you can make it for just one minute. If at the end of that minute, you still have a craving to smoke, repeat to yourself again, "I choose to not smoke for one more minute." If at the end of that second minute, you still have a craving to smoke, repeat to yourself, "I choose to not smoke for one more minute." Usually, after the third minute, the craving will begin to wane. That's a form of CBT. Altering your thinking will alter your behavior. You see, as a smoker, habitual use (the behavior) alters our thinking (*I can't live without smoking*). If you can change your thinking (*I choose not to smoke*), it can change your behavior (you quit smoking).

On a long trip to Hawaii, a ten-hour direct flight from Atlanta, I watched a TED lecture by Harvard social psychologist Amy Cuddy, who uses the well-known maxim "Fake it till you make it." Through her research on nonverbal expressions, she provides insights into how our bodies influence our behavior. Cuddy's research reveals that by paying attention to nonverbal cues—such as crossing your arms—and then doing things to change them, you can actually change your mind and how you perceive yourself, not just how others perceive you.[4]

Cuddy basically says that testosterone (the hormone that governs confidence) and cortisol (the hormone that affects stress levels) both contribute to our confidence. In her study, Cuddy found that high levels of testosterone and low levels of cortisol help us feel more powerful. Conversely, high levels of cortisol can increase anxiety and reduce our confidence. Cuddy and her team observed that power poses (arms open, chin up, hands on hips) produce higher levels of testosterone than the more hesitant poses (slumped posture, shoulders in, eyes downcast) and that certain body movements or postures, even for as little as two minutes, produce changes in hormones. In other words, your body changes your mind.

While some have criticized Cuddy for stating that one should fake it, other research also highlights the effectiveness of making changes in your behavior, which lead to changes in your emotional well-being. For instance, Karen Kleiman writes about several psychological researchers and their repeated conclusions. One of them, J. D. Laird, "conducted two experiments in which he manipulated participants' facial expressions without their knowledge while they viewed cartoons. This experiment tested the hypothesis that if an individual's mouth is manipulated into the form of a smile, it would change his or her perception of a humorous video clip."[5]

Kleiman also writes about a similar experiment in 1988, in which researchers "hypothesized that participants who were led to smile would judge the cartoons as funnier than participants who were led to frown." The researchers told the participants "to hold a pencil between their teeth while performing a task that involved rating the degree of humor in cartoons. Holding the pencil in the mouth this way forced the individuals to smile. Try it, you'll see. The pencil can be lengthwise between the teeth, or hanging down from the tip between your teeth. Either way, you get the forced smile. Other participants were instructed to hold the pencil between their lips without touching the pencil with their teeth and this force[d] the muscles to contract resulting in a frown." Perhaps unsurprisingly, the smiling participants rated the cartoons as more humorous than the frowning participants.[6] More research by scientists at the University of Kansas shows that "smiling during brief periods of stress may help reduce the body's stress response, regardless of whether the person actually feels happy or not."[7]

Now, let's get back to Amy Cuddy. In her TED lecture, she concludes that our bodies do, in fact, change our minds, which is why we might assume a power pose or hold a pencil between our teeth. She takes it a step further by stating that our minds change our behavior, which is a cognitive-behavioral approach. Ultimately, our behavior changes our outcomes, which is to say, don't just fake it until you make it but "fake it till you become it."[8]

One only needs to make small tweaks to their behavior, but those small tweaks can lead to big changes. What is interesting is that the Bible teaches the same principle. Jesus said, "So now I am giving you a new commandment: Love each other. Just as I have loved you, you should love each other" (John 13:34, NLT). Jesus was not commanding us to feel love toward another. There are things that Jesus can command us to do: act in certain ways or talk in certain ways. But how can He command us to feel? A feeling is something that either we have or we don't. What He is commanding us to do is to act lovingly toward one another. He can command us to do that. So when we tell people to fake it, what we mean is: Don't wait until you feel love toward your spouse before you start behaving lovingly toward them. Do the opposite. Start acting loving toward your spouse, and loving thoughts will begin to form in your mind; and eventually, those thoughts will lead to loving feelings.

Furthermore, Jesus said, "But I say to you, love your enemies, bless those who curse you, do good to those who hate you, and pray for those who spitefully use you and persecute you" (Matthew 5:44). Again, Jesus cannot command us to feel love toward our enemies, but He certainly can command us to act lovingly toward them. Look at all the loving actions (not feelings) He tells us to do: *bless* them instead of cursing them, *do good* to them, *pray* for them. Those are all actions. He's not asking us to feel loving toward our enemies, but He is commanding us to act lovingly toward them because He knows that when we start acting lovingly toward them, we will eventually begin to think lovingly—and ultimately we will begin to feel love toward them.

What often happens at home is the opposite. Over time we entertain negative thoughts about our spouse, we resent things they have done to us, and we compare them to other people. In fact, it seems that all we notice is their faults. When we do that, little by little, our love for them erodes: "For as he thinks in his heart, so is he" (Proverbs 23:7). Negative thoughts lead to negative feelings, and negative thoughts and feelings are often accompanied by negative words and actions. On the other hand, positive thoughts lead to positive feelings: "He who earnestly seeks good finds favor, but trouble will come to him who seeks evil" (Proverbs 11:27). Act lovingly toward your spouse, and you will begin to think lovingly. Eventually, you will feel lovingly toward him or her.

This concept was not foreign to the writers of the New Testament. The apostle Paul spoke about the value of thinking about positive things: "Finally, brethren, whatever things are true, whatever things are noble, whatever things are just, whatever things are pure, whatever things are lovely, whatever things are of good report, if there is any virtue and if there is anything praiseworthy—*meditate* on these things" (Philippians 4:8; emphasis added).

Paul then concludes with these words: "The things which you learned and received and heard and saw in me, these *do*, and the God of peace will be with you" (Philippians 4:9; emphasis added). Paul makes it clear that we must *do* those things. Positive actions lead to positive thoughts and positive feelings.

In one of our couples' retreats, we received one of the most beautiful, encouraging letters ever. Here's the entire text:

At one time in our marriage there were a number of annoying habits that bothered me a lot every time they occurred. I mentioned them, but they never changed. Eventually, I prayed to God to change my spouse. God answered my prayer, but not in the way I expected. Instead of changing my spouse, God changed *me*. God changed me, so that I focused on my spouse's positive, endearing qualities instead of focusing on the little things that annoyed me. I found that the things that once grated on me no longer had any effect and I hardly noticed them. By choosing to focus on the positives, today I am more in love than even when we were first married.

If you have come to the place in your relationship where you don't feel those romantic feelings for your spouse and all you see in them are things you don't like, fake it. In other words, act toward them as if you're madly in love with them. Treat them as if they are the most special person in the whole world. Do those things for them that they thoroughly enjoy. Bless them in every way you can, do good to them, and pray for them. If you do these things, you may find, as the author of the letter did, that your perspective of your spouse will change, and you will see them with different eyes. Author Gary Thomas writes, "If you will start to see your spouse as God sees your spouse, if you will cultivate the affection God already has for the person to whom you're married, your relationship will never be the same."[9]

So perhaps the biggest change we need in our marriage is a change in ourselves. Eddie Espinosa wrote the song "Change My Heart, O God" and recalls in his own words the story behind the song:

The year was 1982. I had been a Christian since 1969, but I saw a lot of things in my life that needed to be discarded. I had slowly become very complacent. I acknowledged my complacency, and I prayed to the Lord, "The only way that I can follow you is for you to change my appetite, the things that draw me away. You must change my heart!"
. . .

Shortly thereafter I was in my car on the way to my work, feeling a desire to draw near to God and with the wrestling still going on in my heart. Suddenly, a melody and some words began to flood through my mind. As I stopped at a stop sign, I reached for something to write on. The first thing I found was a small piece of yellow paper, which, by the way, I still have, and began to write as rapidly as I could. It was like taking dictation. I wrote the words on the paper, and kept the melody in my mind.[10]

Espinoza wrote, "Change my heart, O God! May I be like you."[11] So often, we recognize that change is needed, but we fail to take the necessary steps to make that change happen. How do we put our desire into action—so that change is reflected in our day-to-day living?

CONSTANTLY CHANGING

As we said earlier, both husband and wife will change over the course of their lives. In fact, "biologists tell us that every seven years we have totally replaced all the cells in our bodies with new ones."[12] Our ideas, dreams, and hobbies evolve over the years: "While research shows that personality tendencies (like introversion/extroversion) remain fairly constant throughout our adult lives, we still do change."[13] Each of us is truly a work in progress.

In addition, as you go through the years, you will discover that various stages in life bring about a need for change. Things such as an unplanned pregnancy may cause an abrupt change in your life plans. Job offers in another part of the country may mean that relocation becomes a necessity. And the approach of your retirement years or failing health automatically brings about new discussions and transitions. Yes, life has a way of throwing curveballs (some expected and some unexpected), and we find ourselves in a constant state of change.

CHANGING OURSELVES

It's far too easy to point the finger at our spouse and point out all the areas where *they* need to change. After all, it's their problem, and therefore they are the one who needs to do the changing. But is it possible that, if we would change our hearts, our actions, and our attitudes, in the process, we would see them differently?

Ah, but here is where it gets tricky. You see, some changes are natural and occur without us even having to consciously make any attempts to change. Other changes, such as changing our hearts, our attitudes, or our behavior—well, that's a completely different story.

The story is told of a woman who went to see a very prominent divorce attorney. She was at the end of her rope and had decided to file for divorce. She told the lawyer that she wanted to pay back her husband for all the years of pain he had caused her and wanted to hurt him as deeply as possible with all the details in the divorce settlement.

The wise attorney replied, "Well, if you really want to hurt him deeply, here is what we will do. I want you to go home and do everything possible to shower your husband with attention. Cook his favorite meals, compliment him daily, tell him specific things you admire in him. Do this for the next three months. Then come back to see me, and I will have the divorce papers ready for you to deliver to him. After doing all that, he will be so deeply in love with you that those divorce papers will hurt him to his very core."

She decided that she liked that plan and could stand doing all those things (even if she didn't feel like it and even if he didn't deserve it) for the next three months. She had lived with him for all these years, so another three months to put her plan into action would be worth the end result of hurting him deeply.

Three months later, the attorney called and told the woman the divorce papers were ready to be picked up. She replied, "Are you kidding me? Why would I ever want to divorce this man? He is the best husband any woman could ever want. He is kind and considerate. I love him dearly. You can rip up those divorce papers."

You see, her loving actions toward him had changed her thinking. And it had also changed her husband. She realized that she had been focusing on all the negative and had failed to see all the good! Sometimes the person we need to change the most is ourselves.

Ellen Kreidman explains that you can create love every day by acting in a loving way and not worrying about whether you are feeling loving![14] You see, the woman in the story did not feel loving, yet she acted in a loving way. She made the decision to act loving, and her feelings soon followed the loving actions.

WHAT DOES THE BIBLE SAY ABOUT CHANGE?

The need to change ourselves is usually not something we are ready to admit. It's easier to look at others and make a list of everything they need to fix. If asked, we can whip out a list of things that our spouse needs to change. But if transforming our marriage begins with us, how do we initiate that process? What words of advice does Scripture have that will assist us in changing ourselves? Let's look at the passages we mentioned earlier and see how we can translate these verses into actions:

- "A new commandment I give to you, that you love one another; as I have loved you, that you also love one another" (John 13:34).
    o Practice loving actions, even if you do not feel very loving.
    o Love and appreciate your spouse!
- "But I say to you, love your enemies, bless those who curse you, do good to those who hate you, and pray for those who spitefully use you and persecute you" (Matthew 5:44).
    o Pray for your spouse by asking God to bless them.
    o Don't attempt to get back at them.
    o Remember that two wrongs never make a right.
    o Pray for your spouse's well-being.

- "For as he thinks in his heart, so is he" (Proverbs 23:7).
  - Identify what you focus on in your marriage.
  - Be aware that your thoughts will take root in your heart.
  - Make a list of all the positive traits your spouse has. How do they make a positive contribution to you and to your marriage?
- "He who earnestly seeks good finds favor, but trouble will come to him who seeks evil" (Proverbs 11:27).
  - Seek to find the good, and you will find it!
  - If you look for what is wrong, you will certainly find it.
  - Notice when your spouse does something nice and let them know.
- "Finally, brethren, whatever things are true, whatever things are noble, whatever things are just, whatever things are pure, whatever things are lovely, whatever things are of good report, if there is any virtue and if there is anything praiseworthy—meditate on these things" (Philippians 4:8).
  - Meditate on the positive, focus on that which is good. All too often, we find ourselves making a list of all the negatives in our spouse. Why not make a list of all the things that we appreciate and love?

God desires for your marriage not only to survive but also to thrive. Thriving begins as we practice the habit of asking God to convict us of where *we* need to change while looking for the positives in our spouse, praying for our spouse, and acting in ways that show our spouse they are loved and appreciated.

SMALL TWEAKS MAKE A BIG DIFFERENCE

Mom used to say, "Don't make a mountain out of a molehill." Don't make an issue bigger than it really is. Yet the opposite of that simple childhood admonishment is something that we often do in our marriages. If we stop to analyze our "issues," we may discover that they are not so big. It's true! Most marriage breakdowns are not caused by the *big* things. Of course, big things do happen—but overall, they are not the reason behind the majority of divorce cases. Instead, if we focused on changing the small things, we would see big returns in our marriages.

Shaunti Feldhahn, a leading researcher in relationships, discovered these simple things that can make a big difference:

1. *What a wife can do*: Look for things for which you can say, "Thank you." . . . Women wonder, *Does he really love me?* . . . Men wonder,

Does she really appreciate me? So your sincere appreciation for the little day-to-day things he does ("Thank you for changing the light-bulbs that were burnt out") makes your man feel, down deep, *She cares about me.*

2. *What a husband can do*: Reassure your wife that "we're okay" when you are displeased—especially if you have to pull away and get some space. Because most women have that subconscious question, *Would he choose me all over again?* some painful feelings are triggered in conflict. Saying, "I need some space for a few hours, but we're okay" reassures her.

3. *What both of you can do*: Whenever you are hurt by your spouse, look for the more generous explanation and act as if that is the real one—because it probably is. One of the most important things that the happiest spouses do differently is to refuse to believe the worst of their mate's intentions. If you think, *He knew how that would make me feel, and he said it anyway*, that translates to *He doesn't care*: and it's downhill from there. But more than 99 percent of people deeply care about their spouse—and a huge reason why some couples are struggling is that one or both partners doesn't believe it. Changing your assumption to *I know he loves me; he must not have known how that would make me feel* will make everything about your response different.[15]

Feldhahn goes on to encourage, "Yes, some marriages face problems that are extremely complex to solve, but those are rare. Most of the time, seeing that you can accomplish a great deal with a few simple changes will give you the hope that having a good marriage might not be so hard or complicated after all."[16]

WHAT NEEDS CHANGING?

We have talked about changing our focus. We have suggested that instead of focusing on what we want to change in our spouse, we should change our own behavior and attitude toward our mate. But also, we should look at what specific changes need to be made in our relationship so that our marriage will be healthier and stronger. Erin McDowell lists twenty positive changes you can make in your marriage (if you have been reading this book carefully, you will recognize them as concepts we have covered):

1. "Start focusing on what's right instead of just what's wrong in your relationship. . . .
2. Connect physically, even if it's as simple as a 30-second hug. . . .
3. Show appreciation for your partner. . . .

4. Have a weekly 'State of the Union' meeting. . . .
5. Don't leave the moment it gets tough. . . .
6. Get more sleep. . . .
7. Establish 'rituals of connection' that you know you can depend on. . . .
8. Remodel your house—in particular, your bedroom. . . .
9. Take note of your social media and phone use, and whether they may be negatively affecting your relationship. . . .
10. Befriend other couples. . . .
11. Make a conscious effort to have more fun together. . . .
12. Take the time to reminisce and laugh together. . . .
13. When giving feedback, take the blame out of your sentences. . . .
14. Avoid toxic behaviors when you're arguing. . . .
15. Take a breather when arguments get too heated. . . .
16. During an argument, empathize and apologize. . . .
17. Make sex and other forms of physical intimacy a priority. . . .
18. Seek professional help for your relationship struggles. . . .
19. Seek therapy and education for yourself, as well. . . .
20. Follow the golden rule and treat your partner how you would want to be treated."[17]

Lists like this one seem daunting, but if you focus on making just one change, you will see your relationship changing for the better. You're probably already doing some of these things to one degree or another. For now, make changes in the areas where you know things could be better. You can add other areas as you see changes happening. Since we have already dealt with most of these in previous chapters, we won't talk about them all again. Instead, let's focus on a few we have not covered elsewhere.

"Have a weekly 'State of the Union' meeting."

How about setting aside a regular time for a marriage checkup? Ask your spouse for feedback not only on what you're doing well as a couple but also where you could improve. If you do it on a weekly basis, it won't be seen as a "problem only" meeting. Quite often, McDowell points out, "people only receive 'feedback' from their partners in the midst of heated arguments," when it is said in a hurtful manner. Instead of leaving it for one of those moments, couples should plan to have a "State of the Union" meeting during a dispassionate moment "where they are both prepared to discuss in a noncombative way what's working in their relationship and what isn't."[18] It could also be very affirming to you and your relationship to know things are going well and that you may just need a few minor adjustments. It's better to find that out early instead of waiting until it becomes a full-blown problem.

Always start with words of appreciation for each other. Researchers John Gottman and Sybil Carrère "discovered that they could predict the likelihood of a couple's divorce by observing just the first three minutes of a conflict discussion." Evidently, the couples who ended up divorced "started their discussions with a great deal of negative emotion and displayed far fewer expressions of positivity than those who stayed together six years later." The couples who ended up getting divorced were negative and critical toward the other person. The research also "revealed that those discussions will end on the same note they begin." It is always better to begin with what Gottman and Carrère call a "soft start-up." As they explain, "A soft start-up, at its most basic function, serves to protect both you and your partner from feeling either attacked or defensive. It's a proven way to bring up a legitimate disagreement, concern, issue, complaint, or need without blaming your partner or judging their character."[19]

As a reminder, begin the conversation with words of appreciation for each other. Don't immediately follow that up with *but*, because it will simply cancel out everything nice you have just said about your spouse. You may complain, but don't blame. Make statements that start with *I* instead of *you*. Be polite and appreciative, and don't store things up.

"Don't leave the moment it gets tough."

According to McDowell, most couples tend to show a decline in marital satisfaction after the "honeymoon phase" is over, but a research study also indicates that after the twenty-year mark, many marriages have improved. Couples in the study experienced "an increase in shared activities such as recreational activities, eating dinner, or visiting friends together."[20] Similarly, Linda Waite and her colleagues conducted research to determine if "unhappy spouses who divorced reap significant psychological and emotional benefits." Their surprising discovery was that they did not. One of the surprising conclusions of their study was that "two out of three unhappily married adults who avoided divorce or separation ended up happily married five years later. Just one out of five unhappy spouses who divorced or separated had happily remarried within the same period."[21]

The point is that some couples give up on their marriages too soon. If they would just make a few adjustments and seek professional help, they could live happily together until death separates them. The grass may look greener on the other side of the marital fence, but many find that once they are on that side, the first side was better. Don't leave your marriage when things get tough. Fight for your marriage until it becomes the satisfying one you desire.

"Get more sleep."

Couples who don't get enough sleep tend to be more tired, cranky, and argumentative, and they "experience more unhappiness in their relationship," says McDowell. She cites one study conducted by leaders at several renowned universities, in which the researchers concluded that " 'when both partners slept less, couples interacted in a more hostile way than when at least one partner slept more.' "[22]

One of the reasons some couples don't get enough sleep is because they have a television set in their bedroom. Journalist Joshua Becker writes, "Removing the television from your bedroom results in more sleep and better sleep." He goes on to list seventeen other benefits he and his family experienced whey they removed the television set from their bedroom as a thirty-day experiment. Among other things Becker and his wife discovered were that they had more conversation, they had better sex, they were exposed to fewer advertisements at their weakest moments, they spent more time reading, and they usually went to bed at the same time. Becker continues, "Children with televisions in their bedrooms score lower on school tests and are more likely to have sleep problems. Also, having a television in the bedroom is strongly associated with being overweight and a higher risk for smoking."[23] So, your marriage benefits, your children benefit, and your family benefits by not having televisions (or any technology) in the bedrooms.

"Establish 'rituals of connection' that you know you can depend on."

Those rituals of connection could be as simple as sitting down to enjoy breakfast together—at the table—before leaving for work. Spending those few moments in the morning to talk about what's scheduled for the day, what the other has planned, the people you each will meet, and other day-to-day topics can be a good way to connect and keep each other in mind throughout the day. Plan to sit down again for dinner to review the events of the day and talk about the future. Share feelings and concerns, joys and challenges. Have a weekly date or simply cuddle each night for a few minutes. The point of establishing those rituals is to set that regular pattern of connectivity so that other things don't interrupt your time together.

"Remodel your house—in particular, your bedroom."

McDowell points out something interesting: "A recent survey by Porch found that couples who remodeled their homes had an increase in marital satisfaction, particularly if they chose to make-over their bedroom."[24] We get so used to things being the same that we become complacent. Perhaps a small change, such as a fresh coat of paint or different pictures on the wall could be a refreshing change. It doesn't have to be a major, dramatic change, and you may not have to do it all yourselves either. Sometimes just simply moving some pieces of furniture around is all you need to bring a new freshness to your life.

"Befriend other couples."
Friendships are not forced but develop naturally. Sometimes, however, we do need to go out of our comfort zone a little and reach out to others. Perhaps you can invite another couple to go for a walk or come to a cookout in your backyard. Don't try to make it fancy and complicated; rather, make it relaxing and comfortable. The point is to enjoy your time together, not to do something to impress the other couple with who you are or what you have.

"Take the time to reminisce and laugh together."
A study conducted by the *Journal of Social and Personal Relationships* found that couples who took part in exciting activities together, such as doing physical activities or trying something new, were happier than those who simply engaged in pleasant activities, such as eating dinner together or watching a movie.[25] That's not to say that having dinner together is not a positive experience, but sometimes we need something a little more active and out of the ordinary.

"Follow the golden rule and treat your partner how you would want to be treated."
When we think of the golden rule, we usually think of other people. We want to treat others as we would like to be treated. But we don't always make that application to our spouse. McDowell quotes counselor Kristen Scarlett, who poses some important questions: " 'Are you treating your partner as you would want to be treated? Or as you would treat your best friend? Are you showing him/her respect? Are you really listening? Are you stating your own needs and asking what they need? Taking inventory is an excellent first step in making improvements.' "[26]

CONCLUSION
If it is clear that some things must change in your marriage, try starting with yourself rather than focusing immediately on all the ways in which your partner could change. You may be surprised by the power that changing *your* attitude, your perspective, and your behavior has on influencing your feelings about the relationship. You may also be surprised at the impact it has on indirectly "changing" your partner.

Changing ourselves sets off a chain reaction that enables us to see the good in the other person. It transforms not only us, but it also transforms the other person into a beautiful creation. The chain reaction effect kicks in as the contagion spreads to your mate, and they, in turn, begin to reciprocate. If you truly desire to make a change that will have a lifelong impact on your marriage, focus on the little things, such as making her feel loved and making him feel appreciated.

If you are now at the point of admitting that change is needed in your marriage, you can respond by either resigning yourself to a marginal marriage by trying to change your spouse, or you can partner with God to change yourself. After being married for thirty-eight years, we can tell you that partnering with God to change yourself always yields the best results.

---

1. Lauri Przybysz, "Changing Your Spouse—and Yourself," For Your Marriage, accessed August 18, 2020, https://www.foryourmarriage.org/changing-your-partner-and-yourself/.

2. "Psychotherapy," National Alliance on Mental Illness, accessed August 17, 2020, https://www.nami.org/About-Mental-Illness/Treatments/Psychotherapy#:~:text=Cognitive%20behavioral%20therapy%20(CBT)%20focuses,self%2Ddestructive%20behaviors%20and%20beliefs.

3. Adventist Wellness Center, "The Five-Day Plan to Quit Smoking," accessed August 18, 2020, https://www.adventistwellnesscenter.com/uploads/6/4/2/5/6425808/five_day_plan_to_stop_smoking.pdf.

4. Amy Cuddy, "Your Body Language May Shape Who You Are," filmed June 2012 in Edinburgh, Scotland, TED video, 20:47, https://www.ted.com/talks/amy_cuddy_your_body_language_may_shape_who_you_are#t-8082.

5. Karen Kleiman, "Try Some Smile Therapy," Psychology Today, August 1, 2012, https://www.psychologytoday.com/us/blog/isnt-what-i-expected/201208/try-some-smile-therapy.

6. Kleiman, "Try Some Smile Therapy."

7. Catharine Paddock, "Smiling Reduces Stress and Helps the Heart," Medical News Today, August 1, 2012, https://www.medicalnewstoday.com/articles/248433#1.

8. Cuddy, "Your Body Language."

9. Gary Thomas, A Lifelong Love (Colorado Springs, CO: David C. Cook, 2014), 33.

10. Lindsay Terry, "Story Behind the Song: 'Change My Heart, O God,'" St. Augustine Record, November 19, 2016, https://www.staugustine.com/living-religion/2016-11-19/story-behind-song-change-my-heart-o-god.

11. Terry, "Story Behind the Song."

12. Przybysz, "Changing Your Spouse."

13. Przybysz, "Changing Your Spouse."

14. Ellen Kreidman, The 10 Second Kiss (New York: Dell, 1998).

15. Shaunti Feldhahn, "Small Changes Make Big Differences," Shaunti Feldhahn, June 26, 2014, https://shaunti.com/2014/06/marriage-month-daily-tip-13-small-changes/. This quotation has been edited for clarity and style.

16. Feldhahn, "Small Changes."

17. Erin McDowell, "20 Positive Changes to Make in Your Marriage, According to Experts," Insider, July 18, 2020, https://www.insider.com/changes-to-make-in-your-marriage-according-to-experts.

18. McDowell, "20 Positive Changes."

19. Ellie Lisitsa, "How to Fight Smarter: Soften Your Start-Up," The Gottman Institute, March 15, 2013, https://www.gottman.com/blog/softening-startup/.

20. McDowell, "20 Positive Changes."

21. Linda Waite et al., *Does Divorce Make People Happy? Findings From a Study of Unhappy Marriages* (New York: Institute for American Values, 2002), 4, 5.

22. McDowell, "20 Positive Changes."

23. Joshua Becker, "18 Good Reasons to Get the TV Out of Your Bedroom," Becoming Minimalist, accessed August 18, 2020, https://www.becomingminimalist.com/18-darn-good-reasons-to-get-the-tv-out-of-the-bedroom/.

24. McDowell, "20 Positive Changes."

25. Charlotte Reissman, Arthur Aron, and Merlynn R. Bergen, "Shared Activities and Marital Satisfaction: Causal Direction and Self-Expansion Versus Boredom," *Journal of Social and Personal Relationships* 10, no. 2 (May 1, 1993): 243–254, https://doi.org/10.1177/026540759301000205.

26. Kristen Scarlett, quoted in Erin McDowell, "20 Positive Changes to Make in Your Marriage, According to Experts," Insider, July 18, 2020, https://www.insider.com/changes-to-make-in-your-marriage-according-to-experts.

Chapter Eleven

Gray and Stay

*God made husbands and wives to become one body and one spirit
for his purpose—so they would have children who are true to God.
So be careful, and do not break your promise
to the wife you married when you were young.*
—Malachi 2:15, NCV

President Ronald and Nancy Reagan left a lasting testament to the world of a love that stood the test of time. At a luncheon in Nancy Reagan's honor in 1988, Ronald Reagan stood up and made a speech to express his love and appreciation to his wife. Theirs was a love story spanning half a century, and the affection of this classic American couple comes alive as you read the words President Reagan spoke in honor of his First Lady: "What do you say about someone who gives your life meaning? What do you say about someone who's always there with support and understanding, someone who makes sacrifices so that your life will be easier and more successful? Well, what you say is that you love that person and treasure her."[1]

Love like this is what most of us dream of when we are young. Perhaps we saw such a relationship in the lives of our grandparents or our parents. We watched and were amazed at how much they were alike, how they completed each other's sentences, how they laughed as they remembered something from the past, how they held hands, and how they looked at each other with such love.

Our parents didn't live together to a ripe old age. Unfortunately, my (Claudio's) father died of a heart attack at the age of fifty-one and after only twenty-eight years of marriage. And my (Pam's) father died from brain cancer at the age of sixty-three after thirty-seven years of marriage. Both our parents' marriages ended only with the death of our fathers. Of course, their deaths filled us with sadness. However, at the same time, our parents taught us a lesson of commitment to each other, to their marriages, and to their families until they took their last breaths.

Unfortunately, this is not the case with everyone today, as there is an emerging trend of people late in life whose marriages are ending—not because one of the spouses dies but because they have chosen to end it through divorce. In fact, there's a term that has been coined for this trend: gray divorce. What is gray divorce? The term *gray* refers to the color of the hair of the older people who are divorcing after being married for many years. "Gray divorce refers to divorces involving spouses who are older than fifty years of age and therefore are typically members of the Baby Boomer generation. Even though the overall divorce rate has declined over the past 20 years, it has doubled for the segment of the population over age fifty."[2]

REASONS FOR GRAY DIVORCE

Why would a couple who have invested the larger part of their life in growing a family and building a future together decide to divorce? At a time when their future is more secure, and they have so much to lose, why give it all up? When they can play such an important role in the physical and spiritual growth of their grandchildren, why send such a negative message about marriage? Marguerita Cheng writes that there may be several reasons why people in their golden years of life choose to leave the marriage and why gray divorce seems to be increasing (the final two reasons are our own):

1. *Financial management.* All your life, you have worked hard, saved, invested, and planned for your retirement. Now you reach the golden years and find out there isn't enough to live comfortably. Perhaps you didn't save enough, or you or your spouse have not been careful about how you spend money, but the fact remains that you may have to continue working or work at least part-time to supplement what you receive from the government or your retirement account. The dreams of traveling, visiting the children and grandchildren, are all gone.

   As Cheng explains, "Financial matters are the primary issues that arise during a grey divorce. . . . Couples who struggle with debt or constantly fight about finances often end up divorcing." Perhaps one of the spouses has been the primary breadwinner and has been the one to make the financial decisions for the family. They may resent having all of the burden on them throughout the years, and their spouse may resent not having much of a say in how the money is spent. Ironically, how much husbands and wives make can adversely affect their relationship. Cheng further explains, "Research has shown that marriage grows stronger when the husband increases his earnings; conversely, the marriage more often fails if the wife's earnings increase."

2. *Growing apart.* Many couples focus a lot of their attention on raising their children—so much so that they neglect their relationship. Once the children leave the nest, they find themselves with very little else in common. They find themselves legally together but emotionally far apart. It is as if the glue that kept them together has dried up, the spark they once had is gone, and they find no good reason for staying together in a lifeless, loveless marriage.

3. *Infidelity.* With easy access to technology, many older people are initiating or maintaining illicit relationships without even leaving their homes. Unfortunately, many of these relationships continue to develop and end up in emotional and physical affairs. There are dating sites that cater to married people wanting to hook up with temporary sexual partners. "Older men may start finding younger women attractive," Cheng says. "The same could apply to older women who are attracted to younger men." Yes, technology is a contributing factor to gray divorce.

4. *Better health and life expectancy rates.* You would think that the fact we are living longer would be exciting news. But Cheng explains, "Older people have stopped shying away from the idea of divorce after drifting away from their partners because they still believe they can find happiness." She adds that marriages may suffer when spouses find themselves in different states of health in their senior years: "Access to great health care and the availability of activities to keep an individual mentally, physically, and psychologically active have encouraged people to seek partners who suit their interests and attitudes when their marriage partner has failed to stay healthy, fit and active."

5. *Addictions.* While we may think that having an affair is the only form of unfaithfulness, addictions are too. Cheng observes, "An individual could be addicted to drugs, alcohol, gambling, or pornography, and these addictions might derail a marriage." As an example, Cheng describes spouses who "bet and lose all their assets and must start from scratch because they choose to gamble instead of providing for their future and family." That can strain a relationship to the breaking point.[3]

6. *Postponed divorces.* In some marriages, one or both spouses are not happy in their relationship but have decided to remain in it for the sake of their children, because it is more financially advantageous, or because they would be embarrassed to tell their family or church. When these circumstances change (e.g., when their children leave home, when they stop attending church), it encourages them to take the step of seeking a divorce.

7. *Retirement.* Some couples, having both worked all their life separately and having spent large portions of their time apart, suddenly find themselves spending most of their time together and don't know how to navigate those troubled waters. For many couples, retirement is what they have been looking forward to and preparing for; but for others, retirement becomes unbearable, so they choose to go their separate ways.

A BIT OF GOOD NEWS

Although we listed some of the reasons why a couple that's been married for many years chooses to end the marriage in divorce, there may be others. The good news is that the divorce rate is still not all that high for those over the age of fifty. While divorce has doubled over the past thirty years, and the rate has risen much more dramatically for gray Americans than for those under fifty, the divorce rate for those over fifty is still half the rate of those under fifty.

GRAY DIVORCE'S FALLOUT

Elsewhere in this book, we told you that the best gift you can give your children is your marriage. Children of divorce are the most disadvantaged in every way—socially, spiritually, financially, educationally, and the list goes on. When we make such statements, people think that the only ones who may suffer the repercussions their parents divorce are young children. However, even adult children experience a great loss when their parents divorce. Cheng writes, "The process of adapting to the change in family dynamics can be difficult. The children are accustomed to a single-family unit, and they now must deal with a split family. Children may be trapped between their [parents'] feuds and may be forced to take sides, which is not very pleasant. Older children have problems adapting to their parent's dating life or the new family they choose to start."[4]

Adult children must adapt to a new reality, which can be excruciatingly painful for many years. As Kathy McCoy explains, "Adult daughters may tend to blame fathers for a gray divorce, and . . . changing family dynamics—like newly divorced mothers becoming more dependent on their children—can also negatively impact parent and adult child relationships."[5]

The financial aftermath of gray divorce can also have lasting consequences: "Dividing property that was accumulated during the marriage can be complicated because life insurance policies, Social Security benefits, investments, and retirement benefits must be considered."[6]

After the death of their former spouse, those who divorce later in life may experience long, lingering grief. And even though they didn't consider going back to their former spouse, the grief of lost memories and unfinished history together may go on for a long time.

AN OUNCE OF PREVENTION IS WORTH A POUND OF CURE

Benjamin Franklin's axiom "An ounce of prevention is worth a pound of cure" is as good today as it was then, particularly when it comes to gray divorce. According to McCoy, "The biggest risk factor for gray divorce is not a life transition (like an empty nest), but one's marital past. According to a recent study, those who have been divorced before are more likely to divorce again, and those in marriages of shorter duration are more likely to divorce."[7]

One of the reasons we wrote this book was to help couples enjoy a happy marriage until death parts them. We pray that the principles presented in these pages may help prevent decisions that could destroy a lifetime of memories as you enter this "graying" time of life. An ounce of prevention today will be better than a ton of sorrow later.

Naomi Cahn and June Carbone writes about several studies: "They found that several factors were related to staying married. Couples who owned property together were less likely to divorce. And wealthy couples had a higher probability of staying together. . . . 'Financial security' was a 'protective factor' against a later-in-life divorce." Cahn and Carbone quote the research, saying, "The odds of divorce were roughly 38 percent lower for those with over $250,000 in assets compared with couples whose assets ranged from $0 to 50,000."[8] Practice good stewardship and financial principles now, so this does not become a reason for the demise of your marriage.

What can you do to prevent becoming another statistic in the rising number of gray divorces? Now that the kids are gone, it is important that you and your spouse are willing to share new interests and embrace each other's hobbies. Even if it's an activity or hobby that you have never tried before, why not give it a chance?

While we still long to have that romantic spark, what is most important in the long haul is to cultivate a true friendship with each other. Think about it—after retirement, you will be spending more time together. If you don't enjoy spending time together now, it will be even harder to do for extended periods every day!

In happy, healthy, successful long-term relationships, remembering the "little things" can make all the difference in the world. These are spouses that help each other with small, routine things, who show appreciation, and add occasional surprises keep their relationship fresh and their love blooming.

Don't forget that healthy older couples do, in fact, have active sex lives! And they also value being in good shape physically. So even if you have physical challenges that prevent you from the same physical intimacy you were once able to enjoy, include the simple pleasures of touch in your daily repertoire.

Remember that complimenting your spouse regularly and showing your appreciation for their presence in your life continues to make deposits in their emotional Love Bank. Everyone wants and needs to feel that they are valued and loved—particularly by those closest to them.

Also, keep in mind that even old cars need an occasional tune-up. Even if you don't have any presenting issues or problems, going to a couples' retreat or scheduling a few couples' counseling sessions can enhance your relationship and prevent future problems.

While you may think everything's going well in your marriage, make sure your spouse is doing OK—even if you don't see a problem. Instead of assuming all's well, why not ask them? It's better to know so you can take steps to fix the problem than to ignore it and let it wreak havoc when you least expect it.

Think about it from a different angle: Throughout your married life, you have been putting out many fires—births, deaths, debts, jobs, illnesses, and so on. You have now reached an age where a lot of those fires have been put out and are in the past. Why not stoke the fire between the two of you that may have started to go out? Don't wait until after the kids are gone and you two are all alone. Do it now while the embers are still burning, while you have things holding your relationship together.

It seems that as we get older, we stop thinking too far into the future. True, most of our life may be behind us, but that doesn't mean we have to stop living today or planning for tomorrow. Sit down and have a real conversation about what you expect for the next ten or twenty years. Not many newlyweds have such a conversation (though they should). But you are older and more mature, so spend some time thinking, dreaming, and planning for your future together.

STRENGTHENING YOUR RELATIONSHIP NOW

Throughout this book, we have said several times that love is not only a feeling but also a decision. It's a conscious decision we make. So how can we ensure that we make the right decision—to stay together until death do us part? How can you make sure you don't add to the rising number of couples going through gray divorce? Scott Means suggests three simple actions that could potentially reduce the risk of your marriage becoming part of that dreadful statistic later in life:

1. *Recommit to your marriage's higher purpose.* Remember that marriage is not just about you and your own happiness. Marriage is not just about love, although we hope that is a big component. But marriage serves a higher purpose in God's plan of salvation. It is intended to help each partner prepare for the second coming of

Jesus (please review the section titled "The Purpose of Marriage" in chapter 1). We've also said that your marriage is the best gift you can give your children. It is through your commitment to each other and to your kids that they learn the same lesson and can make the same decision. Remember that marriage is not just a legal union but a covenant—a covenant between you, your spouse, and God. What does breaking that covenant teach your children, your grandchildren, and others?

Perhaps you can have a ceremony to recommit to your wedding vows. Make it a special celebration and invite your children and grandchildren to serve as the witnesses of that recommitment. The message you will be sending them is one of love, security, and permanence.

2. *Realize that marriage is not all about you.* Those on the verge of divorce have, at times, asked us, "Don't I have the right to be happy?" Happiness is not a right, something we are entitled to. It, too, is a choice. Yes, some circumstances may knock us down; but we can choose how we react to those events. For us, the better question is: What about your kids? They didn't choose to be born into this world, into your family. You owe it to them to give them the warmth and stability of the home. Means suggests we ask ourselves several questions we're not naturally inclined to ask:

   • "Instead of asking, 'What's in it for me?' ask, 'How can I bless you?' "
   • "Instead of asking, 'What are my rights?' ask, 'What is the right thing?' "
   • "Instead of asking, 'What will advance my cause?' ask, 'What will enhance my marriage?' "
   • "Instead of asking, 'What can I get?' ask, 'What can I give?' "

3. *Every day, choose to make your marriage a high priority.* Again, this is a choice you can make. But perhaps you have taken each other for granted and have grown apart, one day at a time. Like the frog in the kettle, the water in which you have been swimming got hot a little at a time, without your realizing it. Or perhaps you have been so focused on your career that you neglected to plan for your future together. Then again, perhaps you have been so focused on your children that you've failed to nurture the bedrock of your family— your marriage. So, now, while you still have time to turn this ship

around, as it heads toward the rocks of disaster, choose to make your marriage a high priority.[9]

CONCLUSION

Solomon and his bride progressed through their relationship, from dreamy infatuation to love and marriage, through the difficulties and challenges of married life to the joys of passion and intimacy. As the Song of Solomon comes to a close, his wife tells him,

> Set me as a seal upon your heart,
> As a seal upon your arm;
> For love is as strong as death,
> Jealousy as cruel as the grave;
> Its flames are flames of fire,
> A most vehement flame.
>
> Many waters cannot quench love,
> Nor can the floods drown it.
> If a man would give for love
> All the wealth of his house,
> It would be utterly despised (Song of Solomon 8:6, 7).

As this couple reaches their latter days of love and marriage, they understand the value of that lifetime commitment. It is a covenant (a seal on their heart), a love stronger than death, a fire that no water can quench. We pray that as you near, or reach, the latter stage of your marriage, your love and commitment may shine brightly.

---

1. "Remarks at a Luncheon Honoring Nancy Reagan at the Republican National Convention in New Orleans, Louisiana," August 15, 1988, *Public Papers of the President of the United States*, vol. 2, *Ronald Reagan* (Washington, DC: United States Government Printing Office, 1991), 1079.

2. Jo Craven McGinty, "The Divorce Rate Is at a 40-Year Low, Unless You're 55 or Older," *Wall Street Journal*, June 21, 2019, https://www.wsj.com/articles/the-divorce-rate-is-at-a-40-year-low-unless-youre-55-or-older-11561116601.

3. Marguerita Cheng, "Grey Divorce: Its Reasons and Its Implications," *Forbes*, February 26, 2019, https://www.forbes.com/sites/margueritacheng/2019/02/26/grey-divorce-its-reasons-its-implications/#273b7a434acd.

4. Cheng, "Grey Divorce."

5. Kathy McCoy, "7 Key Facts About Divorce After Long Marriages," *Psychology Today*, September 25, 2018, https://www.psychologytoday.com/us/blog/complicated-love/201809/7-key-facts-about-divorce-after-long-marriages.

6. Cheng, "Grey Divorce."

7. McCoy, "7 Key Facts."

8. Naomi Cahn and June Carbone, "Who Is at Risk for a Gray Divorce? It Depends," Institute for Family Studies, May 1, 2017, https://ifstudies.org/blog/who-is-at-risk-for-a-gray-divorce-it-depends.

9. Scott Means, "3 Ways to Avoid 'Gray Divorce,'" YourTango, July 31, 2012, https://www.yourtango.com/2012158038/3-ways-avoid-gray-divorce.

Chapter Twelve

The Second (or Third) Time Around

This I recall to my mind,
Therefore I have hope.
Through the LORD's mercies we are not consumed,
Because His compassions fail not.
They are new every morning;
Great is Your faithfulness.

—Lamentations 3:21–23

There are many reasons why you may find yourself in a second (or even a third) marriage. Some of the reasons may have been out of your control and due to no conscious choice on your part, such as the death of your former spouse or adultery or abandonment on their part. Perhaps you walked away from your marriage because you were in an abusive situation or for a plethora of other reasons. In some cases, only you, your spouse, and God know the reasons. But whatever the reason, here you are! And the important thing now is to work on your current marriage and make of it what God intended.

IS A SECOND MARRIAGE DOOMED TO FAILURE?

You will not have to search the internet very long to discover the gloom and doom related to second marriages. But don't believe everything you read. Most internet sources state that you have a 60–70 percent chance of ending up in a divorce. Wow! That's not only discouraging—it's also *false*. Shaunti Feldhahn, a leading researcher in this area, spent eight years delving deep into all the marriage and divorce data. She writes the following:

> I discovered that the sources routinely quoted for the "60/70 percent of second marriages end in divorce" stat don't exist. The truth isn't perfect, but it *is* much better: according to the Census Bureau (2009), 65 percent of women are still married to their second spouse—and the 35 percent who aren't, includes widows! So, when you really boil it

down, probably closer to 30 percent of second marriages have ended in divorce.

Of course, any amount of divorce is too high, but you need to shift your thinking to realize that if you're entering into a second marriage, it would be unusual if you didn't make it.[1]

Did you get that? That high statistic that we always hear quoted about second marriages failing and ending in divorce is simply not based on fact. It is an urban legend. We hear it so often that it has become commonly believed to be true. Perhaps we have even repeated it to ourselves and others. However, your chance of success is high, and it's higher yet if you commit your second marriage to God. That is not just good news; it is great news!

STUMBLING BLOCKS OR STEPPING-STONES

Many who have gotten married for the second or third time will tell you it was the right choice for them. Brittany Wong interviewed ten couples to ask them to share why they consider their second marriage good, perhaps even better than the first one. Mind you, we are not believers in divorce, except in some special cases, which we have mentioned several times throughout this book. We believe in the permanence of marriage as God intended it. In fact, we wonder if the couples Wong interviewed, and all couples, had taken their own words seriously, whether they might have been able to improve their first marriage—but that is all in hindsight. We include their responses for those whose marriage ended, perhaps as a result of the death of their spouse, because they left an abusive relationship, or because their spouse chose to end their relationship, and they now find themselves afraid of taking this important step again.

For those who had a good first marriage, it doesn't mean you will forget your first spouse. The ideal would be that you were blessed with a good first spouse and now are also blessed with a good second spouse. For many, the second time around is better. Here are the reasons given by these ten couples as to why they feel their second relationship is even better than the first:

1. *"You're not looking for someone to complete you."* Perhaps youth, immaturity, or an idealistic view of marriage had led you to believe that the person you were marrying would meet all your needs and complete you. That is to say that being single, you were incomplete. As one of the responders in Wong's article said, "Now I know that it takes work, sacrifice, perseverance and a *major* sense of humor." Perhaps with experience and maturity, you come to understand that you need to be you, and you need to be happy and content with who

you are instead of trying to find a person to make you happy and make you whole. As another respondent stated, "Be yourself while looking for love again. So many women change themselves into the woman they think a guy wants them to be. Be you and you'll find the right person."

2. *"You know that you can't change your spouse."* Because so many go into marriage with an idealistic view of how their spouse should be, they may try to change them into that image from the moment they say, "I do." After being married for some time, they realize that the person they married is who they are, like it or not. With a second marriage, you may have a more realistic view and may not go into marriage with the hope of changing your spouse. As another of Wong's interviewees explained, "My second marriage is infinitely better because I am not looking to change my spouse (and there are no illusions that he could change me). It's so refreshing to be in a relationship where I know who I am, he knows who he is, we accept and love each other for who we are—faults and all."

3. *"Authenticity and honesty come a little more naturally."* Some people try to maintain a personal facade, or they are protective of themselves, which keeps them from being completely transparent, honest, and vulnerable with others. Here's how one interviewee put it: "If I hadn't had the disastrous first marriage, there's no way I'd be as patient, sympathetic, motivated or as levelheaded as I am now in my second marriage. It's my most deep and honest relationship. That transparency has encouraged my current husband [to] be honest about his needs as well."

4. *"Marriage #1 has changed you for the better."* While we should not enter marriage expecting to change our spouse, we should go in willing to make accommodations and compromises in our relationship with them. What we often learn after being married for several years is that we have changed, hopefully for the better. I (Claudio) believe that I am much more patient and mellow that I used to be. I am not yet where I should be, but I have come a long way thanks to a very patient, tolerant, and forgiving trio of women in my life. Some people don't come to realize that until they are in their second or third marriage. One of the couples interviewed by Wong offered some great advice: "If you're looking to remarry, forgive yourself and forgive your ex—our failed marriage was 50 percent your doing and 50 percent your ex's. Forgive, find inner peace and let it *go*. You deserve happiness, love and a second chance."

5. *"You know what marriage is really like, warts and all."* People who have never been married before bring into their relationship a certain amount of idealistic distortion, looking at their spouse and their marriage through rose-colored glasses. After the honeymoon is over and day-to-day life removes the scales from their eyes, they may begin to see the reality of marriage. They learn that being married to someone they love and who loves them is wonderful but not necessarily a bed of roses. Perhaps the bed of roses still has some prickly thorns. The second time around, people usually come into the marriage with a more realistic view and are better prepared to deal with the differences between them. One of the couples in the article explains that on their (second) wedding day, "the air was heavy, it seemed like there was so much more to lose. But it was also brimming with the magic that comes with second chances. I guess it feels heavier because we know things the second time around. Good things and bad things. But we also know what works and what makes it better. We have grown. We made our vows to each other in the voice of the people we are, not the people we want to try to be."

6. *"With age—and a tough divorce—comes great wisdom."* Many people marry so young that, before they have had a chance to mature and experience life, they often make decisions based on feelings alone. But age and maturity help them appreciate so much more in life that, the second time around, they may be able to base their decisions less on feelings and more on solid reasoning. It does not mean that they will have no feelings, being solely pragmatic or ignoring their emotions, but that they will not rely primarily on them. Again, one of the spouses interviewed talked about her own experience: "In the aftermath of my divorce, I had the opportunity to look very carefully at the man I chose the first time and how I had changed since I had met him ten years prior. I looked at the mistakes I made and our incompatibilities because I was determined that I would not make the same mistakes again. I know for sure that I appreciate my second husband much more because of what I went through with the first one; it was a life lesson."

7. *"You realize that marriage is a choice you have to make every single day."* Having lived through one good marriage—or a failed relationship—hopefully makes you very intentional about making sure you do it just as well—or better—the second time around. Here's a very good insight from a second-time-around spouse: "A second marriage is an eyes-wide-open experience; you know what kinds of work are involved

and say 'yes' anyway. Plus, you endured a worst-case scenario and not just survived, but thrived! A second marriage means you've let go of the 'perfect spouse' ideal, embraced your imperfections and found the unique 'must haves' you need in a life partner."

8. *"You know what you want."* At an early age, we may have had a long list of things we wanted in a spouse, and much of that list may have been external attributes (their looks, their voice, and so on) and not the deepest internal qualities (such as compassion, commitment, and others). Being married for some time, we begin to notice and appreciate more of the qualities that really matter. A second-time-around husband told Wong, "Divorce teaches you that you can be content by yourself and that it's not worth going forward with something if you're hesitant. I never thought I would marry again or have any more kids, but I met my current wife and fell madly in love with her. There is nothing I am hesitant about anymore, except being away from her for too long!"

9. *"You've taken ownership of what you did wrong the first time around."* For those of you whose first marriage has ended, hopefully you have taken the time to carefully examine what happened and how you may have contributed to the relationship's demise. In some cases, you may have been the victim of a manipulative, controlling, or abusive spouse, for which you can't be held responsible. But in most cases, both spouses are responsible for at least part of what caused the end of their marriage. Taking ownership of your part helps you forgive both your ex-spouse and yourself and make appropriate changes the second time around—so that you don't repeat the same mistakes. One of Wong's interviewees explained it this way: "Nobody goes into their first marriages thinking they're going to get divorced. But it happens. So if you are brave enough to try again, marriage is only better the second time around if you learn from your earlier mistakes. Both partners are older and, hopefully, wiser. And both know what they need from each other and what to do to make the relationship work."

10. *"You're incredibly picky—and that's a good thing."* Perhaps a better description is that you are much more careful and cautious the second time around. Again, if you had a good first marriage, you want to do it right the second time around as well. If your first marriage ended in divorce, you will want to make sure this one stands the test of time. That's why taking some time before embarking on a new relationship is wise. As one of the couples interviewed advised, "Learn how to live without a partner and figure what you need from your next-time

partner in that time. Marriage *is* better the second time around."[2]

GETTING MARRIED AGAIN (FOR THE LAST TIME)

If you are married for the second (or third) time around, the best thing you can do now is to consider this marriage permanent and irreversible. In other words, make the decision that this will be the last time you marry because this one is forever. Here are the reasons why:

- *You will be more likely to work through challenges.* Deciding before-hand that this marriage is forever makes you more likely to work through the tough times and solve problems. You will have rough patches, but when you have the attitude that divorce is not an option, then you learn to manage conflict and deal with those rough patches.
- *It creates a sense of success.* Permanence in marriage helps you create a sense of success in your relationship and identity. The failure of your previous marriage may have left you feeling alone, discouraged, and with a sense of failure. Knowing that this one will last a lifetime brings a sense of security you may not have felt before.
- *You will be a positive example for your children.* Marriage for a life-time establishes a powerful example for your children and family. Your children have experienced a loss and may or may not have witnessed a Christ-centered marriage. Now you have another oppor-tunity to change that and show them one.

Perhaps husband-and-wife authors David and Lisa Frisbie summarize the remarriage commitment best in *Happily Remarried*:

> When a husband and wife insist their remarriage is permanent and irreversible, they have taken an important step toward longevity and faithfulness. Knowing that each partner is committed, come what may, helps each person feel safer and more secure.
> For those who have experienced the dissolution of a prior marriage, it is vitally important to reconnect with the " 'til death do us part" dimension of the commitment. When both members of a remarriage understand there is no escape clause—no way out, no option other than staying together—a powerful and positive signal is received in the subconscious mind of each partner.[3]

BLENDING THE FAMILIES

What is a blended family? According to the Sociology Dictionary, it is "a family consisting of two or more adult partners and their children together with their children from previous relationships either living with them or nearby."[4] We also use the term *stepfamily* to describe these relationships.

Also, according to the preceding definition, stepfamilies come about not only from previous marriages. Many have had children without ever getting married, so a stepfamily can often happen in a legal first marriage because of children previously born or adopted.

The blender is used frequently in our home. We use it to make smoothies, blending ingredients together so that they become a smooth mixture with all the fruit blending together as one. Blending families is not always so smooth. The process of blending a family is not quite as easy as pushing a button on the mixer. In fact, maybe we should not view this process as being in a blender, because each individual that makes up the stepfamily as a whole still maintains their individuality. Blending, in this case, is the process of living and working together as a family unit.

WHAT'S YOUR COOKING STYLE?

One of the most recognized experts in the area of blending families, Ron Deal, describes the process some stepfamilies use as they bring together the different ingredients in their home (adults and children) to "cook" their family. He uses the image of various cooking methods used to mix ingredients:

1. *The blender.* As mentioned earlier, we like to throw all of the ingredients into a blender, and the expected result is a smooth mixture. Probably the most common term used today for stepfamilies is *blended families*, but that term assumes that the process of blending is done or completed. As Deal explains, "Those of us who specialize in stepfamily therapy and education do not use the term 'blended family' simply because most stepfamilies do not blend—and if they do, someone usually gets creamed in the process! When cooking, blending is a process by which you combine ingredients into one fluid mixture: think of a fruit smoothie or a cream soup. Rarely can it be said that a stepfamily becomes 'one' in a relational sense. More realistic is a process by which the various parts integrate, or come into contact with one another, much like a casserole of distinct parts."

2. *The food processor.* In order to blend as quickly as possible, Deal says these families attempt to "chop up one another's history." Deal explains: "A classic example of this mentality is the adult who demands

that the stepchildren call their stepparent 'daddy' or 'mommy.' It is as if the child is told, 'We've chopped up your real dad and thrown him to the side. This is your new dad.' Some parents actually think their children will buy that."

3. *The microwave.* Anyone who watched television during the 1970s remembers *The Brady Bunch*. For those who have never watched, it is the story of the ideal stepfamily. Mike Brady had three sons, Greg, Peter, and Bobby. Mike married Carol, who had three daughters: Marcia, Jan, and Cindy. If that were not enough, they also had a lovely housekeeper, Alice, and a dog. While every episode had a measure of drama, the Bradys were the ideal stepfamily. They had their regular childhood spats, but by the end of the show, everything was worked out and everyone was happy. Of course, not only did every family want to be like the Bradys but also every stepfamily thought they *could* be like the Bradys until they got married and were surprised that it wasn't as simple as that television show made it out to be. Deal expounds on the microwave approach: "These families refuse to be defined as a stepfamily and seek to heat the ingredients in rapid fashion so as to become a 'nuke-lier' family (pun intended). They avoid labels like stepfamily and the implication that they are different from any other family. People tell me they resent being called a stepfamily because it makes them feel second-rate. There is nothing inherently wrong with being a stepfamily; it is neither better nor worse than other family types, just different."

Deal goes on to observe that stepfamilies and biological families do exhibit some differences: "No matter how desperately you may want your stepfamily to be like a biological family, it simply cannot be. It is true that every stepfamily has aspects that are reflective of biological families. But every stepfamily also has unique characteristics that differ from biological families. Some parts function the same; some don't."

4. *The pressure cooker.* We love using our pressure cooker. All you do is throw in all of the ingredients, and in a matter of minutes everything is perfectly done. This type of stepfamily tries to do the same. They add all their ingredients from each family—things such as memories, rituals, values, and preferences—in hopes that they will all fuse together. "The family is under great duress, and since expectations are so high, the lid often blows off the pot," Deal notes. One example Deal offers is when "stepfamilies assume that the answer to every conflict in holiday ritual is to combine the traditions. It's important that stepfamilies understand that combining rituals works sometimes, but pressuring

people to be okay with the combination can sabotage the results."

5. *The tossed salad.* A tossed salad is a sort of quick, carefree way to look at stepfamilies. You simply put in all the major ingredients and toss them to your liking, even as you serve yourself. "The ingredients keep some of their integrity," says Deal, "yet are expected to fit together with the other pieces." For example, writes Deal, "When one child is spending time at their other home, remaining children often believe they can play with the absent child's toys or belongings. Children should be taught that even though someone is temporarily away from one home, the absentee's stuff is not free game. Respecting one another's possessions is important because it teaches people to honor others; it also communicates belonging to the child who is spending time at the other home. 'You may be at your dad's house, but you still have a place here.' "

6. *The Crock-Pot.* All of the preceding cooking styles are good when we prepare a meal, but each may be problematic when trying to blend a family. Ron Deal recommends stepfamilies consider the Crock-Pot style: "Stepfamilies choosing this style understand that time and low heat make for an effective combination. Ingredients are thrown together in the same pot, but each is left intact, giving affirmation to its unique origin and characteristics. Slowly and with much intention, the low-level heat brings the ingredients into contact with one another. As the juices begin to flow together, imperfections are purified, and the beneficial, desirable qualities of each ingredient are added to the taste. The result is a dish of delectable flavor made up of different ingredients that give of themselves to produce a wondrous creation."

Keep in mind that the two most critical relationships in any stepfamily home are the marriage and stepparent-stepchildren relationships. If every stepfamily were like the Bradys, they would come together in perfect harmony from the beginning. From the first time the two families meet, they get off on the right foot, they like each other, and it is as if they had always been together as one family. In reality, no matter what "cooking" method you choose for your newly formed family, it will take time—a fair amount of time—before you will begin to have the sense that you are indeed a family.[5]

In another article, Deal explains that bonding in stepfamilies can take a great deal of time and effort:

General stepfamily integration and bonding with a stepchild hardly ever happens as quickly as adults want it to.[6]

Fast families may accomplish this in four years, if the children are young and the adults are intentional about bringing the family together. However, slow families . . . can take nine or more years. In my experience, very few adults come into their stepfamily believing it will take this long. They want a quick, painless blending process.[7]

The sad reality is that if it takes between four and nine years for the newly constituted family to feel like they are one, many may never get to this point and, instead, give up two or three years into their experiment. In the meantime, children in those families go through a plethora of emotions resulting from the dissolution of their own parent's marriage; the joining of one or both of their parents to new spouses; the battles for power and control in every direction; the dynamics between new siblings, stepparents, step-grandparents, and other relatives; and then, after all of that, they might end up having to leave people they have just begun to develop new relationships with. That's why getting married for a second or third time should be a decision made carefully, slowly, and prayerfully.

DISCIPLINING THE CHILDREN

Perhaps one or both of you have biological children from your previous marriage. This creates a quandary as to who plays the role of disciplinarian. You may even hear the child say to the nonbiological parent, "You are not my boss."

Indeed, parenting for a remarried couple can be especially challenging. Terry Gaspard of The Gottman Institute notes, "For the most part, first-time couples usually have the opportunity before the arrival of children to become familiar with some of their differences in raising children, and even to resolve some of them. This isn't usually the case for remarried couples who may find themselves immediately clashing over ways to educate, discipline, and care for the children in their new stepfamily."[8] Not only that, but when children spend some of their time in your home and some at the other parent's home, where their idea of discipline may be different than yours, the child is at a loss as to who to listen to, what to do, where to do it, and how to do it. Imagine a child in the middle of such a situation!

Gaspard goes on to explain that "it's common for stepparents to feel like an 'outsider' in their own home. Many stepparents react by doing their own thing while their partner spends time with the kids. If both partners are parents who respond by spending more time with their biological kids and less time with their stepkids, this tendency toward separation in the stepfamily increases. If an us-and-them scenario develops, it will undermine the family and the remarried couples' relationship."[9]

So where do you begin? This is a new role that you've never held before, and you certainly did not take a course to prepare. Here are some tips to keep in mind as you navigate your new role as a stepparent:

1. *Biological parent equals primary disciplinarian.* It's important for the biological parent to be the primary disciplinarian. This may be hard to accept, but it will save you a lot of unnecessary pain. Your role is to be supportive and work on developing a positive relationship with your stepchild. The older the child is when you marry, the more important it is to follow this advice.

2. *Practice patience.* "One of the most important lessons parents can learn about stepfamily life is that stepparents had best proceed slowly," writes Gaspard. "Take your time in getting to know your stepchild." If you can win the child's respect first, love will often come later. Gaspard goes on to say, "Even if you don't hit it off with your stepchild, you can still develop a working relationship built on respect. If your stepchild does not warm up to you right away, that doesn't mean you have failed." Permit your stepchild or stepchildren to set the pace for the relationship, such as in what to call you (as long as it's respectful) and how much affection they display toward you. It may take time, so "being patient and having a sense of humor can help you get through some rough spots."[10]

3. *Communicate with your spouse.* Communicate with your spouse and discuss sensitive issues in private, away from your children or stepchildren. Discuss things together, such as "family rules, roles, chores, and routines with the kids"[11] ahead of time.

4. *Keep a united front.* "Presenting a united front to your children and stepchildren with your spouse is very helpful to the formation of a healthy stepfamily," Gaspard says. "This action requires respect, caring, and lots of love."[12] It's okay to disagree but never do so in front of your children or stepchildren.

5. *Hold regular family meetings.* It's a good idea to hold regular family meetings. This is a way to help everyone feel like they have input. However, don't forget to maintain a united front during these meetings.

6. *Build new traditions.* Each of you, along with your children, have traditions that existed before the other came into the picture. Why not create new traditions that you can take into your future as a new family?

7. *Don't neglect daily family worship.* Nothing will unite your families like daily family worship. Set a time each day and be faithful in keeping

that appointment. Make sure that all family members understand that this time spent together is nonnegotiable. Gear these worships to the age of the youngest child in the family, make them interactive, and make sure they're fun. It should be a time each member of the family looks forward to each day. It is another opportunity to grow together as you invest time in uniting two families!

Stepfamily expert Ron Deal shares some very practical discipline dos and don'ts for stepparents. As he says, "At best new stepparent authority is fragile and easily shattered. That's why these do's and don'ts must be a priority":

- Do make sure the biological parent has your back. Biological parents must communicate to their children an expectation of obedience to the stepparent and be willing to back up the stepparent's actions. When disagreements occur, settle them in private.
- Do strive for unity in parenting. Discuss behavioral expectations, boundaries, consequences, and values. Bring your parenting philosophies in line.
- Don't be harsh or punish in a way inconsistent with the biological parent.
- Do focus on relationship building. This is your long-term strength.
- Don't unilaterally change rules or try to make up for past parental mistakes or failings.
- Do listen to the child. If they draw into you sooner than expected, don't look back. Use the relational authority offered you.
- Don't get impatient. It often takes years to bond and develop a trusting love-relationship with children. Be persistent in bonding with them.
- Do communicate with the biological parent a lot! If uncertain, find parental unity before engaging the children.[13]

There's a lot more that we could say about stepfamilies. Entire books have been written about this special family dynamic. We recommend you read Ron Deal's book, *The Smart Stepfamily*, as it is full of very practical information and ideas. Also, visit his website at www.smartstepfamilies.com.

NOT ALL GLOOM AND DOOM
We know all this sounds very pessimistic and scary; we don't intend for it to.

However, it is good to know these things and be prepared to deal with them before they cause problems for your new relationship. But it is not all gloom and doom. Many stepfamilies do succeed and go on to have very good, positive relationships and lasting memories. Brittany Wong writes:

> Sorry, all you nuclear family kids: there are just some things that only kids who grew up in a stepfamily can understand.
>
> Case in point? The 22 things below, which prove life in a blended family is nothing short of an adventure—a uniquely awkward but ultimately wonderful adventure.

1. The bathroom is never yours. The water in the shower may have been hot at some point, but freezing showers have become your new normal.
2. You may be one big happy blended family, but let's be honest— the siblings are divided into two distinct teams: littles and bigs. (Sorry, middle child, you're going to have to choose a side.)
3. You'd like to buy your mom one of those cute Hallmark family tree frames for Mother's Day, but there aren't enough branches.
4. You get called by every sibling's name but your own regularly.
5. Your mom or dad has also, on occasion, called your stepparent by your bio-mom or dad's name. And forgotten that it was your *dad* who liked cheesecake for his birthday, not your stepdad. Oopsie.
6. Vacations are nearly impossible. Thanks a lot, dueling custody agreements.
7. But at least there are two Christmases! #score
8. There's a chore board in your home that features an elaborate matrix of schedules and competing extracurricular activities. The struggle to make sense of that board is real.
9. Your stepparent tried to win you over with Taylor Swift concert tickets when he or she first met you. It didn't work. Treating your mom or dad right did.
10. Industrial-sized boxes of cereal for breakfast *again*?
11. You were a little peeved when your stepbrother stole your birth order position in the family. You wanted to be the baby in the family forever. FOREVER.
12. If you never see another set of bunk beds again, it will be too soon.
13. You get "but you look nothing alike?!" stares every time you introduce your stepsibs to new friends. (You could introduce them as "my stepbrother" or "stepsister," but how weirdly formal is that?)

14. You can't find your beloved little cropped blazer anywhere . . . until you see your stepsister wearing it in a Facebook pic from her little brother's graduation.

15. You have shouted, "You're not my real dad/mom!" at some point in your life.

16. When you're older, one of your stepsibling's distant cousins asks to be set up with you. Awkward much?

17. You were shocked at how lax your stepdad's house rules were for your stepsiblings—and you better believe you lobbied hard for the same house rules when you all moved in together.

18. There's always that one relative who buys you something awesome for the holidays (hello, 3D printing pen!) but something crummy for your stepsiblings.

19. You're embarrassed to admit you've given serious thought as to which member of the Kardashian-Jenner crew you are.

20. You've uttered a sentence that goes something like this: "Oh, she's my stepbrother's mom's stepdaughter's aunt."

21. Your parents, stepparents, stepsiblings, and half siblings may drive you crazy at times, but at the end of the day, you're proud to call them family.

22. And let's not forget the joy that is having two of each holiday. #blessed.[14]

You can tell that some of these items were written with tongue in cheek, but they do reflect the general feeling that many in stepfamilies share. If you are in such a situation, we pray you, too, will have success, joy, lots of love, and good memories in your stepfamily.

CONCLUSION
Above all, the key to making a second marriage a success is to commit the marriage to God and rely on Him for the grace and strength needed. Regardless of the situation in your previous relationship, it's time to turn the page and focus on your current spouse. Make of this marriage all that God intended.

---

1. Shaunti Feldhahn, "Second Marriages: 3 Things You Need to Know," Shaunti Feldhahn, December 8, 2017, https://shaunti.com/2017/12/second-marriages-success/; emphasis in original.

2. Brittany Wong, "10 Reasons Marriage Is Better the Second Time Around," HuffPost, March 16, 2015, https://www.huffpost.com/entry/second-marriages-are-better-_n_6865506; emphasis in original.

3. David Frisbie and Lisa Frisbie, *Happily Remarried* (Eugene, OR: Harvest House, 2005), 44.

4. "Blended Family," Sociology Dictionary, accessed August 19, 2020, https://sociology dictionary.org/blended-family/.

5. Ron Deal, "How to Cook a Stepfamily," Smart Stepfamilies, accessed August 19, 2020, https://smartstepfamilies.com/smart-help/learn/stepfamily-living/how-to-cook-a-stepfamily.

6. James Bray, *Stepfamilies: Love, Marriage, and Parenting in the First Decade* (New York: Broadway Books, 1998), cited in Ron Deal, "Smart Stepparenting," Focus on the Family, January 1, 2002, https://www.focusonthefamily.com/parenting/smart-stepparenting/.

7. Ron Deal, "Smart Stepparenting," Focus on the Family, January 1, 2002, https://www.focusonthefamily.com/parenting/smart-stepparenting/.

8. Terry Gaspard, "Navigating the Challenges of Stepfamily Life," The Gottman Institute, June 26, 2018, https://www.gottman.com/blog/navigating-challenges-stepfamily-life/.

9. Gaspard, "Navigating the Challenges."

10. Gaspard, "Navigating the Challenges."

11. Gaspard, "Navigating the Challenges."

12. Gaspard, "Navigating the Challenges."

13. Ron Deal, "Stepparenting Do's and Don'ts," Smart Stepfamilies, accessed August 19, 2020, https://smartstepfamilies.com/smart-help/learn/parenting-stepparenting/stepparenting-do-s-and-don-ts.

14. Brittany Wong, "21 Things Only People Who Grew Up in a Blended Family Can Understand," HuffPost, updated May 6, 2014, https://www.huffpost.com/entry/blended-family-_n_5255640.

Chapter Thirteen

"Find Us Faithful"

I will perpetuate your memory through all generations;
therefore, the nations will praise you for ever and ever.
—Psalm 45:17, NIV

J ust as the earth experiences spring, then summer, then fall, and finally winter, our own life cycle has its seasons. It's true that, usually, we have our favorite seasons; but, like it or not, those seasons are part of the cycle of life, and one follows another. We can't stop them, delay them, or accelerate them.

It's good to contemplate how each season prepares us for the one to follow. For example, proper planning and planting in the spring will enable us to reap the benefits of the autumn harvest. In many ways, our marriage follows suit as it goes through seasons. Each season prepares us for the next, and what happens in previous seasons will impact the final harvest that is reaped. The important thing to keep in mind is that, regardless of the season in which we find ourselves, we must be faithful to God, faithful to our marriage, and faithful to our family. In doing so, we will leave a legacy that will continue from season to season and from generation to generation. Let's look at each of the seasons of marriage.

SPRING

One may argue that spring is the foundation upon which all the other seasons are built. During this season, you make decisions that impact how each of the other seasons will unfold, so it's crucial to understand this bedrock of life. Just spend a few hours with a farmer, and they will tell you the importance of spring. In this season, a great deal of thought goes into deciding when to prepare the fields, when to plow and till the soil, which seeds will be planted, and when to apply fertilizer to ensure the best crop yield. It is the time to make sure all of the equipment and tools are in the best condition and ready for use.

The season of spring is a time of joy and excitement in your newfound relationship. Butterflies flutter within you, and the sweet perfume of blossoms fills the air. You look forward to each date as a couple. You go through the premarital preparation, plan your wedding, go off on that dream honeymoon, and relish your days as a newlywed couple. So let's explore some phases of life that could be equated with springtime:

- *Friendship phase.* During the years of adolescence, the teen years, the best choice one can make is to develop good friendships. It may be among these friends that deeper relationships form and even lead to marriage. Friendships will be your pillar of courage and strength during the good, the bad, and the ugly days of life. The wise man wrote, "The sweet smell of incense can make you feel good, but true friendship is better still" (Proverbs 27:9, CEV).

- *Courtship phase.* From the various friendships you have developed, perhaps you tried to take some into deeper relationships. Most have not worked out. As the saying goes, there was not enough chemistry between you. But somewhere along the way, you met someone that sparked your interest. You enjoyed their company and felt comfortable with them. Day by day, a little at a time, the relationship deepened, you became more vulnerable with each passing moment, and trust began to strengthen. Perhaps you began to dream and fantasize about how things might be if you were married: "Oh, that he would kiss me with the kisses of his mouth! For your caresses are more delightful than wine" (Song of Songs 1:2, CSB). Physical attraction becomes an emotional attachment, and you begin to hope, wish, and pray that this may just be the one God has chosen for you.

- *Premarital phase.* Don't rush through springtime! Enjoy this season, for it's a time of development and maturation. If you take a tiny rosebud and try to force it open, you will destroy the beautiful rose. If you cut open a cocoon before nature determines the right time, you will kill the life inside. Nature teaches us the important lesson of patience. Hold on, step back, and wait for a moment. The Bible advises, "Do not stir up or awaken love until it is ready!" (Song of Solomon 2:7, NRSV). After all, "there is a time for everything, and a season for every activity under the heavens" (Ecclesiastes 3:1, NIV).

  So now you have taken your relationship to a new level. You have decided it is the right time to make the first commitment by becoming engaged. It is a signal to each other, and to others, that you are seriously moving in the direction of marriage and a lifetime together. You may want to read the first chapter of this book again and be reminded of the important steps you need to take during this time before you say, "I do."

- *Newlywed or honeymoon phase.* The newlywed season of your married life can be one of joy, discovery, and fun. Having said that, you are also learning what it means to live together and function as a team on a day-to-day basis. You are adapting to each other's quirks and habits, adopting new practices, leaving some things behind, and looking forward to new experiences. It can be a scary time—but also very exciting.

Successful marriages require intentionality. That honeymoon will fade all too quickly unless we focus on meeting each other's needs. Remember, it is in this season of spring that all the preparatory work is done to yield a bountiful harvest. Perhaps Paul has the best advice for newly married couples: "Be completely humble and gentle; be patient, bearing with one another in love. Make every effort to keep the unity of the Spirit through the bond of peace" (Ephesians 4:2, 3, NIV).

Little by little, things begin to fall into place. New routines become part of everyday life. The single life is but a memory, and we can't see ourselves ever returning to that again. The season of spring is beautiful. It's full of promise for the future, for exploration of what may come, and for planning new adventures together.

SUMMER

Summer is no time for the farmer to relax. Days are spent weeding the fields, making sure the plants have adequate water, and keeping the insects and other plant-eating animals at bay. There is pruning as well as aerating the soil that needs to take place. Those plants are growing rapidly, but they still need a farmer's watchful and caring eye.

In the same manner, summer is the season of your relationship where growth is at its peak. Yes, there may be pruning to be done, but there are also feelings of happiness, satisfaction, accomplishment, and connection. It's a time to reap the benefits of hard work, to experience upward mobility in your career, and maybe have the joy of welcoming a new baby into your home. It is the time to work together as a team to fulfill all the dreams you talked about during springtime, such as buying your first home.

As writer and podcaster Zaid K. Dahhaj puts it, "Summer is an exciting time of your life. Seeds of action are planted and then come to fruition, benefiting the people you serve. This motivates you to work harder, to plant more, and to strive to be perennially generative."[1] You may find yourself attempting to keep summer alive as long as humanly possible. Let's look closer at what happens in our lives during the summer season:

- *Family growth.* An especially important and exciting area of growth during this season may be in the size of your family. This marks a transition in your marriage as two become three or four or more. Parenting skills are added to the mix, and decisions about discipline and other child-rearing concerns become frequent conversation topics.

  While it is a wonderful time of growth, it may also be very stressful. Marriage elation tends to decline with the birth of each child. Family life assumes a new normal. Much as farmers need to prune the plants, parents must sort through the challenges of discipline. Just as each plant is different, each child is different. As the Bible reminds us: "Our earthly fathers correct us, and we still respect them. Isn't it even better to be given true life by letting our spiritual Father correct us?" (Hebrews 12:9, CEV).

- *Career growth.* It is usually during this season when the most growth takes place in your personal and family life. One of those areas is career growth. You may begin to climb the corporate ladder, and decisions about how to balance career and family come into the picture.

  Today's culture has made this season even more challenging, as we find the office following us around on our cell phones and other electronic devices. We must discover ways to still be faithful to our families while maintaining work responsibilities. Keep the boundaries between work and family intact. Don't blur those lines. Prioritize your relationship. If your work forces you to put family second, you may need to rethink your career possibilities. God, family, and career—in that order!

The days of summer bring enjoyment, outdoor activities, vacations, picnics, yard work, and the smell of fresh fruit. All too soon, those long summer days begin to get shorter, and the temperature begins to cool down. The sunny summer days quickly fade into the beautiful colors of autumn.

AUTUMN

Autumn is here at last for the farmer. It's time to harvest and enjoy the fruitful bounty of all that they have worked so hard for. It's still a lot of work, but in the process of all that hard work, they finally see the rewards of their labors.

In life, summer often fades into fall before we are prepared. What is it that we have worked so hard for? What rewards of our labors shall we reap? If you live in an area where fall colors are vibrant, then you know that few things are more beautiful than the bright oranges, reds, and yellows of the autumn leaves.

In our Western culture, we prize youth and vitality. Aging is often not celebrated or seen as a lovely time in one's life, so we dye our graying hair, get plastic surgery to erase the wrinkles, and attempt to artificially keep summer going when we really should be experiencing and celebrating autumn. In going hard all the time and trying to push back the years, we often miss out on the beauty that autumn and winter have to offer. As we enter the autumn of our lives, we are often unwilling to embrace it. The signs of aging that emerge during this season may seem to give way to winter all too quickly.

Fall is often a time of mixed emotions. As children leave home and we find ourselves with an empty nest, midlife crisis sets in, menopause happens, retirement occurs, and the joy of grandparenting surrounds us. Let's break these issues down a bit and further explore the season of fall:

- *Empty nest.* This season of life seems to creep up on us before we realize what has happened. We find ourselves helping our "baby" pack up their belongings and head off to college or to a job across the country. The house is eerily quiet, and, all too often, couples find themselves relearning how to live together without the children. Perhaps the entire household has centered on the child, and once the child is removed, there exists this vacuum.

   This new experience does not have to be sad, however. The couple can now spend undivided time together and, with more free time, they can enjoy a period of reliving old memories and learning new things. They can find new ways to experience and appreciate life, to grow closer, and to take more satisfaction in what they have accomplished through the years.

- *Menopause.* Some of the changes in the autumn of our life are emotional. Others are physical, such as menopause. Menopause is a natural and normal part of life, but often we are caught off guard when it happens, and we have not educated ourselves about what to expect from this phase of life.

   According to gynecologist W. David Hager, "Menopause is defined as 12 months of going without a menstrual period. The most common symptoms are hot flashes, sweating, increased irritability and mood changes, sleep disturbances, difficulty concentrating, and thinning of hair on the head."[2] Of course, every woman is different, and that period of twelve months may last much longer for some. As if this were not enough, vaginal dryness resulting in painful intercourse often occurs, leading some couples to experience issues with sexual intimacy.

   "A woman can often benefit from the care of a qualified medical professional, who can provide information about menopause and treatments for discomforting symptoms," Hager says. "Similarly, the counsel of a licensed therapist or a pastor can be valuable in dealing with relationship issues. Research shows, however, that only about 20 percent of women feel comfortable enough to discuss their symptoms with their health care professional, and many women struggle through this time without the support they need."[3]

Don't miss that startling statistic. It means that 80 percent of women suffer in silence and are uncomfortable discussing things that are part of the normal season of life. Why should we be embarrassed to talk about something that is perfectly normal? There is support, and there is available help with some of the most annoying symptoms of menopause if we just speak up. Just think—it may help your marriage if you do!

- *Midlife crisis.* While the ladies are dealing with hot flashes, or as I (Pam) call it, "their personal summer," men are also dealing with physical changes. For many, there is a decrease in testosterone. They begin graying or losing their hair, their muscle tone weakens, and their energy levels may decline. While the physiological changes are taking place, men will also notice some psychological challenges. "It's normal for men to enter a period of deep introspection and re-evaluation of their life somewhere between the ages of 45 and 60," writes Catherine Wilson for Focus on the Family Canada. "Although it's a passing phase, it's usually a long one, lasting for months or even up to five years. Some men experience relatively little angst, while for others, the confusion and inner turmoil ushered in by midlife is a thoroughly wretched experience."[4]

This midlife crisis not just brought on by the mental realization that a man is in his autumn season. Wilson writes that there is a physical reason for it, as well: "Falling levels of testosterone can impact a male emotionally as well as physically. The first signal that a man is approaching midlife might not be a change he sees in the mirror; it might just be a slow slide into an increasingly gloomy mood that he doesn't understand and can't seem to shake off."[5] Some men try to deal with it by buying a nice sports car, changing hairstyles, or working harder on their physique. Unfortunately, others try to cope by seeking liaisons or full-blown relationships with other women, which is devastating to their marriages and families.

Once again, just as with menopause for a woman, experiencing some of the signs of middle age is normal for a man. You are not alone, and, yes, there is support and help for you if you seek it. Speak to your medical professional, to a counselor, or to another trusted man. This period can be a time for reevaluating what is important in your life and what matters most. Make it a time to renew the commitment to your mate and to God.

- *Retirement.* In autumn, says Dahhaj, "the focus is less on doing and more on allowing and reaping the benefits of what you sowed during the summer. It is time to attend to yourself and the people in your life—to give them care. Enjoy your relationships. The people around us are the greatest gifts life has to offer."[6]

  If you have been making appropriate plans for this season, you may have your house paid off, you may have no debts, and you, hopefully, have sufficient funds in your retirement, bank, and investment accounts to retire comfortably. If, for whatever reason, you reach this point in your life and you still have major pending financial responsibilities, you may be facing working beyond your retirement age or retiring with a lower income than you anticipated. Some must supplement their retirement income by continuing to work at least part-time. If you're still young enough, make good financial decisions, so you can enjoy the autumn season of your life comfortably and with your family.

- *Grandparenting.* This may be one of the best things that happen during this season. We find ourselves pouring all our energies into this new little baby who gives us renewed life and strength. At the same time, it can bring some challenges if we are not careful. For example, too many grandparents forget that the baby is not their child, and they are not the primary custodians (unless the court has mandated it). It may be easy to have conflicts with our adult children as we try to tell them how to raise our grandchildren. (For more on this topic, you may want to check out our book, *Grandparenting: Giving Our Grandchildren a GRAND View of God*, available on Amazon.)

Yes, autumn is a lovely time in our lives. The key is to enjoy the season and all that it offers. Relish all the beautiful moments of color that the autumn breeze brings.

WINTER

Winter on a farm is a time for the farm to rest. It is a time when the soil lies beneath the snow and ice (at least in the northern climates) and gets ready for the coming year. The soil is worn out and needs time to renew itself to begin the cycle of life again when spring arrives. At the same time, farmers will tell you that spring is on their minds. They are thinking ahead about the next season of crops.

Wintertime in our life may not be associated with joy, as it brings about the issues of aging, loss, grief, death, and bereavement. Sure, we would like to skip or eliminate this season altogether and stay in a perpetual state of summer or fall. However, the thing about seasons is that one follows the other, and time marches on. Let's plunge deeper into some of these aspects of winter and see if perhaps we can break through the chill to find moments of warmth, caring, love, and even some rays of sunshine:

- *Aging.* It's during this season that we all long for the springtime of youth. We miss the youthful feelings that came with our honeymoon phase and the joy of anticipation of our new life together. As our aging becomes apparent, we find ourselves spending time, energy, and resources on dealing with the issues that it brings. Our bodies slow down and ache where they didn't earlier in life, and we become more vulnerable to sickness. Yes, it's easy to focus on all we can't do during this time in our life. However, what would happen if we counted our blessings and focused on all we have been able to do?
- *Grief and loss.* It was during the season of spring that you joined your lives together and became intertwined. But then because of the death of your spouse, suddenly, and for the first time in decades, you find yourself alone, without your life companion by your side. Some are still young and in good enough health, and they may choose to remarry, which could be a blessing in many ways.

  The experience of loss and grief can be overwhelming to some. Navigating the waters of older age on their own, perhaps having to move from their home to a care facility—it all may be a heavier burden than some can manage. We all have heard of people who lose their spouses and shortly afterward, they themselves die. Their lives have become so intertwined through the years that with the passing of one, the other doesn't have the will or desire to continue living. They truly die of a broken heart. Others are more resilient and go on to live on their own for many more years, giving their children and grandchildren good memories, joy, and laughter.
- *Preparing for death.* Facing your own mortality and preparing for it is a normal and healthy part of this season. It is a very positive step to face mortality as a normal process and make appropriate preparations so that the burden will not fall in our children's laps when the time comes. Having a good conversation with our children to talk about such things as advanced directives, power of attorney, funeral arrangements, and a will can make the transition for you and your

children a lot easier than if your children have to do it. Remember this biblical advice:

> To everything there is a season,
> A time for every purpose under heaven.
>
> A time to be born,
> And a time to die;
> A time to plant,
> And a time to pluck what is planted (Ecclesiastes 3:1, 2).

The only thing that you can be certain of that is the same in everyone's life is change. Change occurs as one season of our life merges into the next. Just as we reach the winter of our lives, others are moving closer to autumn, others are just in their own spring or summer, and the cycle is repeated, generation after generation. It is important to see the beauty, blessings, and opportunities in each of the changing seasons of our life.

No matter what season of life you are in, embrace it and celebrate what it has to offer. Every season has a lesson to teach and presents us with opportunities to pass on those lessons to other people. The important thing is to walk with God in every season of our life!

Also, ask yourself what you are leaving for the next generation. While winter may seem dark, bleak, and cold, it comes to an end just as spring returns. Winter, too, serves a purpose. The soil rests in order to prepare for spring. Winter snows leave the soil moist and ready for the next planting season. It is winter's legacy to the next cycle. What is yours?

"FIND US FAITHFUL"

What legacy will you leave after winter ends? What is the most important inheritance you will leave? Your family's homestead? Money? Boats? Cars? Those things will rust with time. However, there is something that will stand the test of time and last into eternity. We love the message in the words of the song "Find us Faithful." It speaks of those who follow in our footprints. It is a prayer that "the lives we live" may "inspire them to obey."[7]

Remember that the farmer begins preparation in springtime. Begin preparing now for the legacy you will leave. Have you considered that passing on the legacy of faith and reflecting Jesus in your marriage is perhaps the best inheritance you could leave for those that come behind you? A Christlike home will sustain your marriage today and tomorrow and will be a lasting legacy for the generations that follow.

THE BEST GIFT

Are you a gift giver? Do you enjoy picking out that perfect gift for your child? We certainly do. In fact, we collect little gifts all throughout the year as we travel. We tuck these treasures away until Christmas and can hardly wait until they are unwrapped, each one chosen especially for each of our children. Even the Bible talks about giving good gifts to our children when it says, "If you, then, though you are evil, know how to give good gifts to your children, how much more will your Father in heaven give good gifts to those who ask him" (Matthew 7:11, NIV).

As parents, we enjoy giving our children gifts that bring smiles to their faces. But too often we discover that the gifts we have given are discarded, forgotten, or broken. Think about that last birthday present or Christmas present you gave your child. Is it still as cherished as it was on the day it was unwrapped?

We tend to give material gifts that do not stand the test of time. However, is there a gift that you could give to your children that would last forever? Is there a gift that will not break, be discarded, or be forgotten? In fact, is there a gift that will linger far beyond the years you will live on this earth? We would like to suggest to you that the gift of your marriage is indeed such a gift! We know some of you may argue with us and tell us that the best gift we can give our children is their faith in God. We say, yes, but where do they learn that faith? Isn't it at home? Don't they observe it in your life and in your marriage? How can they believe in a God who could not even keep their parents' marriage intact? And how can they believe in your faith if you couldn't make it evident in your marriage?

Fathers, you are teaching your daughters about what to look for in a husband. You are showing them that common acts of courtesy matter, such as pulling out the chair for your wife or opening the car door for her. As you honor your role as spiritual leader of the home, you show your daughters the importance of seeking a godly man. And for your sons you model the biblical view of a husband loving his wife in the same way as Christ loved the church. Your sons will emulate your behavior.

Mothers, in the same manner, you teach your little boys what to look for in a wife. You are caring, kind, and compassionate as you demonstrate love each day. And for your daughters you model the biblical view of a wife respecting her husband. Your daughters will emulate your behavior.

Do not underestimate the role that your marriage has in the future of your children. They are learning how to show love, manage conflict, and forgive. These relationship lessons will stay with them throughout their lifetimes and have a great impact on their futures. Are you modeling the type of spouse that you want for your son or daughter? Do you want your son to treat his wife the way you treat his mother? Do you want your daughter to relate to her husband the way you relate to her father? You see, these things matter because, like it or not, you are modeling relationships to your children, for better or for worse!

PRAY FOR YOUR CHILD'S FUTURE SPOUSE

They were just babies, and yet there we were praying for their future spouses. We didn't wait until they were old enough to choose a spouse; we were praying from the time they were little girls. Choosing a spouse is one of the most important decisions your child will ever make. The more important the decision, the more it should be lifted up in prayer. So be sure to bathe this one in prayer, even though they are too young to think about it.

As our daughters grew and matured into young adults, it was important for them to hear us audibly praying for them, as our words served as a constant reminder of what they were to look for in a spouse in the not so distant future. Here are some ways in which we prayed for our daughters' future spouses. We prayed for a husband who

- leads his family as God directs;
- is a prayer warrior himself;
- understands what it means to be the priest of his family;
- is kind, caring, and patient;
- has the ultimate goal of his entire family being together in heaven; and
- loves our daughter as Christ loved the church.

Following God's direction in this all-important decision will ensure that the legacy of a good marriage continues for generations to come. Other than the decision to accept Christ as their personal Savior, marriage is the most important decision our children will make in their lifetime. Make it a matter of prayer, no matter how young they are.

OTHERS ARE WATCHING TOO

Modeling a Christ-centered marriage in every season of your life not only impacts your own children—but also many others are watching and observing, even when we think no one sees. For some, you may be the only positive image of marriage that they will ever see. Perhaps they only know dysfunction and brokenness in their own family. What an opportunity we have every day!

We were coming out of a restaurant to get into our parked car. As usual, Claudio proceeded to open the car door for me. As he was doing so, another car pulled into the parking space opposite us. The driver, a man, leaned out of the car window and said, "My wife is very impressed to see that you open the door for your wife." At that precise moment, the passenger (obviously the man's wife) opened her own door, stepped out, slammed it shut, and stomped into the restaurant. Obviously, the man had completely missed his wife's hint. He would have scored so many points if he had told her to sit still and then proceeded to open her door for her!

That incident reminded us that others are watching. We sometimes do things out of habit, without realizing that someone else—perhaps someone that we do not even know—is watching our interactions. And keep in mind that it's not about the big things. You can be a positive role model to others in the small things, such as holding hands while you are walking in the neighborhood, putting an arm around your mate's shoulder, whispering in your spouse's ear, giggling together, or opening a car door for your spouse.

PASSING ON A LEGACY

Your marriage must be built on a strong faith foundation—one that will not crumble when tested by trials, one that is not easily destroyed, and one that stands tall as a testament to God. Is it your desire to leave a lasting legacy of faith that will stand the test of time? Consider Jesus' words: "Therefore whoever hears these sayings of Mine, and does them, I will liken him to a wise man who built his house on the rock: and the rain descended, the floods came, and the winds blew and beat on that house; and it did not fall, for it was founded on the rock" (Matthew 7:24, 25). If that is your desire, here are some ways you can focus on a Christ-centered marriage, building on the Rock in every season of life:

- *Remember, marriage is a covenant.* "Your family will never be stronger than the covenant that established it," states Dennis Rainey.[8] Your marriage is not based on a piece of paper that you signed on your wedding day or one that is filed in the courthouse. Rather, it is a covenant relationship that you established by your promise, "Till death do us part." It involved you, your spouse, and God. That strand of three is one that is not easily broken. It represents a holy vow!
- *Pray together each day.* Rainey notes that "daily prayer keeps us from building walls between each other. And it builds bridges across chasms that may have widened between us during the day."[9] Pray with and for each other audibly every day. One of the sweetest sounds is the sound of your spouse's voice praying for you.
- *"For better or for worse."* Marriage has rough spots and difficult moments in every season of life. There are times of job loss, illness, financial challenges, and the death of loved ones. It is so important that

a husband and wife stick together and remain united during those times. We must stand together—looking to God to grant us wisdom in decisions and praying that He will guide us through them all.

- *Seek what makes your spouse happy.* In this book, we have devoted two whole chapters to this topic (one for men and one for women). Have you discussed these two chapters together? Have you shared your top needs with your spouse? If not, we encourage you to do so and then strive to meet the other's needs. Ask these questions of your spouse:

  - "What can I do to help you feel more loved, more respected?"
  - "What can I do to help encourage you toward achieving your goals and dreams?"
  - "What practice would you like to see me improve or develop?"
  - "What mutual goal would you like to see us accomplish together?"

- *Listen!* It would have been easier to comply had we said, "Talk" instead of, "Listen," but perhaps we should stop and listen for understanding before speaking. Good communication begins with good listening!
- *Take the initiative to manage conflicts.* There's a reason why Scripture admonishes, "Do not let the sun go down while you are still angry" (Ephesians 4:26, NIV). God knows that if we allow issues in our marriages to fester, it gives Satan an opportunity to divide us. Is there any unmanaged conflict in your marriage? Are you harboring any bitterness? Take the initiative to work through the steps to manage conflict. Approach it in a way that would honor Christ, and don't sit back and wait for your spouse to do it. It's just as much your responsibility as it is theirs.

Give your children the best gift—the gift of your marriage. Our God-given responsibility as parents is to impart not just our knowledge of God to our children but to give them an example—a vision of a healthy marriage. "Remember," Dennis Rainey writes, "your marriage and family are the headwaters of your legacy. Your legacy begins at home. What occurs downstream . . . will only be as deep as the source."[10]

TURNING ASHES INTO BEAUTY

Perhaps some of you are reading this and thinking that you have already ruined your legacy. We have good news for you! We have all messed up at some point in time—every one of us! So, don't be so quick to give up, because even our disappointments can teach life-changing lessons. God can turn the broken pieces of our lives into a beautiful legacy.

Not long ago, we took a trip to Israel. While there, we wanted to purchase some special olive wood candlesticks. As we looked over the vast number on the shelf, some stood out. These were the ones with visible knots in the wood. Though often considered imperfections, the knots created beautiful patterns of color that encircled the olive wood. Those were the ones we picked. Those "defects" in the wood made the finished candlesticks all the more beautiful. It's the same with our lives. All the challenges from the past have made us what we are today. Those flaws can assist us in becoming the beautiful creation God desires.

Rest assured that passing on the lasting legacy of a good marriage does not mean that you must have a perfect marriage! We can promise you that no one reading this book (including its authors) has a perfect marriage. No relationship is perfect—every marriage and every family have flaws. The good news is that God is a restorer of broken things. It is in forgiving, starting over, and learning from our past mistakes that we glean some of life's greatest lessons. Here are some important reminders:

- *Don't skip over challenges.* All too often, we want to share our success stories but skip the "bad parts." Did you ever stop to think that those times of challenge teach some of the greatest lessons? Tell your children and grandchildren about the moments when you had to lean on God to sustain you. Share the tears as well as the joys—because when your children face the ruts in the road of their own lives, they will reflect on the precious conversations they had with you.
- *Teach the importance of prayer.* Tell your children over and over again about the importance of prayer. Relate to them the times that prayer made a difference in your relationship.
- *All relationships need forgiveness.* A Christlike marriage means saying, "I'm sorry," and it means exhibiting a forgiving spirit. Model this forgiving spirit and teach your children and grandchildren that forgiveness is a decision that impacts their future well-being.

When you model trusting God despite the challenges that each season brings, you will leave your family with a wonderful legacy. What is more valuable than that? You can be living proof that God Himself is the Giver of life and joy. Our messes become masterpieces in the hands of the God, who has the power to transform hearts and lives. Teach your children and grandchildren how to handle life's disappointments by handing those hurts to God and allowing Him to turn ashes into beauty.

CONCLUSION

The next time you are tempted to think that staying married doesn't matter, think again. It matters because you are passing on a legacy of faith and family that has a lasting impact on future generations. Your family tree is rooted in your marriage. The success of your marriage matters for generations to come, so don't tread lightly upon its value.

Every marriage leaves a legacy, one that can be painfully destructive or wonderfully life giving. The challenge for each of us is to think beyond our present moment of busyness. We each need to be mindful of the long-term consequences of our marital behavior. Through the choices we make in our marriages, we create a profound impact on the lives of all those around us.

No, we are not perfect, and that means our families will not be perfect either. Leaving the lasting legacy of a good marriage doesn't demand perfection. It only demands that day by day and season by season, we place ourselves, our marriages, and our imperfect families in the hands of a perfect God!

You are indeed writing your legacy. The only question that remains is what that legacy will be. The legacy of your marriage will outlast anything typically written in a will. It lasts far beyond things that decay over time, such as a home, a car, or family heirlooms.

Oh Lord, may You indeed find us faithful. May we reflect the type of relationship that You intend between a husband and a wife. And, after our days on this earth are finished, may our children find that we have been faithful to You and to our marriage vows. May they see in us the same sacrificial love that Jesus exemplified.

As our autumn and winter seasons draw nigh, may we be mindful of our children and grandchildren, who are in the springtime of their lives. And may we leave a lasting legacy of faith that continues from season to season and from one generation to the next!

1. Zaid K. Dahhaj, "Why Understanding the Seasons of Life Will Ease Your Suffering," Medium, February 27, 2018, https://medium.com/@zaiderrr/why-understanding-the-seasons-of-life-will-ease-your-suffering-32ad7381c634.

2. W. David Hager, "What Husbands Need to Know About Menopause," Focus on the Family, January 26, 2018, https://www.focusonthefamily.com/marriage/what-husbands-need-to-know-about-menopause/.

3. Hager, "What Husbands Need to Know."

4. Catherine Wilson, "Recognizing Your Husband's Midlife Struggles," Focus on the Family Canada, accessed August 19, 2020, https://www.focusonthefamily.ca/content/recognizing-your-husbands-midlife-struggles.

5. Wilson, "Midlife Struggles."

6. Dahhaj, "Ease Your Suffering."

7. Jonathan Mohr, "Find Us Faithful," (Jonathan Mark Music and Birdwing Music, 1987).

8. Dennis Rainey, "What Will Be Your Legacy?" FamilyLife, accessed August 19, 2020,

https://www.familylife.com/articles/topics/marriage/staying-married/husbands/what-will-be
-your-legacy/.

9. Rainey, "What Will Be Your Legacy?"

10. Rainey, "What Will Be Your Legacy?"